This Is Our Message

This Is Our Message

Message

Women's Leadership in the
New Christian Right

EMILY SUZANNE JOHNSON

OXFORD
UNIVERSITY PRESS

Oxford University Press is a department of the University of Oxford. It furthers the University's objective of excellence in research, scholarship, and education by publishing worldwide. Oxford is a registered trade mark of Oxford University Press in the UK and certain other countries.

Published in the United States of America by Oxford University Press
198 Madison Avenue, New York, NY 10016, United States of America.

Library of Congress Cataloging-in-Publication Data
Names: Johnson, Emily Suzanne, 1984– author.
Title: This is our message : women's leadership in the new Christian right /
Emily Suzanne Johnson.
Description: New York, NY : Oxford University Press, [2019] |
Includes bibliographical references and index.
Identifiers: LCCN 2018016560 (print) | LCCN 2018039917 (ebook) |
ISBN 9780190618940 (updf) | ISBN 9780190618957 (epub) |
ISBN 9780190618964 (online content) | ISBN 9780190618933 (cloth) |
Subjects: LCSH: Christian women—United States—Biography. |
Women conservatives—United States—Biography. |
Christian conservatism—United States.
Classification: LCC BR1713 (ebook) | LCC BR1713 .J645 2019 (print) |
DDC 277.3/08209252—dc23
LC record available at https://lccn.loc.gov/2018016560

Contents

Acknowledgments

EIGHT YEARS AGO, I sat down at my computer and began to organize the thoughts that would eventually become this book. Now I find myself opening a blank document once again and hoping that I can adequately express how grateful I am to the many, many people who helped make this project possible.

This book began as a dissertation at Yale University, where I benefited from the guidance of extraordinary mentors. My admiration for Joanne Meyerowitz's work convinced me to apply to Yale in the first place, and once I was there, she became the best mentor that anyone could ask for—rigorous, supportive, and always pushing me to dig deeper and to make the project better. Kathryn Lofton arrived at Yale at just the right moment; without her, this particular project would not have been possible. She is a seemingly tireless scholar and mentor, who taught me how to think about the study of religion in new ways. I am so grateful for her many readings and re-readings of these chapters and for her professional guidance on issues large and small. Beverly Gage, George Chauncey, Skip Stout, and Jon Butler also offered deeply valuable advice that helped to shape this project and my approach to scholarship more broadly.

I was also lucky to be part of an especially supportive cohort of graduate students, many of whom have become lifelong friends. Sarah Koenig, Sarah Bowman, Marie-Amelie George, Briallen Hopper—it is difficult to imagine my life, much less this project, without you. Devin McGeehan Muchmore, Claudia Calhoun, Natalie Prizel, Mattie Fitch, Sara Ronis, David Minto— all of you have left your impact on this book and on my scholarship. Thank you—all of you—for all of your reading, your advice, your insights, and for the examples of your own scholarship and writing.

As I completed the dissertation, I spent a year as a fellow at the John C. Danforth Center on Religion and Politics at Washington University in St. Louis. This gave me the opportunity to encounter another group of wonderful mentors, whose support and advice has been so meaningful in shaping this project and especially its transition from dissertation to book. R. Marie Griffith and Darren Dochuk offered their own deep insights into the politics and culture of twentieth-century evangelicalism, along with writing advice and warm encouragement. The guidance and support of Leigh Eric Schmidt, Mark D. Jordan, Laurie Maffly-Kipp, Lerone Martin, Rachel Lindsey, and Anne Blankenship were so valuable. And to Rachel Gross, my fellow dissertation fellow, officemate, and friend—thank you for every draft that you read, every idea that you helped me to work through, and every coffee date you organized as we worked toward the finish.

There have been so many others who have offered their advice and support as this project has developed into its current form. Michelle Nickerson, Rebecca L. Davis, Kate Bowler, Kathleen Belew—thank you! I am grateful, too, to my editor Theo Calderara for his insights and guidance.

This project would not be what it is without the generosity of those who agreed to speak to me about their lives and experiences: Marabel Morgan, Bruce Barbour, Hugh Barbour, and Theo Van Der Meer. Thank you, too, to Marilyn Gordon and David Greendonner at Baker Books for going above and beyond in finding sales records and catalogue data for me to use. Thank you to Concerned Women for America for welcoming me and allowing me to look at past newsletters and publications. Thank you to all of the archivists who helped to make this work possible: Bob Shuster at the Billy Graham Center Archives; Becky Schulte and everyone at the Kenneth Spencer Research Library at the University of Kansas; Mary Nelson at the Wichita State University Special Collections; Edward Fields at the University of California Santa Barbara Special Collections; everyone at the Stonewall National Museum and Archives; and Darrin Rodgers, Glenn Gohr, and everyone at the Flower Pentecostal Heritage Center.

Of course, I could not have accomplished any of this without the support and encouragement of my family. Mom and Dad, you introduced me to my love of learning, and you have always encouraged me. Dan, you're a pretty great brother. Auntie Suzie, you are my biggest cheerleader. Thank you! And to my wonderful extended family—Grandma, Papa, and so many others, thank you for supporting and inspiring me. To my partner Sean thank you for reading drafts and listening to ideas, for your encouragement and understanding, for always making life better.

And, finally, a postscript, to my cats: Lennie, you are a perfect writing partner, curling up on my lap and forcing me to sit still for hours. Sophie, your aggressive cuddling and insistence on walking across the keyboard were honestly not super helpful, but I still love you quite a lot.

This Is Our Message

Introduction

IN SEPTEMBER 1983, Beverly LaHaye gave a press conference in Washington, DC, to announce that her four-year-old lobbying group Concerned Women for America (CWA) was about to become a force to be reckoned with in the nation's capital. "This is our message: *The feminists do not speak for all women in America*," she asserted.[1]

From its new home in Washington, LaHaye promised that CWA would continue to fight against the notion that all women supported a feminist agenda, including things like legal abortion, sex education in public schools, and acceptance of nontraditional families. Struggling against the idea that social conservatism was "antiwoman," LaHaye sought to prove that the religious right actually represented the true interests of most American women.

Nationally prominent women like LaHaye played pivotal roles in building and sustaining the modern religious right as it coalesced into a self-conscious national movement in the 1970s and 1980s. They focused predominantly, though not exclusively, on issues designed to appeal to women in their roles as wives and mothers. In doing so, they helped to ensure that gender and sexuality would be the central issues around which the developing movement revolved. They positioned themselves against contemporary feminism and insisted that feminism did not represent the interests of all women. As they sought to make Christian conservatism more appealing to women, the very fact of their leadership demonstrated that the movement was more than just a network of angry white men upset at losing their privilege in the face of gains by feminists and civil rights activists.

White women's grassroots support was critical to the success of conservative movements in the United States. In the decades following the Second World War, conservative women organized opposition to changes in the public schools, including the introduction of sex education, the elimination of mandatory school prayer, and desegregation. They spoke out against perceived communist influence and government overreach in their communities, which they discerned in programs to fluoridate water, to expand mental health services, and to vaccinate children against polio. They rallied other women by organizing coffee meetings in their homes, by publishing and distributing newsletters, and by repurposing their Christmas card lists for the distribution of political literature. They were active in parent-teacher associations and they ran for positions on their local school boards. They famously campaigned as "Goldwater Girls" in 1964. Across the country and across a broad range of issues, right-wing women organized, energized, and helped set the agenda for a developing conservative populism that emphasized small government, "colorblind" meritocracy, and the protection of traditionalist social values.[2]

However, we know a great deal less about the ways in which these movements fundamentally relied on women's leadership at the national level. Where the names of some nationally prominent conservative women are widely recognized, they tend to be understood as lone figures in a movement characterized by male leadership and female grassroots support. These women's individual contributions have been understudied, but more than that, the movement's reliance on women's national leadership has been overlooked.

Focusing on the massive mobilization of conservative evangelicals in the 1970s and 1980s, this book asserts that women's national leadership in the New Christian Right was not anomalous and that it was not accidental. In fact, the national prominence of conservative women was critical to the development and success of the modern religious right. In the particular case of evangelical conservatism, women's national leadership was a function of the movement's development through existing church networks and through a growing evangelical subculture that emphasized women's special authority on issues related to family and sexuality. Understanding women's national leadership in this movement, then, is necessary to understanding the history of the movement and its continued influence.

Postwar Conservatism and the Rise of the New Christian Right

The conservative populism that propelled the New Right in the second half of the twentieth century was grounded in an ideology of meritocratic individualism, which found especially fertile ground in postwar suburbs and among middle-class white suburbanites. In the wake of the Second World War, and in the context of the Cold War, booming American industries moved their operations out of large cities to cut costs and to reduce their vulnerability in case of a Soviet attack. Federal subsidies encouraged industrial decentralization and funded infrastructure including highways and bridges that made suburbanization possible. Homeowners' associations and mortgage brokers (including the federally managed Home Owners' Loan Corporation) enforced policies that encouraged neighborhood segregation and resulted in a cycle that afforded white middle-class families the opportunity to move to suburban enclaves while keeping lower-income, predominantly African American and Latino residents trapped in deteriorating cities whose tax bases were quickly eroding.[3]

Particularly in the Sunbelt South, which benefited disproportionately from the wartime and postwar industrial boom, a developing "homeowner politics" emphasized individual striving and condemned government overreach, but overlooked the federal funding and government policies that made suburbanization possible. At the same time, a "color-blind" approach to race politics countered the forceful racism of segregationists while ignoring the systemic issues that contributed to racial disparities and a widening opportunity gap.[4] During the 1950s and 1960s, suburban homeowners organized to resist taxation and to ensure that their values were reflected in their children's public school curricula. After the Supreme Court ruled school segregation unconstitutional in 1954, these parents also fought against policies that would bus their children to inner-city schools and bring students of color into their neighborhoods. For many, these single-issue campaigns became the foundation of a lasting interest in broader political action on the local, state, and federal levels.[5]

At the center of these concerns lay a particular vision of the white, suburban, middle-class family as the bedrock of American life. The notion of "parents' rights" became a rallying cry for groups increasingly concerned with protecting the autonomy of the nuclear family against government intervention and liberal education models. In the late 1960s and 1970s, various movements on the left began to mount direct challenges to the male-breadwinner model that was implicit in the traditionalists' family ideal. Gender and sexuality became key sites of struggle that stood for broader understandings of national identity and contrasting visions for the future of the nation. During the 1970s in particular, in mass media and political rhetoric, the family became the dominant symbol for anxieties about national military, economic, and social decline. In this context of rapidly changing cultural and political landscapes, conservative opposition to abortion, gay rights, and contemporary feminism helped to define a new right-wing populism that combined free-market economics with an emphasis on social issues, under the expansive rubric of "family values."[6]

Across the country, and particularly in the thriving Sunbelt South, flourishing evangelical ministries were essential in spreading this conservative
vision.[7] In the years following the Second World War, church attendance
across the United States was on the rise, with particularly dramatic and sustained growth in socially and theologically conservative denominations.[8] In
the Sunbelt suburbs, new migrants from the South fused their religious
traditions with a new gospel of wealth that contributed to the development of
"a creative conservatism, animated by free market and family politics, racial
moderation, and a determination to defend the autonomy of their churches,
neighborhoods, and nation."[9] Beginning in the 1970s, the rapid proliferation
of specifically religious political organizations—including Concerned Women
for America, the Moral Majority, and the Heritage Foundation—brought religious reasoning to the center of conservative rhetoric and helped to define
a new emphasis on social issues that would become a dominant force in
conservatives' political ascendancy.

The expansion of evangelical influence during the postwar decades was not
limited to churches. Throughout the last half of the twentieth century, conservative Christians built national networks supported by intensive investment
in educational institutions, print media, and broadcasting. The founding of
National Association of Evangelicals in 1942 fostered a spirit of collaboration
and community building among conservative Christian churches from divergent denominations across the country.[10] This was also the period that saw the
birth of the Christian bookstore, which became ubiquitous in American cities
and towns. The growing availability of conservative Christian magazines,
newsletters, books, and music helped to establish a shared national culture
among far-flung believers, immersing them in a worldview that increasingly
fused Christian faith with right-wing politics. This subculture disseminated the
theology and politics of Christian conservatism to believers across the country
not only in churches and in explicitly political forums but also in Christian educational institutions and media including radio, television, magazines, and
books. Filtered through a growing national network of conservative Christian
ministries and media, religious doctrine and political commitments gradually
became inseparable for a generation of right-leaning Christians struggling to
make sense of their place in a rapidly changing world.[11]

"Ladies, Not Libbers"

The New Christian Right's emphasis on "traditional family values" was in
part a response to political movements on the left—including gay liberation
and second-wave feminism—and in part a rearticulation of long-standing

theological traditions that proclaimed gender hierarchy to be God-given, and the nuclear family to be the essential building block of a healthy nation. These ideals often limited women's contributions within their communities, but women were never only passive recipients of patriarchal theological mandates. Over the centuries, Christian women have continually negotiated subtly shifting theologies of gender and family while also carving out positions of authority for themselves. The history of women's leadership within American Protestantism has been dominated by the figures of the itinerant preacher or missionary, the maternalist reformer, and the Christian wife and mother. These have sometimes been discrete categories, but they have often overlapped with each other and with the political realm. Aimee Semple McPherson, for example, made her name as one of the most famous American evangelists of the 1920s, and often used her celebrity and her multimedia empire to champion political candidates and causes.[12] In the 1970s and 1980s, conservative Protestant women wove together elements of all these precedents—knowingly and unknowingly—as they established new forms of cultural and political authority in their own communities and on the national stage.

During the decades of New Christian Right ascendancy, in the context of a movement centered on defining and preserving traditional gender roles, no ministry headed by a solo female preacher gained national renown. Yet prominent women did emerge within the movement, and they drew on many of the same justifications for their work that had characterized the rhetoric of female evangelical preachers for centuries. Female preachers have long emphasized a special calling from God to justify their authority while also implicitly acknowledging the strangeness of their role. Many insisted on their initial unwillingness to preach and some even narrated experiences of serious illnesses that were cured only when they agreed to follow God's call.[13] These stories invariably underscored that the speaker had wanted to conform to prevailing ideas about women's limited roles in church and society but that God had forcefully compelled her into the public sphere. Similarly, prominent women in the New Christian Right often highlighted their initial trepidation about stepping into either leadership or politics. Nearly all of them related in great detail the prayers to God and conversations with husbands and (male) pastors that tortuously, finally convinced them to take on these responsibilities.

For at least two hundred years, female preachers in the United States have also drawn attention to the particular feminine qualities that made them ideal religious leaders. Drawing on contemporary understandings of women's roles, female preachers in the nineteenth century argued that women's innate morality made them strong religious authorities while their natural affability made them particularly adept at preaching. They also emphasized their marginality as a boon to their authority, drawing in particular on examples of Old Testament prophets and early church martyrs as quintessential outsiders. Similar strategies have deep roots in the history of women's activism. Nineteenth-century reformers and suffragists argued that women's active political engagement would "clean up" corrupt governments and shift diplomatic priorities toward peacemaking.[14] Postwar conservative women asserted that women's status as political outsiders made them ideal reformers and populist visionaries.[15] In the New Christian Right, nationally prominent women emphasized their concerns as mothers and wives in framing their political priorities. They also drew on the notion of conservative women as political outsiders to characterize their goals as noble and family-centered in contrast to the politically motivated machinations of cynical feminists.

Female preachers and political activists provided two templates for women's political leadership in the New Christian Right; traditions of women's lay authority within the church offered another. Despite a pattern of women's preaching stretching back over three centuries, female preachers have always been a small minority among conservative Christian women. Persistent efforts to preserve traditional gender roles in official church hierarchies have tended to limit women's official leadership in these contexts, but have also made room for women's authority in other arenas, particularly as Sunday School teachers, foreign missionaries, and the leaders of Bible study meetings for other women. Women have always made up the majority in American Protestant pews, and their leadership in these arenas was often necessary for churches to run smoothly. Over time, many denominations adopted the general rule that women could serve in positions of leadership as long as they did not claim authority over men of an equal or superior social or economic class.[16]

As evangelical churches experienced explosive growth in the second half of the twentieth century, specific evangelical women's ministries also expanded. Growing evangelical churches began to host targeted ministries for a variety of demographic groups, with women commonly organizing Bible studies, retreats, luncheons, and mentorship programs dedicated to women's interests and needs. These endeavors offered women unique spaces within their churches to organize and lead a wide range of programs and events, though often limited to an emphasis on wifehood and motherhood.

Women's parachurch organizations, unmoored to any specific church, also flourished during this period. Annual women's conferences hosted by denominations and interdenominational groups proliferated, often hosting female authors and speakers who built careers as public figures in these forums. The largest and best known of these groups is the Women's Aglow Fellowship, which was founded in 1967 and grew through the 1970s and 1980s to include annual conventions, a dedicated magazine, and hundreds of local chapters with regular meetings throughout the year. As ethnographer and historian R. Marie Griffith has argued, these spaces have served to educate women in traditionalist gender norms while simultaneously providing opportunities to air grievances, build support networks, and negotiate the boundaries of those norms.[17]

The growth of national women's ministries like Aglow were accompanied by a more general expansion of evangelical women's culture in the second half of the twentieth century. As evangelical ministries proliferated during this period, so too did conferences, books, periodicals, and other products specifically for evangelical women. This development was an outgrowth of evangelical women's church ministries as well as a canny strategy on the part of Christian merchandisers seeking to expand and compete in an increasingly saturated marketplace. Christian publishers led the way, diversifying their catalogues to include a variety of niche genres written by and for laypeople. In particular, editors increasingly sought out women to write on issues related to gender, family, and the home.[18] These books built on the success of growing national women's ministries and offered conservative Christian women an alternative to contemporary feminist communities and ideas. The genre proved profitable for Christian publishers, and the production of evangelical nonfiction written by and for women grew throughout the twentieth century.

These were not the only outlets of evangelical women's culture during this period. In 1978, the evangelical publishing company Fleming H. Revell began distribution of *Today's Christian Woman*, marketed as the "first ever full-sized Christian feature magazine for women."[19] That same year, televangelist Tammy Faye Bakker introduced *Tammy's House Party*, one of the first Christian television programs that catered to a specifically female audience. Some of these developments were directed by men, including the editors at major Christian publishing houses who sought out female authors beginning in the 1950s and launched *Today's Christian Woman* two decades later. But women were also prominent figures in a culture that relied on and promoted women's expertise. Christian celebrities like Dale Evans Rogers and Anita Bryant, authors like Marabel Morgan, and broadcasters like Tammy Faye Bakker played essential roles in shaping the development of an evangelical women's culture that in turn helped to shape the rhetoric and priorities of the broader evangelical movement.

As with women's ministries, these other aspects of Christian women's cultural production during this period served to socialize women into traditionalist gender roles while also providing space for women to negotiate the boundaries of traditionalist gender systems. In publications, broadcasts, discussion groups, and conferences, evangelical women discussed their difficulties conforming to the doctrine of wifely submission, which instructed women to submit to their husbands just as their husbands should submit to God. Prominent evangelical women during this period subtly redefined that doctrine even as they propagated it. By the late twentieth century, many evangelical ministries had moved away from a strict emphasis on submission and toward a doctrine of complementarianism, which asserts that men and women have different but equally important roles and emphasizes their mutual submission to God.[20]

The explosive growth of a national subculture of conservative evangelicals—reading the same books, attending the same conferences, and listening to the same mail-order tapes—had significant consequences for the development of the New Christian Right. It created new kinds of opportunities for men and women to claim authority and national recognition among conservative evangelicals. For women in particular, the expansion of evangelical women's ministries on a new scale and in new media brought expanded opportunities to claim leadership roles in their communities without overstepping the bounds of conservative Christian womanhood. Even more significant, this subculture helped to lay the groundwork for the New Christian Right by establishing new national networks of conservative Christians and by inculcating them in the political assumptions of the developing movement, even in purportedly apolitical spaces.

This ability to reach audiences outside of explicitly political forums was particularly important during a decade in which the bounds of the political realm were hotly contested. The New Left of the 1960s distinguished itself in part through its insistence on the political significance of practically everything. As leftist identity movements proliferated throughout the 1970s, each developed new understandings of the ways in which systems of inequality were perpetuated in everyday encounters and mundane personal choices. Perhaps best captured in the contemporary feminist mantra "the personal is political," the central emphasis of these movements was that systemic oppression persisted not only through formal political mechanisms but also in the family, the workplace, and the home.

At the same time, many Americans resisted the incursion of political rebuke into their everyday lives. The rhetoric of an embattled "Silent Majority," popularized by President Richard Nixon in 1969, captured a mood of alienation from these contemporary social and cultural changes. This language of conservative disaffection was not new to the 1960s, but it bore new resonances in the context of a rapidly shifting political landscape that seemed to draw everyday life into the political realm and to make it increasingly difficult to find refuge from political battlegrounds.

Although conservative movements had been active in the United States across the twentieth century, a new conservative populism mobilized millions in the 1960s and 1970s because of its appeal to a large cadre of people who were not initially interested in political involvement and in fact resented the creeping infringement of politics into their personal affairs. This story is a vital part of the development of modern conservatism, but it is a story that cannot be fully captured by looking only in the archives of political parties and activist groups. Evangelical subculture offers one window into the development of conservative mobilization outside traditional political spaces during a historical moment in which this was especially significant.

Nationally prominent women in these subcultures helped to shape the gender politics of a burgeoning movement. In deciding whether to claim explicitly political roles, they also contributed to a shifting understanding of the relationship between religion, family, and politics in the late twentieth-century United States. Some prominent women actively denied their political involvement while others stepped decisively into the political sphere. Yet all of these women engaged in politically charged debates over issues such as gender roles, reproductive rights, and the role of the government in family life. As authorities within evangelical subcultures, they helped to shape the political priorities of a developing movement, and they were able to reach audiences that were politically engaged as well as those that were not. Their work offers insight into the rise of the New Christian Right in the 1970s and women's complicated roles within it. In particular, their careful choices about when and whether to acknowledge their work as political helped them to maintain their authority in conservative communities without overstepping their bounds as women. These choices helped them to galvanize conservative Christians and to mobilize those who were uncomfortable with contemporary cultural changes but also uneasy about thinking of themselves as political activists.

THIS BOOK TRACES the lives of six nationally prominent conservative women, each of whom exemplifies a larger theme in the history of women's roles within the modern religious right. These chapters are organized roughly chronologically, though with significant overlap, based on a key moment in each woman's life: the publication of Marabel Morgan's breakout advice manual *Total Woman* in 1973, Anita Bryant's anti-gay-rights campaign beginning in

1976, Beverly LaHaye's establishment of CWA in 1979, Tammy Faye Bakker's stardom in the 1980s, Sarah Palin's vice-presidential campaign in 2008 and Michele Bachmann's presidential bid four years later. Each of these women played an important role in shaping the priorities of the modern religious right and in mobilizing other women in support of conservative campaigns. They struggled with how to understand their roles as leaders and how to define their relationship to the political sphere. Their lives and work offer critical insight into the developing gender politics of the religious right and into women's leadership within one of the most vocal and most successful antifeminist movements in American history.

I

Marabel Morgan Defines
"The Total Woman"

IN JANUARY 1978, an article published in the *Washington Post* and syndicated across the country announced that author Marabel Morgan "just may be, without knowing it, the most avant-garde feminist in America today."[1] The statement was unusual and intentionally provocative, aimed squarely at the controversy surrounding this writer of Christian marital and sexual advice. Following from the success of her evangelical marital manuals, Morgan had become a symbol of a developing argument against contemporary feminism and in favor of a new vision of traditionalist gender roles. But while she was more typically portrayed—as the same article put it—as a "pariah of the feminist movement," Morgan consistently insisted that her work had no political intent whatsoever. Instead she maintained that she was no more than a "naïve" housewife who, while agreeing with some basic feminist principles, wanted to make sure that other women could find fulfillment in their domestic and familial roles.[2] For *Washington Post* reporter Sally Quinn, this philosophy marked Morgan as an unintentional "avant-garde feminist" because, as Quinn put it: "Marabel Morgan has left the women's movement behind. Honestly."

The Christian publishing house Fleming H. Revell published Morgan's first and most influential book, *Total Woman*, in 1973. In simple language and an upbeat tone, Morgan explained how she had transformed a disappointing marriage into one that was both exciting and gratifying. She encouraged women to stop nagging their husbands and to focus instead on changing themselves, to adapt to their husbands' needs and then watch how their husbands became more attentive to them in return. She also emphasized the sexual aspects of marriage, encouraging wives to spice up their marital sex lives with arousing costumes, erotic games, and other strategies designed to

break up boring, even sexless, routines. Perhaps most notorious was her suggestion, given during one of her many talk show appearances, that wives try
greeting their husbands at the door wearing nothing but Saran Wrap.[3]

The book attracted millions of readers, but also scores of vocal detractors.
Morgan's critics argued that she promoted cynical manipulation rather than
equitable communication between partners, and they accused her of setting
women back by decades, even centuries.[4] Mass media coverage of her work,
from *Time* magazine to the *Phil Donahue* show, often pitted Morgan against
contemporary feminists, both figuratively and literally. In her talk show
appearances throughout the 1970s and 1980s, Morgan frequently sat opposite guests who represented contemporary feminist groups and who argued
that Morgan's vision of marital relationships was archaic and toxic. In 1974,
Total Woman appeared on the *New York Times* bestseller list with the short
description: "All right, girls—shape up for your better halves (advice to the
unliberated)."[5]

Throughout her career, Morgan has maintained that she had no intention
of making a political statement with her work and that she was surprised by
the political attention she received. Yet in spite of herself, Morgan quickly became a key figure in debates that would shape enduring perceptions of the
feminist movement, the modern religious right, and the relationship between
them. Whether she intended to or not, Morgan made an important political
claim precisely by insisting on her disinterest in political matters and by positioning herself as neither a feminist nor an outright opponent of feminism.
Instead, she represented herself as part of a cohort of ordinary housewives
who neither needed nor railed against the contemporary feminist movement.
In doing so, she ceded the ground of angry activism to her feminist opponents
and added weight to conservative populists' appeals to "normal" Americans,
against the specter of militant atheism, communism, and proliferating social
movements on the left. Even more significantly, Morgan reached a broad community of women who—like herself—did not necessarily consider themselves
politically engaged or even interested in political engagement.

In this sense, reporter Sally Quinn's description of Morgan as an "avant-
garde feminist," however tongue-in-cheek, illustrates exactly the political
framework against which Morgan tried to situate herself. While contemporary feminists battled patriarchy in homes, offices, and mass media across
the country, conservative Christian women in turn began to feel embattled
by feminists whose political language spoke past them and seemed to den-
igrate their most deeply held beliefs. As the women's movement gained
traction in national media, many commentators began to evaluate the work

of prominent women in relation to feminist goals, as either feminist or distinctly not. In this context, Morgan resisted feminist claims to speak for all women, not only by asserting that feminism did not speak for her but also by refusing to be placed on a political spectrum that measured women's public contributions against feminist definitions of women's best interests. In other words, she insisted that she was neither feminist nor antifeminist, even as that neutral ground eroded around her. In this way, she helped to define the New Christian Right's rhetoric of ambivalence toward the political realm and to disseminate its political assumptions about gender and family to large audiences who were not necessarily seeking out political engagement.

From "Cloud Belt" to Sunbelt

In 1970, Marabel Morgan was an upper-middle-class housewife living in Dade County, Florida. She was the mother of two young daughters and the wife of a prominent attorney. She had left behind a difficult childhood in the Ohio "cloud belt"—as she put it—and recently started a new family in sunny Miami.[6] And Marabel Morgan was miserable.

Three decades earlier, Marabel Hawk had been a small girl living in Mansfield, Ohio.[7] By 1942, when Marabel was six years old, her father had left and her mother was remarried, to a man whom Marabel describes as her "wonderful, beloved daddy."[8] When I interviewed her at her home in 2012, Morgan told me in more detail than her books reveal that her home life during this time was never stable. Within two years, Marabel's mother had initiated divorce proceedings against her second husband, based in part on the advice of a Ouija board. The divorce was never completed and Marabel's stepfather died in 1950 when Marabel was in the ninth grade. In the interim, her mother's mental health deteriorated: "I came home from school one day in the third grade and all the blinds were pulled down and she had gone upstairs to bed. She wouldn't come down. She stayed upstairs for six years," until the day that Marabel's stepfather died.[9]

In high school, Marabel won a scholarship to Ohio University in Athens, about 140 miles away, but her mother would not allow her to accept it, demanding instead that Marabel—her only child—stay to care for her. Marabel gave up the scholarship but quickly decided that she needed to leave Mansfield and attend college after all. She went to work at a local beauty shop, where she spent four years saving the $900 that she needed for a single year's tuition at Ohio State University, located in Columbus, just seventy miles from her hometown. Morgan would later say that it was during this time that she gained her independence.

Marabel had grown up with little religious influence in her life aside from her mother's and an aunt's interest in séances and "the occult," and it was during her time as a beautician that she became a "born-again" Christian. In the retrospective language of evangelical Protestantism, she later described searching for something that would make sense of her life and bring her out of a place of "spiritual darkness." In our 2012 interview, she recalled: "I asked all of my customers, 'What do you believe?' Nobody seemed to believe anything, except after a couple of years this wonderful lady came into the beauty shop. . . . She said, 'Oh honey, it's so simple. God loves you.' I'd never heard that." The woman bought Marabel a Bible and began taking her to Sunday services and Wednesday prayer meetings. Marabel later reminisced: "My life had been marching along in the dark, literally, and I was on His path, the path of light. It changed my life."[10]

The conversion narrative is a central genre in evangelical Protestant life, affirming each believer's belonging in both earthly and otherworldly communities.[11] Told and retold in church meetings, Bible studies, and proselytizing attempts, the conversion story structures the individual's identity and sense of belonging while also reaffirming the central assumptions of the faith community. Morgan's desperate searching for God and her grateful conversion by a true believer affirm the project of evangelism itself, not as an intrusion upon people with their own systems of belief but as a gift to those who do not know God and who must want to, whether they realize it or not.

Morgan's particular narration of her own life history also speaks to American evangelicals' sense of place in the shifting religious landscape of the 1960s and 1970s. Morgan's experience of a world made up of a salvific true believer, a handful of desperately sad occultists, and a large group of people who, like her, had nothing to believe in was not only one story told in isolation but rather a reflection of a dominant evangelical narrative about a nation awash in secularism and sinister new religious movements. Such perspectives lay at the heart of the evangelical project and contributed a central tenet of the New Christian Right: that particular conservative theologies could form the basis of national stability, both in terms of collective morality and individual emotional health.

Marabel was twenty-four when she enrolled at Ohio State University, taking a year of home economics and interior design before her funds were spent. During spring break, she visited an aunt in Fort Lauderdale where she experienced the darkness-into-light metaphor of her conversion experience in a very literal sense: "Having lived in Ohio, which was in the cloud belt, I was depressed most of my youth. When I hit the sun and the beach I thought, 'Oh, this is heaven.'"[12] She made friends with a student at a local Bible college, a type of institution that Marabel had never heard of but that appealed to her desires to explore her new faith and to stay in the Sunshine State. The following year, she moved to south Florida and enrolled in Florida Bible College (FBC), where she joined the choir and worked for the local chapter of Campus Crusade for Christ, an organization founded in 1951 to support Christian college students and to evangelize on college campuses. When Morgan joined in 1960, Campus Crusade for Christ was entering a period of explosive growth. By 1970, it would be one of the most significant parachurch organizations of the twentieth century, reaching thousands of college students each year with its particular brand of evangelical Christianity and anticommunist politics.[13]

It was also at FBC that Marabel Hawk met Corabel Morgan, the popular choir director who offered informal counseling to girls at the school. They became close, and soon Corabel was writing to her son Charlie—who was away at Wheaton College in Illinois—about this "nice little girl" whom he should get to know. According to Marabel, Charlie made a "mental note" to resist his mother's matchmaking efforts, but the two quickly hit it off when he returned to Miami over a school break. Within a year, Charlie had enrolled in law school at the University of Miami and within two years, in 1964, the couple was married.[14]

Total Woman Seeks Perfect Marriage

Marabel had high hopes for a "perfect marriage," although she later admitted that as a result of her own childhood experiences, her "knowledge of what that entailed was nil." She expected an "all-American Cinderella story" in which "marriage was ruffly curtains at the kitchen window, strawberries for breakfast, and lovin' all the time." Yet within a few years, Morgan realized that she and her husband were no longer laughing, or even really speaking with one another. In between occasional spats of bickering, their relationship was merely "polite." And so, according to Morgan, she resolved to change. "Being mediocre in any area of life never appealed to me, and least of all, in marriage," she later wrote; "I didn't want a marginal marriage; I wanted the best."[15]

Morgan traced these problems, in part, to her own past. "My mother . . . nagged one of [her husbands] to death, literally," she told me, "It was all I'd ever known." When Morgan came across a passage in the Bible that instructed her to "do all things decently and orderly," she reflected that she "had never seen anything like that, decent and orderly. It was chaos in my life."[16] She also considered the period of independence between leaving her mother's house and setting up her own family home to be a part of the problem. Although she valued this experience, she said, it became a source of conflict when she began to have to share decision making with another adult rather than being the sole director of her own affairs: "For nine years I had worked before I was married at 28. I had been a hairdresser. I was a strong independent woman. And I was not about to go into a marriage with a man telling me what to do. Instead, I was telling him what to do."[17] As Morgan tells it, she soon learned the error of her ways. At the same time that contemporary feminists publicly encouraged "strong independent women" to work toward gender parity in the home, Morgan would insist that someone had to take charge in the marital relationship. Drawing on her own experiences to bolster the theological contention that "God planned for woman to be under her husband's rule," Morgan would come to assert that a "Total Woman" was ideally a submissive wife.[18]

As she developed this philosophy, Morgan read everything that she could about marriage, relationships, and human psychology. She later reported: "I read until I felt cross-eyed at night." She "took self-improvement classes" and read marriage manuals alongside her Bible.[19] According to her often-repeated account, she applied the principles that she found in these wide-ranging texts, and she began to change. She nagged Charlie less and complimented him more. She attempted to follow scriptural advice to "respect and honor [her] husband."[20] And according to Marabel, Charlie responded almost immediately. He became more open to Marabel's suggestions and he was more affectionate toward her, both at home and in public. Their friends began to notice, and soon Marabel was sharing her tips with a group of girlfriends who began to meet in her living room on a regular basis.

These girlfriends told others, and demand grew. Soon Morgan was teaching her "Total Woman" classes in living rooms around Miami, charging fifteen dollars in tuition for eight hours of instruction.[21] Morgan recalls that she and her friends came up with the name of the course as a tongue-in-cheek reference to Total cereal: "All my friends were on it [the task of naming the course], and we decided we'll call it the Total Woman, which was so funny because there was a breakfast cereal then called Total. We said that's what it encapsulates, what we're trying to say."[22]

The reference is not insignificant. Total cereal was marketed at the time as a nutritional powerhouse that could help solve remarkably gendered problems in the consumer's life. A 1970 print advertisement for the brand featured an attractive white woman with unrealistically skinny arms washing a window above the headline: "Keep up with the house while you keep down your weight."[23] Another advertisement in the same series featured a slim (though not unreasonably slim) white man swinging a golf club above the headline: "Keep up your game while you keep down your weight."[24] The "Total woman" of the cereal advertisement, as Morgan realized, was not unlike the "Total Woman" that the advice author imagined: beautiful, hardworking, and focused on domestic duty. Though her ideas may seem retrograde to modern readers thinking through the lens of contemporary gender politics, this example illustrates that Morgan was informed by a much larger cultural context in which such representations of women were the overwhelming norm.[25]

Morgan's attraction to the idea of "totality" also had roots in evangelical theology, wherein a person is said to be made whole by his or her relationship to God. Indeed, Morgan's *Total Woman* offered a dual narrative of conversion: from despondent nag to satisfied wife on one hand, and from unhappy sinner to devoted (or more devoted) Christian believer on the other. In our interview, Morgan stated firmly that non-Christian women could benefit from the "Total Woman" course, though she also recognized the abundance of Christian language in the book: "I have some Jewish friends, for instance, who love the book, which was amazing to me because I have a lot about Jesus in there. They say, 'We just gloss over that part and do the principles.'" Nonetheless, Morgan wrote her books in an overarching evangelical language that assumed readers would at least accept the Bible as a reasonable source of wisdom and Jesus as a moral role model. Similar assumptions were also apparent in loaded rhetorical questions such as: "If you've lost the love for your husband, why not ask God to restore it?"[26]

Morgan also ended each of her books by asking readers to make or renew a commitment to God, a move that mirrored the traditional "altar call" at the end of evangelical revivals.[27] In *Total Woman*, Morgan's central self-improvement metaphor asked each reader to imagine herself as a house, to introspectively straighten out her inner life and improve her "curb appeal" through bubble baths and the application of various beauty regimens. In the penultimate chapter, Morgan drew peripheral religious themes to the center of her message: "So far in this book, we've taken your old house, the fragmented you, and painted the outside . . . and done some redecorating," she wrote, "All we need now is the power. Without a power source for heat, for light, for life, your shell is nothing more than a glorified outhouse." She spent the remainder of this chapter narrating her own conversion experience as a model for readers, describing God as "the world's greatest power" who, in her own life, had "turned on all the lights, brighter than I had ever seen."[28] In our interview, Morgan recalled that this metaphor was an effective evangelistic tool in "Total Woman" classes, in which she would draw "a cute little outhouse" on a flip chart to illustrate her point: "That seemed to strike a nerve, the picture of a glorified outhouse, doing all these things but without the power. A lot of women trusted the Lord."[29] This last sentence also recalls the rhetoric of the evangelical revival, in which the language of "trusting the Lord" is used to describe experiences of conversion and recommitment that ideally occur at the end of the meeting. Marital and spiritual revival were both central goals of the Total Woman program.

Total Woman, Inc.

Among Morgan's first pupils in her nascent Total Woman classes were twelve wives of Miami Dolphins football players, whom Morgan knew because her husband's law firm represented some members of the team. In 1972, a year before *Total Woman* was published, when the Dolphins became the first National Football League (NFL) team to complete the regular and playoff seasons undefeated and win the Super Bowl, Morgan gained some playful local acclaim. "People were saying, 'It's because their women are 'Total Women.' They've made these men into big gladiators and they're just going out and trouncing everyone in sight,'" Morgan recalled. "Of course, I knew it was because of [head coach] Don Shula, but it was fun to have people say this."[30]

Another prominent student of Morgan's early classes was the Top-40 singer and evangelical author Anita Bryant, who was among the first to insist that Morgan make a book out of her ideas. Soon after, Bryant introduced Morgan to her publisher at Fleming H. Revell.[31] In 1973, the company produced a small run of five thousand copies of *Total Woman*. The 188-page book of marital advice comprised personal anecdotes and religious references alongside quotations from news stories and Western canon authors ranging from William Shakespeare to Robert Louis Stevenson.[32] As she had done in her workshops, Morgan began the book with what would become a standard retelling of her own marital experience, including her early disappointment and her resolution to make her marriage everything that she had wanted it to be.[33] She drew heavily on personal experience throughout the book, sharing anecdotes from her own marriage and from the lives of former Total Woman pupils. She also borrowed widely from other self-help literature, including evangelical marital and parenting advice by evangelical luminaries Tim LaHaye and James Dobson, alongside bestselling secular advice manuals like *How to Win Friends and Influence People*.[34]

As an author, Morgan took pains to identify herself with her readers, both by opening up about her own marital difficulties and by acknowledging that her advice might be challenging for readers to follow, at least at first. "I can hear you howl," she wrote in *Total Woman*, after encouraging wives to greet their work-weary husbands at the door in sexy costumes: "'She's got to be kidding. My husband's not the type, and besides, we've been married twenty-one years!'" She assured readers that she had been skeptical, too, but that she had also been at her wits' end and willing to try anything. She related the stories of pupils whose reluctance turned to jubilation when they experienced the results of the Total Woman method, including one Southern Baptist woman whose husband came home, "took one look" at his wife dressed in nothing but "black mesh stockings, high heels, and an apron," and shouted: "'Praise the Lord!'" Said Morgan: "He was flabbergasted, but extremely pleased. He could hardly eat his dinner!"[35]

Morgan's advice was accessible and easy to apply; she combined chatty prose with short, numbered lists—often alliterative—and ended each section of the book with "assignments" for her readers, taken from the Total Woman curriculum. Most famously, she encouraged wives to follow the "Four A's" with regard to their husbands: to accept him, admire him, adapt to him, and appreciate him.[36] At the end of the section that introduced these concepts, Morgan included one assignment to ease her readers into each of the four A's. To practice accepting their husbands, for example, wives were to "write out two lists—one of his faults and one of his virtues," and then "Take a long, hard look at his faults and then throw the list away; don't ever dwell on them again. Think only of his virtues." The second list wives could keep, in case they needed inspiration for the second assignment: "Admire your husband everyday" in order to "Put his tattered ego back together again at the end of each day."[37]

Morgan was frequently concerned with husbands' "tattered egos," produced by difficult work environments and worsened by wives' nagging. Downtrodden husbands, according to Morgan, were a common cause of unhappy marriages and even marital infidelity. "Indifference hurts him more than anything," Morgan counseled in a chapter called "Super Sex."[38] She advised: "Don't deprive your husband of sex when he acts like a bear. He may be tired when he comes home tonight. He needs to be pampered, loved, and restored. Fill up his tummy with food; soothe away his frustrations with sex. Lovemaking comforts a man. It can comfort you, too."[39]

Morgan's critics frequently took up statements like these as evidence of a pathological emphasis on men's needs that ignored women's rights in the marital relationship. "One major reason for the hostility toward Marabel Morgan," explained a *Time* magazine reporter in 1977, "is the belief that she preaches a return to those days of unfairness and unequality [sic]."[40] However, this concern with the pressures imposed by the modern workplace can also offer insight into some women's disinterest in the promises of the contemporary feminist movement. If liberal feminists prioritized entry into the job market on an equal footing with men, some women preferred a system that at least ideally kept them out of the workaday world that seemed to cause their husbands so much stress.[41]

Anticipating and responding to another major strand of criticism, Morgan insisted that all things must be done out of sincere love and not for the purpose of manipulating one's husband. In her second book, *Total Joy*, Morgan wrote: "Adapting involves giving. Adapting is not giving for the sake of getting; that's *manipulation*."[42] Emphasizing that a Total Woman had to commit to a total change in attitude, Morgan gave both practical and ethical reasons for women to "be sincere" in their decision to accept, appreciate, admire, and adapt to their husbands. In the first place, Morgan asserted that manipulation simply wouldn't work: "Don't you know when you're being manipulated? So does your husband," she wrote in *Total Joy*.[43] And in *Total Woman*: "His [your husband's] love cannot be aroused by something contrived by a manipulative wife."[44] She also drew on deeper moral and psychological arguments, asserting that Jesus exhorted believers "to give 100 percent with no thought of what you'll receive in return." She also quoted a psychologist who compared the Total Woman concept of adaptation to the principle of the Golden Rule, saying: "What a privilege and advantage it is to be the one to *initiate* a cycle of behavior. This is for strong and honest women, not for weak, conniving, manipulating, hostile, or defiant ones."[45]

Still, Morgan would not have been much of a self-help author if she did not promise benefits to readers who followed her system. After sharing students' success stories, including improved communication with their husbands, more exciting sex lives, and the occasional material gift, Morgan encouraged her readers to give the Total Woman principles a try: "Your husband will love it too. And he will love you for wanting to please him. When his need for an attractive and available wife is met, he'll be so grateful that he will begin to meet your needs. Try it tonight!"[46]

Millions of women did. Within a year of *Total Woman's* publication, the Revell Company contracted Pocketbook Paperbacks to produce a much larger run of the book, and by the end of 1974, *Total Woman* had sold over three million copies, or six hundred times the number of books that Revell had initially printed.[47] The book became a bestseller and Marabel Morgan became a sensation. She received national and international press attention in Christian and mass-market media, including a cover story in *Time* magazine in 1977.[48] She was featured on the popular game show "To Tell the Truth" and she made several appearances on television talk shows ranging from the televangelical *PTL Club* to network programs including *Phil Donahue* and *Dinah* (hosted by singer and actress Dinah Shore).[49]

As the book gained popularity, Morgan was overwhelmed with phone calls and letters from readers as well as requests for Total Woman workshops. When she began to get so much mail that she could not answer it herself, she enlisted a group of friends to get together at her father-in-law's warehouse twice a week to help her respond. Eventually, Charlie drew up the legal paperwork to found Total Woman, Inc. and Marabel moved her base of operations to a dedicated downtown office. There she trained dozens of teachers, who offered Total Woman courses across the country. And though it never again led to an undefeated season, football teams including the Dallas Cowboys and the Green Bay Packers invited Total Woman teachers to present the course to their players' wives.[50]

Over the next twelve years, Morgan published three more books: *Total Joy* in 1976, a *Total Woman Cookbook* in 1980, and *The Electric Woman* in 1985. Each expanded on the ideas put forward in *Total Woman*. *Total Joy* closely paralleled the original book, with Christian marital advice as its central theme. *The Electric Woman* focused less closely marriage and more broadly on general self-improvement and stress relief. *The Total Woman Cookbook* offered recipes and advice geared at romance and family bonding. Though none of these sequels enjoyed the explosive success of the original, Morgan and her Total Woman concept continued to receive widespread media coverage, and Morgan remained a prominent—and controversial—cultural figure for over a decade. She says that she stopped writing after 1985 because she felt that she had said all she had to say and that God was no longer inspiring her to write. "I felt like with *Total Woman*, I was being pushed," she recalled, "and the ideas were just coming. In *Total Joy*, I felt like I was just trying to put it together." Later, she tried to establish an "Electric Woman" course to follow her third book, but, she told me: "Here again it was I [and not God], trying to make it fly."[51]

"The Submission Part was the Real Kicker"

For many observers, especially those outside of conservative evangelical circles, the most jarring part of Morgan's work was her promotion of the doctrine that wives should be submissive to husbands. Yet even as she advocated this conservative theology, she also presented readers with a subtly updated interpretation. In particular, her emphasis on women's agency within submission distinguished *Total Woman* from earlier Christian marriage manuals written overwhelmingly by men.

Morgan very rarely used the term "submission" although this was the term—taken from the Bible—that was most commonly associated with contemporary conservative churches' teaching on gender.[52] Instead, she spoke primarily about "adapting" to a husband's needs and desires. Morgan recalled later that she wanted to emphasize that submission could be a woman's choice, that it did not have to mean "subservience" or inferiority. She acknowledged, though, that this was "a hard distinction" to "put across," especially to audiences not well versed in the subtleties of conservative theologies and shifting approaches to gender roles. Even for her usually like-minded pupils, Morgan noted, "The submission part was the real kicker." "I tried to ease that into my class," she recalled; "I would talk about sex and fun things and then ease into it."[53] Morgan repeatedly emphasized in her books and in interviews that submission was—and even had to be—a woman's choice. "A Total Woman is not a slave," she wrote in her debut book. "She graciously chooses to adapt to her husband's way."[54]

In the same book, Morgan also anticipated that some readers might respond indignantly to the notion of adaptation: "You may think, 'That's not fair. I have my rights. Why shouldn't he adapt to my way first, and then maybe I'll consider doing something for him?'" To those readers, she responded: "I have seen many couples try this new arrangement, unsuccessfully." Their failure, according to Morgan, was in ignoring God's "originally ordained [plan for] marriage," in which men and women, "although equal in status, are different in function."[55] Though Morgan did not name the feminist movement, its specter lurked in her references to "new" arrangements and women's insistence on their own "rights."

At the same time, her conclusion, which emphasized a version of gender equality even within the patriarchal marriage relationship contributed to a newly emerging softening of the submission doctrine and a transition toward complementarianism, with its emphasis on men's and women's different but equal roles in society, and their mutual submission under God.[56] Morgan's work is an early example of this transition, displaying elements of both systems and demonstrating the overlap between them. Morgan's insistence on women's adaptation to their husbands exemplified the older approach to submission doctrine, but Morgan also asserted that equality rather than submission should rule gender relationships outside of the family: "Please note that I did not say a woman is inferior to man, or even that a woman should be subservient to all men, but that a wife should be under her own husband's leadership."[57]

To be sure, Morgan's vision for gender equality was a far cry from contemporary feminist understandings of the same concept, yet this language is significant for what it demonstrates about shifting understandings of traditional gender roles in conservative Christian communities in the years leading up to the New Christian Right's ascendancy. In response to contemporary changes in American culture influenced by the feminist movement, and as a result of the growing number of prominent Christian women contributing to these conversations conservative evangelical gender ideologies were in flux at the very moment that the politics of "family values" were being defined around a purportedly unchanging ideal of traditional family roles.

By the time she wrote her second book, Morgan was even more circumspect about the principle of adaptation. Emphasizing compromise as the default mode for couples, she situated submission less as an overarching characteristic of the marriage relationship and more as a pragmatic last resort. She also noted that her model of adaptation was not the only choice for couples: "If you and your husband have another way of dealing with problems that can't be resolved by compromise, that's great. I've heard some couples agree to use other methods, such as flipping a coin, or alternating the final decision between spouses each time they disagree."

Her frustration with her critics became palpable in her next sentence, however, and Morgan made it clear that these strategies were not equal to God's own plan for marriage: "If such methods as 'keeping score' or a 'game of chance' work for you, then there's no problem anyway. All your potential conflicts will be resolved at the Compromise Level. You can skip the rest of this chapter and go straight to Sex 301."[58] Indeed, Morgan made it clear that while she was not arguing for women's subservience, neither did she believe in these modern arrangements: "Men and women, although equal in status, are different in function. God ordained man to be the head of the family, its president, and his wife to be the executive vice-president," she wrote. "Every organization has a leader and the family unit is no exception. There is no way you can alter or improve on this arrangement."[59] Likely in response to earlier critiques of *Total Woman*, Morgan took an almost defensive tone in *Total Joy* when addressing the idea of submission. Conceding that couples were free to choose any system that worked well for them and underscoring women's authority in the home (as "executive vice-president"), she insisted that the best model for a happy marriage was the only one that God had ordained: a system of male headship based in mutual respect.

In many ways, *Total Woman* represented a reiteration of ideas that had been presented in secular and religious marital manuals over the past several decades. However, its popularity at this particular moment in American history struck a chord with feminists who saw in the book everything that they opposed. At the same time, it also resonated with a population of predominantly conservative, predominantly religious women who felt alienated from a feminist movement that did not seem to make room for their beliefs

or lifestyles. That the book and its sequels were embroiled in controversy despite their author's protestations is indicative of the shifting political landscape into which they were published. Issues of family, sexuality, and gender
were quickly becoming inextricably politically charged as they were linked to
broader public conversations about equality, citizenship, and national identity.
If Morgan found it difficult to stake out an apolitical position on gender and
family in 1973, by the end of the decade it would be nearly impossible to do so.

Even in the mid-1970s, not all conservative Christian women adopted the
same apolitical stance that Morgan chose. Helen Andelin authored her own
Christian marital advice manual, *Fascinating Womanhood*, in 1963. A decade
later she fully embraced the political significance of her work. In December
1975, the *Los Angeles Times* reported that Andelin "claims credit for launching"
a Christian "counterfeminist movement" based on her book and its associated
course.[60] Six months earlier, the *New York Times* had published an article on
Morgan and Andelin that drew heavily on interviews with alumni of the Total
Woman and Fascinating Womanhood courses. While some former students
seemed to support Andelin's antipathy toward the feminist movement (like
Helen Green of California who asserted that "women's liberation has cut men
to pieces"), others argued that "all the Total Woman course is about is happiness in marriage; it is not opposed to and is not a reaction against women's
liberation."[61] For these women, Morgan's insistence on the apolitical nature of
her work was part of what made her concept attractive. *Total Woman* was full
of potentially politically charged concepts, but they were made less objection-
able (for some readers) in their presentation as timeless principles rather than
political arguments. In this way, avowedly apolitical work like Morgan's helped
to develop the assumptions that would undergird the rise of the New Christian
Right and to disseminate these assumptions far beyond the sphere of already
engaged political activists.

Regardless of whether Morgan or her readers wanted to engage in these
political debates, books like *Total Woman* set precedents for women's voices
to shape the politics of gender in conservative Christian communities, both
from explicitly political and purportedly apolitical vantage points. At the same
time, the language that Morgan and others like her used to make sense of
their roles also contributed to women's historical invisibility as leaders of this
movement. Morgan refused to be counted among the political voices speaking
out on issues of gender and family in the early 1970s. Later in the decade, even
women who took on explicitly political campaigns, like Morgan's friend Anita
Bryant, were circumspect in their identification with the political sphere and
reluctant to see themselves as political leaders. In some ways, this reluctance
facilitated feminist movement claims to speak for women writ large. It also

allowed some conservative evangelical women to claim public political roles that did not fundamentally challenge accepted notions about women's proper place in their communities. More broadly, it added weight to Christian Right claims to represent a "normal majority" against a small group of militants who wanted to change—and potentially destroy—the American nation. As feminists and conservative Christians struggled over competing claims to represent a majority constituency against a group of fringe radicals, books like Morgan's helped to make women's voices simultaneously indispensable and largely invisible in the latter camp.

Total Womanhood in a Community of Women

Morgan's success was due in part to her accessible style, her promises of marital happiness, and the sex appeal of her concept.[62] But this success also came at the convergence of three broad cultural trends: the expansive growth of a supposedly apolitical evangelical women's culture, the proliferation of self-help literature in secular and religious contexts, and the growing influence of feminism and contemporary sexual revolutions. In each of these areas, Morgan entered into existing conversations in unexpected and significant ways, including her simultaneous promotion and renegotiation of conservative gender ideologies, her refusal to be marked as either feminist or antifeminist, and her commingling of Christian conservatism and sexual experimentation. In these ways, Morgan's work presented challenges to contemporary cultural categories, demonstrating how even avowedly apolitical conversations about sex and gender helped to frame emerging political rhetoric on these issues.

Conservative Christian women in the 1970s structured a new public authority for themselves around issues of sex and gender—both as proponents of a more modern openness about these topics and as opponents of an increasingly sexualized and permissive culture in which gender distinctions were allegedly eroding. They did so in part through the creation of a specific women's culture within a growing evangelical subculture, making room for women to renegotiate among themselves the bounds of traditional gender roles and the exact meaning of traditional family values. During this decade, as evangelical subcultures expanded nationally, conservative Christian women developed their own niches—in media, courses, and conferences that spanned local and national contexts. They drew on the tradition of evangelical women's ministries—separate spaces within churches where women gathered to minister to other women—and they borrowed from secular women's cultures to produce advice literature, magazines, television shows, and other forums designed especially for Christian women.

In Christian publishing in particular, women began to make inroads in the postwar decades. Though Christian women had long been the primary consumers of Christian literature, including both fiction and nonfiction, it was not until the postwar period that major Christian publishing houses began to recognize the potential profitability of producing books by and for Christian women on a large scale.[63] The Fleming H. Revell Company was a pioneer in this field, publishing books by Marabel Morgan and Anita Bryant as well as other prominent Christian women including Beverly LaHaye, Dale Evans Rogers, and the faith-healing preacher Kathryn Kuhlman. Beginning in the 1950s, in the context of increasing competition from new and growing rivals, Revell sought to expand its reach by producing more books for lay-people. This included a particular focus on courting women authors to write on issues related to gender, family, and sexuality. During the 1940s, fewer than 15 percent of the books published by Revell bore a female author's name. By the 1980s, 34 percent of Revell's books were authored by women and another 11.5 percent by women and men writing together. These changes are displayed in the following chart.[64]

Revell Publications by Gender of
Author(s), 1940–1989

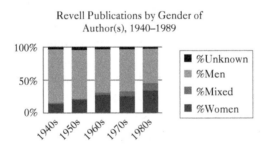

In my interview with Bruce Barbour, an executive editor at Revell during the 1970s and 1980s, Barbour traced this development in Christian publishing to an expansion of women's cultural authority in conservative evangelical communities more broadly, beginning in the 1960s. As evangelical women's conferences, classes, and associations became more common, and as a co-terie of evangelical women—including Marabel Morgan, Anita Bryant, and Beverly LaHaye—gained celebrity within these contexts, it became possible for evangelical publishers to seek out more female authors and to further con-tribute to the development of evangelical women's newfound national cultural authority, albeit within a limited scope. "From a publishing perspective, the thread was that the women were allowed, if you will, by conservative pastors and by the general community of leaders to take a leadership role, a speaking role," Barbour told me, "but only if they spoke to women."[65] In this way, the expanding national subculture of evangelical women rested on the same logic that had structured evangelical women's authority in local congregations and foreign missions since at least the nineteenth century. Evangelical theology lauded women's expertise in the domestic sphere and granted them authority to speak as experts as long as they ministered to other women, to children, and in some cases on foreign mission fields, but did not claim authority over adult men of a socioeconomic status equal or higher to their own.

For evangelical women making a name for themselves in the second half of the twentieth century, the tradition of women ministering to other women on issues related to gender, family, and sexuality was especially salient. The postwar fascination with the domestic sphere dovetailed with developing anxieties about the decline of the American family to make these especially popular topics in secular and Christian mass media alike. As Bruce Barbour suggests, conservative Christian women began to build a subcultural niche around their authority on these topics even before Christian publishers and broadcasters widely acknowledged and promulgated the genre. In the early 1960s, for example, Mormon housewife Helen Andelin, mentioned above, sought to improve a dreary marriage in much the same way that Marabel Morgan would do a decade later. Reading widely in marital advice and scripture, she produced *Fascinating Womanhood*, based in large part on a series of pamphlets produced by the Psychological Press in the 1920s and 1930s.[66] Like Morgan and her Total Woman concept, Andelin fashioned Fascinating Womanhood into both a book and a class, and she reached hundreds of thousands of devotees primarily through word-of-mouth promotion. Unlike Morgan, however, Andelin could not find a publisher for her work and had to self-publish from 1963 until Bantam finally picked up the book in 1980.[67]

Though its success came more slowly than that of *Total Woman*, Andelin's *Fascinating Womanhood* set the stage for Morgan's later work by helping to both build and demonstrate the existence of a market for Christian marital advice written by and for women. When Morgan wrote *Total Woman* in the early 1970s, she benefited from an existing national community of conservative Christian women that helped to promote her book across the country. She was able to find a publisher willing and even eager to gamble on her success based in part on the precedents set by books like *Fascinating Womanhood* and by popular autobiographical advice books written by Christian celebrities like Anita Bryant and Dale Evans Rogers.

When *Total Woman* appeared in 1973, it entered into a newly established and still rapidly expanding Christian women's subculture. *Total Woman* experienced unprecedented crossover success in the secular and Christian markets, making it an especially notable and influential product of that subculture, even as its success relied on these established networks. Morgan and her book received relatively little press attention when *Total Woman* was first released in 1973, garnering more notice late in 1974, after it had been announced as the bestselling nonfiction book of that year. Much of its early success came from women recommending the book to other women, or as *Time* later put it, "a housewives' grapevine."[68] Producing nearly three million sales in the book's first year on the market, this "grapevine" was not only an informal network of Morgan's friends and relatives but also a national community of evangelical women connected through interdenominational classes, national conferences, and other parachurch organizations.

In the context of their socially and theologically conservative communities, these spaces of evangelical women's subculture had the potential to be both empowering and disempowering for the women who participated in them. In particular, conservative evangelical women's groups policed the boundaries of appropriate femininity even as they gave women the opportunity to subtly renegotiate those bounds. The doctrine of wifely submission, central in Morgan's work, offers a particularly striking example: while conservative churches have maintained that biblical mandates (including those related to gender) are unchanging and not subject to cultural standards, most churches have gradually shifted over the past four decades from a strict emphasis on gender hierarchy to an emphasis on husbands' and wives' mutual submission under God.[69]

The Total Woman Is O.K.

Secular self-help was also a growth industry in the late 1960s and early 1970s. Perhaps the most famous example, Dr. Thomas A. Harris's *I'm O.K., You're O.K.*, was first published in 1969 but it did not appear on the *New York Times* bestseller list until April 1972. Three months later, Harper and Row sold the paperback rights to the book for a record $1,000,000, and over the next sixteen months this "lay man's guide to self-analysis" spent a total of seventy weeks on the bestseller list.[70] Alongside it during these years were other emerging classics of the self-help genre, variously emphasizing interpersonal relationships, productivity, and diet. Between 1973 and 1974 alone, prominent examples included *How to Be Your Own Best Friend, You Can Profit from a Monetary Crisis*, and *The Memory Book*, which each spent well over thirty weeks on the list.[71] When Vidal and Beverly Sassoon's *A Year of Beauty and Health* appeared on the list in 1976—preceded by *The Save Your Life Diet* in 1975, *Dr. Atkins' Diet Revolution* in 1972, and *The Doctor's Quick Weight-Loss Diet* in 1968—the *New York Times* editorial staff offered the terse description: "Another how-to exercise, diet, etc., book."[72] Alex Comfort's groundbreaking *Joy of Sex* was described in 1974 as "sophisticated eroticism, but basically just another how-to."[73]

Marabel Morgan's reluctance to embrace a political identity was related to her particular religious and political contexts, but it is also consistent with the self-help genre, which has its own complex relationship with the political realm. The 1970s are sometimes castigated as the "'Me' Decade," a period of intense self-focus and individualism in comparison to an emphasis on collective social change in the 1960s.[74] The expansive proliferation of self-help literature and pop psychology during the 1970s offers some support for this interpretation. But self-help literature often presents its own promises of sweeping social change, however subtle, and however couched in an emphasis on the responsibility of individuals.[75] In the context of a developing late-twentieth-century conservatism that deployed the language of personal responsibility against leftist rights-based movements and government welfare spending alike, self-help manuals like Morgan's were well situated to contribute to a particular politics of gender and family that placed responsible individuals and healthy, normative families at the center of a stable nation.

Morgan's advice emphasized quintessentially personal problems and offered solutions that rested in individual action, but she also considered marriage and family in their broader social contexts. Following a discussion of God's vision for gender roles within marriage, for example, Morgan implied a widespread contemporary failure to adhere to those roles: "The evidence is all too clearly visible. In some cities there are now more people getting divorced each day than getting married." Total Women, Morgan suggested, had the power not only to revitalize their own marriages and socialize their own families but also to revive the institution of marriage itself, to curb the soaring divorce rate, and to save the American family by returning en masse to "God's way" for marriage.[76]

Yet despite this attention to broad social problems, it is unsurprising that Morgan—along with many other authors of marital self-help literature—understood this project to be wholly apolitical. The idea that the domestic and political spheres are completely separate from one another has deep roots in Euro-American culture. In the eighteenth century, as the Industrial Revolution moved paid labor out of the home and into separate workplaces, the domestic sphere gained new significance as a refuge from worldly concerns. Later, the Victorian "Cult of Domesticity" amplified this idea, elevating the home to the status of semi-sacred space.[77]

In the mid-twentieth century, as Morgan was growing up, the home was again receiving special attention as a bulwark not only against politics writ large but also against the specter of communism in particular.[78] In mass culture and political rhetoric alike, the suburban, patriarchal, nuclear family emerged as a powerful symbol of the "American Way of Life." Profoundly steeped in unspoken assumptions about class, race, and gender, postwar depictions of ideal family life were arguably most powerful in the ways in which they denied class barriers, ignored racial inequalities, and naturalized a particular model of gender relations that centered on the male breadwinner and suburban housewife. In contrast to the totalizing ideology of communism, American ideals—symbolized by the middle-class suburban family—were widely represented as the natural outcomes of universal values fully realized by free people: not an ideology, but a "Way of Life." In this context, the family held profound political import that rested precisely on the notion that it was a refuge from and a bulwark against the political sphere.

By the 1970s, this ideal was unraveling. The postwar decades had been its heyday, both culturally and demographically. During the decade immediately following the Second World War, marriage and birth rates soared, while divorce rates and the average age at first marriage dropped.[79] Even so, this normative family was only ever an ideal, and even postwar critics worried about the decline of the American family, apparently disrupted by war and the shift in gender roles that it wrought.[80] After a brief decline immediately following the war, women's workforce participation continued to rise, particularly among white married women and mothers.[81] By the early 1970s, postwar demographic trends were proving anomalous. In the context of stagflation, deindustrialization, and social unrest (evident in phenomena ranging from the counterculture to race riots), as divorce rates rose and birth rates fell, the purported decline of the "American family"—assumed to be a white, middle-class, suburban household headed by a male breadwinner and presided over by a stay-at-home mom—became a powerful symbol of widespread cultural anxieties about the health of the American nation, its economy, and its place in the world.[82]

In this context, marital manuals made up a particularly notable subgenre of 1970s self-help, and their authors offered wide-ranging perspectives on the apparent crises facing the American family. Books like *Open Marriage*, by Nena and George O'Neill—which spent forty-two weeks on the *New York Times* bestseller list in 1972 and 1973—indicated a willingness among millions of Americans to at least entertain ideas about non-normative marriage models, whether out of personal interest or distanced curiosity.[83] The O'Neills did not centrally encourage extramarital sexual relationships but focused instead on flexibility in gender roles, equality between partners, and extramarital sociality.[84] They opposed what they called the "traditional closed marriage contract," which they blamed for stunting individuals' emotional growth, fostering unfulfilling relationships, and contributing to a widespread disillusionment with the institution of marriage. While directly opposing many of Morgan's views on marriage, the O'Neills—like Morgan—cited the rising divorce rate as a critical social problem and they asserted that their goal was to "save marriage" from an impending collapse.[85] More conservative texts like *Total Woman* rounded out a broader conversation about marriage that captured anxieties about gender roles and contemporary relationships, which—depending on the source—sat somewhere on a spectrum between stiflingly rigid and dangerously out of kilter.[86]

Christian Couples Have the Best Sex

Morgan's stance on sexuality was not straightforwardly conservative, however. One of the most fascinating aspects of *Total Woman* is the complicated relationship it reveals between conservative Protestantism and contemporary changes in US sexual culture. On one hand, Morgan's exclusive emphasis on heterosexual marriage and her insistence on the importance of traditional gender roles indicate a rejection of contemporary sexual revolutions, in keeping with the New Christian Right's later campaigns against homosexuality and the widespread "sexualization" of US culture.[87] On the other hand, Morgan's recommendations of sexual costumes and games, and her oft-quoted admonition that "variety is the spice of sex," reflect a willingness to embrace of at least some of the revolutionary approaches to sex that emerged in the 1960s and 1970s.

Morgan presented her marital advice not only as a solution to wives' marital unhappiness but also as a way to keep husbands and children safe from worldly temptations that could lead them into adultery, homosexuality, or feminism.[88] In *Total Woman*, Morgan advised women to remember that each of their children struggled in a "sophisticated, amoral society with unique pressures on his front doorstep that children have never experienced before."[89] Luckily, a Total Woman had the power to protect her children and counteract broader social problems: "If you and your husband express your love visibly and tell your child 'I love you' every day, in his hour of need he may turn to you instead of sex, crime, or drugs."[90] In this way, Morgan connected her promises of domestic bliss to rhetoric about broader social problems that reflected contemporary conservative critiques of sexual revolution, rampant immorality, and youth counterculture.

Morgan, the mother of two daughters, also took time to address the concerns of women who worried that their sons would grow up to be gay. Rehashing the common perception that overbearing mothers and deferent fathers produced gay children, Morgan warned that in a "household off balance" in which the "family leadership was upside down," a son "may identify with his mother and begin to develop certain feminine qualities on a subconscious level." "Physically, he can appear quite masculine," she continued; "emotionally, however, because of his strong attachment to his mother, the door is open to homosexuality."[91]

As in much contemporary conservative literature that addressed homosexuality, lesbians were less visible in Morgan's analysis. Rather than suggesting that the daughters of "mothers who call the shots" would develop homosexual attachments in adulthood, Morgan worried that they would grow up to resent their own husbands and to replicate their parents' dismal marriages. Morgan asserted: "When she grows up she will transfer her resentment toward Daddy to all men, including her husband" and the cycle of "off-balance" marriages would continue.[92] This language may have pointed to the possibility of future lesbianism, but it also closely mirrored contemporary conservative ideas about the unhappy lives of bitter feminists.

In these passages, Morgan repeated common contemporary understandings about how the parent-child relationship could impact children's gender and sexual identities. Drawn from Freudian psychology and early sexology, these ideas gained new life in the postwar period amid contemporary concerns about women's changing roles, a widely reported increase in juvenile delinquency, and a spate of sensationalized sex crimes.[93] Repeated in self-help literature, parenting advice, and newspaper crime coverage, these tropes would not necessarily have seemed like specifically political concerns for most Americans until the gay liberation movement drew increasing attention to the notion of sexual identity as a political issue in the 1970s.[94] Writing at the cusp of this cultural shift, Morgan reproduced notions about sexuality that would soon be central to New Christian Right condemnations of homosexuality, even as she drew on ideas that may have seemed to her to be politically neutral.

As the decade wore on, the religious right would become iconic in its opposition to changing sexual mores, purportedly wrought by the sexual revolution, radical feminists, and gay-rights advocates. Only three years after *Total Woman* was published, Morgan's friend and devotee of the Total Woman course, Anita Bryant, would launch a campaign not only against the nascent gay-rights movement but also against "the alcoholism, the cults, and the promiscuity that pervade our culture."[95]

Yet even as Bryant's emphasis shifted away from the autobiographical domestic manuals that had begun her own authorial career to focus more narrowly on her anti-gay-rights campaign, she took the time to quote an April 1977 *Redbook* survey that had found that "the more religious a woman is, the healthier, *sexier*, and happier she is."[96] Drawing on a salient theme from her early writing, Bryant distinguished between secular sexual revolutions and the sex that God ordained between married couples to be "legal," "beautiful," and even "total."[97] "Despite all of today's frankness about sex," she wrote in 1973, "despite the new so-called freedom, new knowledge, new research on the subject, I just don't believe sex in itself—without love and commitment—can have full beauty. Certainly it would have very little meaning."[98] Echoing a trend that Morgan's books had helped to pioneer, Bryant rejected homosexuality and most aspects of secular sexual liberation, but she also embraced a new cultural openness about sexual pleasure, as long as it remained firmly within the bounds of heterosexual Christian marriages.

Thus, while Morgan's assumptions about homosexuality represented one political priority that would become central for the New Christian Right, she was also at the forefront of a sea change in evangelical attitudes toward marital heterosexual exploration that belies understandings of the religious right as wholly and unproblematically opposed to changing cultural attitudes toward sex the 1960s and 1970s. In 1967, Herbert J. Miles's *Sexual Happiness in Marriage: A Positive Approach to the Details You Should Know to Achieve a Healthy and Satisfying Sexual Life* was the first evangelical sex manual of its kind, pioneering an insistence among conservative evangelical authors that a mutually satisfying sexual relationship was essential to marriage as God designed it.[99] When Marabel Morgan published *Total Woman* five years later, she was still very much on the leading edge of this trend. Though evangelical publications on domestic life, child-rearing, and gender roles were already gaining popularity in the early 1970s, there were still very few evangelical sex manuals on the shelves in 1973. Morgan's success, coupled with evangelical authors' desire to respond to contemporary sexual revolutions within a conservative Christian framework, spurred the rapid proliferation of the genre through the mid-1970s and beyond.

These books ranged in tone from Morgan's peppy guidance—which was often quite vague when it came to the topic of sexual intercourse—to the more clinical and explicit language of Tim and Beverly LaHaye's *The Act of Marriage*, first published by Zondervan in 1976.[100] Morgan couched her sexual advice in a broader discussion of marital adjustment, and she spoke much more frequently about costumes, games, and perfumed sheets than she did about sexual acts themselves. In contrast, the LaHayes used explicit clinical language and anatomical diagrams to instruct couples in the precise mechanisms of heterosexual intercourse. They foregrounded their expertise in pastoral marital counseling and took a much more distanced and authoritative tone than was present in any of Morgan's books. This strategy was typical of books written by Christian couples and men but almost entirely absent in books written by solo female authors.[101] This divergence demonstrates that although the growing interest in books on the subjects of sexuality, gender, and family provided new spaces in which women could claim authority in flourishing national communities of evangelicals, their authority was also limited in scope and in tone by persistent understandings of traditional gender roles.

Despite these important differences, however, books like *Total Woman* and *The Act of Marriage*—along with the many other Christian sex and marriage manuals published in the 1970s—also had a great deal in common. Like Miles in *Sexual Happiness in Marriage*, all of these authors sought to reclaim marital sexuality from discourses of sin and shame and to celebrate it instead as a sacred gift from God.[102] "The Creator of sex intended for His creatures to enjoy it," Morgan wrote in *Total Woman*. "We need never be ashamed to talk about what God was not ashamed to create."[103] The LaHayes agreed: "The act of marriage is that beautiful and intimate relationship shared uniquely by a husband and wife in the privacy of their love—and it is sacred," they wrote. "In a real sense, God designed them for that relationship."[104]

The authors of evangelical sexual advice also insisted not only that Christian couples could have good sex but that they had the best sex.[105] The LaHayes asserted unequivocally that Christians "enjoy it [sex] more on a permanent lifetime basis than any other group of people."[106] Morgan went even further by claiming that truly satisfying sex was possible only for Christian couples. "Spiritually, for sexual intercourse to be the ultimate satisfaction, both partners need a personal relationship with their God," she asserted. "When this is so their union is sacred and beautiful, and mysteriously the two blend perfectly into one. Intercourse becomes the place where man and woman discover each other in a new dimension." On the other hand, Morgan argued that couples whose sexuality was disconnected from religious devotion "may feel restless, dissatisfied, and even destructive."[107] Sexual excitement might be the missing piece in an unsatisfying marriage, in other words, but a real commitment to God was likely the missing piece in an unsatisfying sex life.

Conservative Christian authors of marital advice necessarily drew strict boundaries around permissible sexual behavior even as they expanded its scope. While encouraging a new openness on the topic of sexuality and instructing their readers on a variety of sexual and seduction techniques, evangelical authors made it clear that sacred sexuality could only occur between two married, heterosexual, Christian partners. They also insisted on key biological and social differences between men and women, articulating ideas that would later become central in the antifeminist arguments of the New Christian Right. According to Morgan, sexual difference was essential to God's plan for sexuality. Describing the creation of Adam and Eve, she wrote: "Their human bodies were perfect. No bad parts; they were all good! They fit together perfectly in the exquisite relationship God had planned for them."[108] And it was not only physiological differences that mattered. Often beginning with a biblical account of creation and the scriptural verse "He [God] created them male and female," Morgan and other authors rehearsed common contemporary ideas that upheld a traditionalist gender ideology, focusing in particular on what they understood to be men's natural aggression and easy sexual arousal in comparison to women's natural passivity and their relative difficulty in achieving orgasm.[109]

These intertwined ideas make it clear that the two strands of evangelical sexual discourse in the 1970s—one apparently sex-positive and apolitical and the other explicitly sex-negative and politically engaged—should not be understood as separate, oppositional, or strangely incommensurate. Rather, they worked together to form the basis of a broader evangelical conversation about sexuality that both reappropriated and rejected elements of contemporary sexual revolutions. Domesticating sex—even exciting, experimental, and costumed sex—within marriage was the flipside of renouncing homosexuality and extramarital sexual activity while still remaining culturally relevant in a changing society.

These parallel sexual discourses were also essential in structuring women's authority to speak as experts on political matters as the New Christian Right coalesced later in the decade. As newly prominent authors in an expanding evangelical subculture, Christian women participated in constructing and reinterpreting the ideas about sex and gender that would inform the politics of the New Christian Right. As these topics became increasingly contentious political issues, some women parlayed this authority into roles of political prominence, as we will see in Chapters 2 and 3, which examine the activism of Anita Bryant and Beverly LaHaye. These women and others like them would also develop complex responses to contemporary feminism as the antagonism between the feminist movement and the religious right hardened in the late 1970s. And though she tried to recuse herself from these debates, Morgan helped to set the stage for conservative women's later antifeminist activism in her own writing and through her reactions to feminist critiques of her work.

Conclusion

In the context of shifting definitions of the political sphere in the 1970s, Morgan's work was politically significant in three ways. First, sex and family manuals like Morgan's presaged the "family values" politics of the New Christian Right by making issues of sex, gender, and family central concerns in proliferating conservative evangelical subcultures. Though purportedly apolitical, popular books like Morgan's drew together concerns about cultural change, family stability, and national cohesion that would form the basis of the religious right's political priorities as the movement picked up steam in the late 1970s and 1980s. Such books reached audiences who might not seek out explicitly political groups or literature and trained them in the assumptions of a burgeoning Christian conservative movement, including ideas about the Christian foundations of the American nation, the critical importance of the traditional family, and the normativity of conservative evangelical social values. In the contexts of a decade in which the dominant image of the political activist was distinctly unconservative, and in which a new religious right was emerging despite a long history of ambivalence about direct political engagement, the broad reach of ostensibly apolitical Christian media was particularly vital in developing support for what would soon become a powerful and distinctly political movement of conservative evangelicals.

Second, Morgan both relied on and helped to expand a specific women's culture within the conservative evangelical subculture that undergirded the New Christian Right. Writings like Morgan's conspicuously policed the boundaries of Christian womanhood but also introduced a new conversation, led by women, that explored conservative gender ideologies, expressed these women's particular investment in a system of traditional gender roles, and subtly renegotiated certain bounds of that system. Morgan's work promoted wifely submission but also softened that doctrine in ways that would be critical to the lasting legacy of religious conservatism in the United States.

Third, the national controversy provoked by Morgan's work contributed to widespread and enduring characterizations of the religious right, the feminist movement, and the relationship between them. Morgan was the most prominent writer in a rapidly growing evangelical women's subculture that helped to establish conservative Christian women's authority to speak out in national conversations about sex, gender, and family. Though she always rebuffed politics, she contributed to cultural trends that would help to make women's leadership indispensable in the developing religious right. At the same time, Morgan's defense of her writing as naïve and apolitical facilitated broader characterizations from across the political spectrum of a secular, progressive, and militant feminist movement poised against a backlash led by conservative Christians, who stood for families and "traditional morality" but against feminist conceptualizations of gender equality and women's rights. In other words, her repudiation of politics helped to make conservative Christian women's leadership less visible by inadvertently supporting the notion that politically active women supported feminism while those who did not were simply naïve.

2

Anita Bryant Leads a Moral Crusade

TO HEAR ANITA BRYANT tell it, her political awakening in 1976 was sudden and deeply unsettling. "Never had I taken a public stand on any political or controversial issue," she wrote; "for the most part, my husband and manager, Bob Green, and I have sought to keep our home life as private as possible."[1] Yet Bryant had already enjoyed an active public life for nearly two decades. As a singer and spokeswoman for a variety of national brands, she had built her career on the tropes of down-home Americana, singing at venues including the Super Bowl, the White House, and US military bases abroad. In the late 1960s and 1970s, as the political landscape shifted under her feet, she transformed herself from an uncontroversial pop star into a lightning rod in contentious battles over American values.

Unlike her friend Marabel Morgan, Bryant eventually entered the political realm purposefully and forcefully. In 1976, she became the face of a backlash against proposed gay-rights legislation, first in her local Miami-Dade County and then nationally and even internationally. In January of that year, the Dade County council amended its antidiscrimination code to include protection against discrimination based on "affectional or sexual preference."[2] Encouraged by her pastor and other members of her Southern Baptist community, Bryant led the charge against this change, bringing together a diverse contingent of voters that included conservative Protestants, Catholics, and Jews, whites, Latinos, and African Americans.[3] Her Protect America's Children (PAC) campaign focused in particular on the specter of openly gay teachers. Drawing on popular perceptions of gay men as child molesters, she popularized the idea that "since homosexuals cannot reproduce, they must recruit."[4]

Six months of campaigning ultimately culminated in a countywide referendum that overturned the gay-rights amendment and generated nationwide media coverage for two emerging social movements: gay liberation and the New Christian Right. After the Dade County legislation was repealed, conservative Christian groups from Toronto to California invited Bryant to help lobby against similar laws in their own localities. Bryant, whose performance calendar had lately been packed primarily with business conventions, began to focus instead on political speeches and rallies throughout the United States and Canada. One of the first evangelical spokespeople to make homosexuality into a national political concern, Bryant's early campaigns helped to situate this issue at the very core of the "family values" politics that would come to define the New Christian Right.[5]

Yet although Bryant led a crusade that would become a watershed in the development of the New Christian Right, she expressed a notable ambivalence about the idea of political activism, and this was not unusual. American evangelicals have been active reformers for centuries but have often expressed their moral concerns as separate from or purer than the corrupting world of politics.[6] In the 1970s, male and female leaders of the nascent New Christian Right expressed their inheritance of these traditions in their own ambivalence about the political realm. They typically framed their political vision as a return to normality, couched in a particular idealization of the American past, rather than as an agenda for radical change. Characterizing their political opponents— including hippies, feminists, and liberal judges—as forces bent on tearing America away from its Christian and family-centered roots, conservative evangelical leaders represented their own agendas as almost antipolitical by contrast. Politics meant change in this construction, and conservative Christianity—at least rhetorically—offered a beacon of stability. Where movement leaders did seek change, they asserted that it was only in response to urgent national declension, to attempt to return things to the way they ought to be.

For conservative Christian women entering the political arena in the 1970s, this understanding of what constituted the political realm carried additional meaning. Women's leadership in the New Christian Right relied on the movement's emphasis on the family as the bedrock of a healthy nation. This argument was tied to a traditionalist gender ideology, which generally denied the legitimacy of women's authority outside of the home. At the same time, however, the religious right's emphasis on gender and family issues also politicized the domestic spaces that were the centers of conservative evangelical women's expertise. Women like Bryant built their political authority in these contexts, emphasizing the political importance of their domestic interests and expressing their political engagement as primarily a function of their concerns as mothers and as Christian citizens.

Women's movements across the political spectrum have long used similar maternalist strategies, focusing on motherhood as justification and preparation for political activism. In the second half of the twentieth century, conservative women relied on a notion of "housewife populism," which emphasized women's political marginality as well as their "selflessness, anonymity, and militancy on behalf of their families" to situate women as ideal activists in a developing right-wing populist movement.[7] Prominent evangelical women used this framework in conjunction with the religious right's "family values" rhetoric and its early ambivalence about explicit political engagement. Drawing on contemporary feminist insights, even as they definitively denounced the feminist movement, these women articulated a particular understanding of the relationship between the personal and the political that simultaneously justified their prominence, disclaimed their status as leaders, and expressed a nuanced vision of conservative gender ideology. In other words, they developed a new iteration of conservative maternalism to justify their position not only within the grassroots of a developing conservative movement but also among the ranks of its leadership.

When Bryant began her career in 1959, neither beauty pageants nor Coca-Cola, neither motherhood nor patriotism carried an obvious political charge for the pop singer or her fans. Indeed, such things seemed to them almost quintessentially uncontroversial. By the mid-1970s, however, conflicting ideas about gender, family, and American identity were at the center of explosive national debates. For Bryant and millions of other conservative Christians, this cultural shift challenged deeply held assumptions about American normativity and the bounds of the political realm. In particular, the widespread politicization of such ostensibly private issues as gender and family rendered visible the ideological commitments inherent in assumptions about the family, the nation, and the moral order that had previously gone unquestioned for Bryant and others like her, even as other groups had recognized their political significance much earlier.

Bryant's personal story of politicization in the late 1970s, following a decade of escalating but initially inchoate concern about national moral declension, acts as a kind of microcosm for the New Christian Right as a whole. Her shifting interpretations of the boundaries of the political sphere and her adapting willingness to identify as a political actor parallel the emergence of a newly cohesive and self-aware movement of conservative evangelicals that gained national recognition during the last half of that decade. Bryant's particular concerns—grounded in the rhetoric of maternal responsibility and developing from broader conversations about divinely appointed family roles—demonstrate the mechanisms through which gender politics became central to this movement, in part through the vital role that female leadership played in shaping its political commitments.

Bryant's career also makes it clear that understanding the ways in which conservative Christian women renounced their own authority is as important as understanding the ways in which they claimed it, both to elucidate the gender politics of the New Christian Right and to explain women's historical invisibility as leaders of that movement. Bryant was by no means the first conservative woman to speak out on issues of gender and family, to narrate an abiding concern with American moral declension, or even to connect her faith to a conservative political platform. But she was among the first in this era to articulate, to a broad national audience, the political implications of conservative Christian gender ideology, which many of its practitioners had not yet fully recognized as the basis for a sweeping political agenda. Taking Bryant's experience of sudden political awakening seriously while also understanding its historical context, this chapter helps to explain why a developing rhetoric of "family values" came to resonate so strongly for a large group of conservative Christians who had not previously understood their lives as politically charged. It also helps to explain why and how the emergence of the New Christian Right seemed so sudden to contemporary observers and even movement participants, despite a long history of conservative evangelical political activism.

"The Anita Bryant Story"

Anita Jane Bryant was born on March 25, 1940, in the small town of Barnsdall, Oklahoma. She was a frail baby whose young parents did not expect her to live through the night. According to family lore, her grandfather—whom she would describe in her first autobiography as "not yet a born-again Christian" at the time—nursed her back to health on coffee and whiskey. She would later reminisce: "I'd made a dramatic entrance into an equally dramatic world—the raw, rugged Oklahoma oil country."[8] Bryant would build her popular appeal on this kind of patriotic nostalgia for a not-so-distant American past, located firmly in the heartland and meant to resonate with lower-income and middle-class white Protestants longing for simpler times.

She particularly emphasized the centrality of church and family in her upbringing. Bryant had only one sibling (a younger sister) but she grew up amid a large extended family that included her beloved grandparents, aunts, uncles, and cousins. Yet even in her rosy retelling, Bryant's family life was not uncomplicated. Her parents divorced when Bryant was a baby and remarried each other when she was three years old, only to divorce again ten years later.[9]

At the age of fifteen, Bryant moved with her mother, stepfather, and sister to Tulsa where her mother hoped that the girls would have better opportunities to develop their talents in singing and dance. Bryant's sister quickly decided that show business was not for her, but Bryant—who had been singing in church since the age of three—thrived. By the time she was in her junior year of high school, she was appearing with some regularity on the popular American Broadcasting Company (ABC) radio program "Don MacNeill's Breakfast Club." In 1959, her third-place finish in the Miss America competition brought new opportunities. Unconstrained by the contractual obligations bestowed on the pageant winner, the nineteen-year-old was able to leverage the attention she garnered from the competition into a long and successful career as a performer and corporate spokeswoman.[10] That year, she signed her first recording contract, with Carlton Records, and she recorded four top-40 hits with the label before moving to Columbia Records in 1961.[11] Between 1960 and 1967, she was also a fixture on Bob Hope's Holiday Tours to United States military bases around the world, particularly in Southeast Asia.[12] Her regular performances and color commentary at the Florida Orange Bowl football game and her performance of the national anthem at Super Bowl III in 1969 further cemented her image as an all-American, down-home girl.

In 1960, Bryant married popular Miami disk jockey Bob Green, who became her manager and helped her to build a personal brand based on wholesome American ideals, or as Green would later put it, "God, country, [and] apple pie."[13] Bryant would later relate that she had been attracted to Green because of his commitment to clean living: "Bob Green neither smoke nor drank," she wrote. "Now that's certainly no criteria for decency, nor is it the only character reference—but I considered it most unusual. . . . This Bob Green was beginning to interest me."[14]

Shortly after their marriage, Bryant learned that she might not be able to have children. She would later recount that the "news hit Bob and me particularly hard, for we'd both counted on having a house full of kids."[15] Based on the advice of friends, the couple decided to adopt a child and, in 1963, they brought home an infant son whom they named Bobby. Within a few weeks, Bryant discovered that she was pregnant. She gave birth to a daughter, Gloria Lynn, when their son was only seven-and-a-half months old. Referring to Bobby and Gloria as her "miracle babies," Bryant described their arrival as evidence that "God's planning is perfect, even if ours isn't."[16] Four years later, when Bryant and Green decided to add to their family again, they wanted to replicate their experience with Bobby and Gloria. "'Since we can't order twins,'" Green proposed to an enthusiastic Bryant, "'let's do the next best thing. Six months after you give birth, let's adopt another baby of the opposite sex.'"[17] This plan proved unnecessary; in 1969 Bryant gave birth to twins, a boy named Billy and a girl named Barbara. For Bryant, this second family "miracle" furnished further evidence of God's very direct response to prayer.

The twins' birth was difficult, however, and both Bryant and the premature infants remained in the hospital for weeks afterward. National news media covered the story and Bryant later credited the family's recovery to the prayerful support of fans from across the country, along with the help of her family, her church community, and the prayers of friends including Billy Graham, Senator Mark Hatfield, and President Lyndon Johnson.[18] Bryant's narration of these experiences as miraculous helped to frame and sustain media interest in her family. It also gave her an opportunity to talk publicly about her religious beliefs, including the importance of faith, the necessity of sublimating selfish desires in favor of God's will, and the understanding that God intervenes directly and concretely in believers' lives.

During the 1960s and 1970s, Bryant represented a variety of American brands including Coca-Cola, Kraft Foods, and Tupperware, which all cashed in on Bryant's popularity and wholesome image. After she became a mother in 1963, advertisers tended to represent her as a beautiful, happy, suburban housewife, offering advice to others who were, or who aspired to be, like her. In 1968, Bryant signed a major contract with the Florida Citrus Commission and for much of the following decade she would be best known to many Americans as the "Florida orange juice girl." Seven years later, during the American Bicentennial festivities, a reporter for the *Chicago Tribune* mused: "It's difficult to imagine a Bicentennial prayer breakfast that *wouldn't* have Anita Bryant on prominent display." He continued, "When you invite Anita Bryant for breakfast, she brings the orange juice, and sprinkles it with the fairy dust of unshakeable American optimism."[19]

Toward the end of the 1960s, almost a decade removed from her pageant appearances, Bryant shifted her musical focus from songs about love and heartbreak to numbers that centered on themes of God and country. In 1967, Columbia released three albums of patriotic and Protestant hymns performed by Bryant. In 1970, she signed with the Christian label Word Records, which produced an additional six Anita Bryant albums, including "Old Fashioned Prayin'" and "Anita Bryant's All-Time Favorite Hymns." During that decade, she also joined Billy Graham on his evangelical crusades and, with her husband's encouragement, she began to understand her performance career as a vehicle for sharing her Christian faith: "When I first started witnessing," she wrote, "I began to realize that I'd been missing that joy all those years, that I did so many things out of mere habit, in obedience to God—and *still* missed the real point of Christianity."[20] At the same time, she began incorporating more "patriotic and sacred numbers" into her act, including "The Power and the Glory," "God Bless America," and "The Battle Hymn of the Republic." As she put it, "These songs have become a part of my witness."[21]

Significantly, American patriotism and Christian faith were often inextricably linked for Bryant, and this conflation foreshadowed her later fusion of religious and political commitments in her anti-gay-rights activism. In her first book, written six years before the Dade County campaign, Bryant described her work as a "spokesman for certain American industries" and asked rhetorically: "Where else could a Christian give a witness on stage and sing such songs as 'How Great Thou Art' and 'Mine Eyes Have Seen the Glory'?" Bursting with patriotic pride, she answered: "These fine American companies aren't afraid to speak out for God and country. This is the wholesome, constructive kind of work God led us into when we became willing to trust Him with our lives."[22] Bryant's celebrity rested on patriotic Americana, and for her this was inextricably linked with an implicit understanding of the United States as a fundamentally Christian nation. In turn, she presented her success as a Christian celebrity in secular forums as evidence that American culture and conservative evangelical values were essentially one and the same.

This shift in tone meant that as Bryant's currency as a young pop star began to fade in the late 1960s, the devout Southern Baptist singer was able to shore up a firm following within a growing subculture of conservative evangelical Protestants. Her fusion of patriotic and religious pride echoed the rhetoric of prominent evangelists from Billy Graham to the stridently anticommunist Billy James Hargis. She too became an icon among conservative Protestants, not only as a singer but also as a prolific author. Drawn by Bryant's dedication to conservative Christian values—evident in the songs she sang, the bookings she accepted, and the interviews she gave—the evangelical Fleming H. Revell publishing company offered Bryant her first book contract in 1970 and went on to publish nine books by Bryant over the next eight years.[23] These near-annual volumes of personal biography and domestic advice bolstered Bryant's image as an ideal Christian wife and mother—or at least as someone who strived to be—and they helped to sustain interest and personal investment in Bryant among a conservative Christian fan base. In keeping with Revell's efforts to produce widely accessible nonfiction for a broad audience, these books were small, easy to read, and easy to carry, with covers that broadcast Bryant's evolving self-fashioning as an evangelical celebrity, wife, mother, and eventual activist.

The first of these books, published in 1970, followed the conventions of a typical celebrity autobiography, tracing Bryant's life from her birth in 1940 and highlighting major milestones including her career breakthroughs, her marriage in 1960, and the miraculous arrivals of her four children in 1963 and 1969. Revell relied on Bryant's established celebrity and patriotic brand to draw potential readers. The book's opening blurb promised to reveal the "uniquely American success story" of a well-known singer from humble roots, who was "born to a youthful oil field roustabout and his teen-age bride" in rural Oklahoma. The cover, which featured a wistful Bryant against a hazy background, recalled many of her album covers, making a visual connection to the pop singer with whom readers would already have been familiar.

The next five books, written between 1971 and 1976, are more properly classified as Christian advice manuals, still largely framed as personal anecdote but through snapshots of recent experience rather than comprehensive recounting. Bryant's tone shifted in these books, from the somewhat distanced approach of a celebrity addressing her fans to a more intimate, familiar, and spontaneous style typical of evangelical women's culture.[24] In these books, Bryant variously emphasized themes of marriage, family, and Christian witness, drawing on the evangelical tradition of personal testimony to present her life experiences both as models for emulation and as sources of cautionary example. Using this narrative framework, Bryant situated herself within the long-standing custom of evangelical testimonial, which has for centuries played an enormous role in building individual religious identities and forging bonds in evangelical communities.[25] The testimonial script, which draws spiritual lessons from personal experience, makes each believer's life a site of spiritual significance that should be shared with the rest of the community. The practice of sharing testimony also makes a kind of religious authority available to all congregants, including those who—due to gender, race, age, or other factors—might otherwise lack access to the pulpit. As a result, this practice is closely tied to evangelical women's tendencies to rest their claims to authority in narratives of personal calling from God and to subsume the potential threat of their public speaking by foregrounding their individual experience, couched in feminine and maternal identities.[26]

Bryant's books also reflected the conservative gender and family ideals central to contemporary evangelical women's culture. Like Marabel Morgan, Anita Bryant believed that gender hierarchy within the family was divinely ordained. "God has sanctioned our marriage," she wrote, "and the Holy Spirit dwells within Bob. The Lord expects Bob to take charge of our household, and for me to uphold him in his decisions. This is what I must do, according to the Word of God."[27] Also like Morgan, Bryant experienced some early difficulty with the principle of submission: "SUBMISSION? Baloney! Who does *he* think he . . . *mutter* . . . *grumble* . . . *storm*," she wrote playfully in 1976.

"Sound familiar, girls? Be honest!"[28] But whereas Morgan wrote gleefully about the possibilities of a marriage built on submission, Bryant's tone was more typically one of struggle and resignation. Even her frequent advocacy of submission doctrine belied her ongoing difficulties with putting it into practice: "When I resorted to Christ, He helped me relinquish authority so my husband could assume proper control," she told readers in 1970, immediately before acknowledging: "This may be news to Bob, of course. He thinks I'm still plenty bossy!"[29]

In 1980, Bryant would divorce Green. That year, *Ladies Home Journal* reported based on a candid interview with the singer that "she didn't feel the books were dishonest or hypocritical" despite her ongoing marital problems: "It was only that she wanted to have a happy marriage 'so badly that I'd only share the good parts.' "[30] To careful readers, the tensions in the Bryant-Green household would have been apparent long before the couple's divorce. But Bryant's books exemplify the nuances of evangelical women's culture and the conservative gender ideology it promoted. On its face, this subculture revolved almost universally around the promotion of wifely submission and the protection of traditionalist gender roles. Yet most female authors also expressed difficulty with these concepts and gradually contributed to the shift away from strict emphases on male headship toward an acceptance of women's capacity for leadership, at least in certain circumstances. At the same time, the possibilities for dissent were limited. Though expressions of struggle and even resentment were common, these narratives always built toward a new resolve to enact the principle of submission, even if slightly modified.[31]

Bryant, like Morgan, couched her promotion of submission doctrine in an emphasis on women's agency: "The act of submission is something that happens between equals, something that happens by choice," she insisted.[32] Going further than Morgan, she also critiqued the unbalanced vision of submission that she observed in contemporary churches: "Much has been preached on 'Wives, submit yourselves unto your own husbands, as unto the Lord,' (Ephesians 5:22), but much less, it seems, on Ephesians 5:25: 'Husbands, love your wives, even as Christ also loved the church, and gave himself for it.' " This "wrong emphasis," she argued, helped to explain why "many Christian women today trip over the whole idea of submission."[33] While maintaining that God-given family roles were essential to a healthy society, Bryant also insisted on an interpretation of those roles that emphasized men's responsibilities as much as women's. Even so, she could not buck the doctrine of submission entirely; she may have been able to joke that she sometimes thought the whole system was "baloney" but only if she used her next paragraph to promote some version of it to her readership.

Significantly, the evangelical valorization of this family model rested not only on conservative theology but also on the notion that there had been an epoch in which such ideal Christ-centered families had been the norm. Bryant's earliest autobiography buttressed this assumption by eulogizing that very historical moment as she recalled it. In 1970, for example, Bryant recalled her Grandma Berry as "one of the last of her breed: a remarkable pioneer American woman" who, in contrast to the sometimes-hapless Anita, was "a naturally accomplished wife and mother" and "a genius at the art of living."[34] Similar themes ran through all of Bryant's writing, and served not only to express a pervasive sense of American moral decline but also to establish through her childhood reminiscences a clear example of those lost ideals and proof of their possibility.

In 1973, however, Bryant acknowledged that neither husbands nor wives "come readymade" and she asserted that building up a Christian home "must require more grace and hard work than any other organization on earth."[35] This was intimately tied to her frequent descriptions of submission doctrine as a source of inner turmoil. As she put it in 1976: "Despite all the good words, many of us women have to fight a daily battle about the submission question. It does not come naturally, and I suspect it never will."[36] This tension between the naturalness of traditional gender roles and the difficulty of living up to them was a common theme in Bryant's writing and in evangelical women's culture more broadly. Such tensions between the naturalness and difficulty of living up to conservative gender roles were common in contemporary evangelical domestic advice. For many feminist observers, this apparent contradiction undid the logic of the patriarchal system: how, after all, could something be both natural and difficult to achieve?[37] For conservative Christian women like Bryant, however, this tension was perfectly consistent with their understandings of original sin and contemporary immorality. The performance of God-given gender roles required hard work and self-discipline, as Bryant acknowledged. But this was true for both sexes and not dissimilar to evangelicals' more general striving to live a life as free from sin as humanly possible despite also believing in the inevitability of failure.

These ideas about women's roles and the history of family arrangements also reveal a great deal about women's attraction to conservative gender theologies, which celebrated women's domestic work while also acknowledging that this work can be difficult, all while harkening back to a time in which wifehood and motherhood were universally valorized and perhaps slightly easier. While contemporary feminists sought to improve women's lives by dismantling patriarchal structures that perpetuated gender inequality, conservative evangelical women sought to establish a godly world in which women's roles would be valued and their hard work rewarded.

The Politics of Becoming Political

Bryant's ruminations on gender, family, and the American nation during the 1970s provide unusual insight into her political formation in the years before and during her campaigns against gay-rights legislation. Most of the New Christian Right's leaders were already political figures by the time they earned book contracts, meaning that only their retrospective narratives of politicization have been preserved in the historical record. It is rare to be able to check these narratives against a decade of developing political concerns, but this is possible in Bryant's case. Doing so deepens our understanding of Bryant's personal politicization as well as her own understanding of that process in the context of conservative Christian ambivalence about the political realm. It also underscores the significance of ostensibly apolitical evangelical cultural spaces as sites for developing conservative ideas and identities in the years leading up to the New Christian Right's ascendancy.

Many of the assumptions that undergirded Bryant's later activism were embedded in her writing long before she considered herself to be politically engaged. Over a decade that was critical to Bryant's personal politicization and to the mobilization of the New Christian Right more broadly, subtle shifts in language and emphasis demonstrate how evolving concerns about national cultural changes gradually transformed into an articulable political ideology that helped to mobilize many conservative Christians who had also not previously considered themselves politically inclined. As Morgan had, Bryant also expressed deepening concern about the world in which her children were growing up, beginning with general allusions to American moral decline. In Bryant's case, these ideas eventually developed into the more explicit anti-gay-rights, antifeminist, and pro-family discourse that transformed the pop singer into a prominent political activist.

This evidence of gradual political development contrasts sharply with Bryant's own narrative of sudden political awakening. Based on the content of her six earlier books published over the preceding seven years, this discrepancy seems less the result of a deliberate political strategy on Bryant's part and more likely an indication of the complicated relationship between politics, religion, and personal life that characterized the early rhetoric of the New Christian Right. With the benefit of hindsight, the social conservatism inherent in belief systems like Bryant's seems obvious, but for Bryant and many of her contemporaries, the notion of mixing religious belief, family life, and explicit political engagement was—at least initially—counterintuitive and potentially disconcerting.

Early in her career, Bryant expressed a notable, firm, and sometimes explicit disengagement with political controversy. Writing in 1970, for example, Bryant described her singing performances at both the Democratic and Republican National Conventions during the explosive summer of 1968, but she gave no hint of the bitter clashes that had surrounded that year's campaigns or the violence that had erupted around the Democratic Convention in Chicago. She acknowledged the difference between the two conventions only to say that if she "looked more radiant at the Republican National Convention (RNC) than I did for the Democratic one," it was because she found out she was pregnant on the same night that she performed for the RNC.[38]

In the same book, Bryant expressed admiration for American troops in Vietnam—whom she met as a performer on Bob Hope's USO tours—but she never acknowledged that there existed any domestic controversy surrounding that war. Indeed, she regarded her patriotism—which included a tacit support for the war—as an issue so uncontroversial that it could bring divided Americans together. Warned not to sing "The Battle Hymn of the Republic" in front of a southern audience in the mid-1960s, she argued, "It's a Christian hymn. With all the war in Viet Nam, that hymn sounds completely contemporary." She sang the song, and by her account: "God's message superseded any thoughts of sectionalism, and the words to a classic American hymn suddenly seemed to sing with a new authority."[39] This apparently willful ignorance of political conflict allowed Bryant to maintain a public image centered on the tropes of cheery motherhood and old-fashioned American values while revealing her assumption that those values were inherently Christian, conservative, and patriotic.

Bryant's nationalism, her conservative morality, and her religious commitments would eventually coalesce into an explicit political agenda, culminating in her involvement in the campaign in Dade County, Florida, beginning in 1976. Yet despite her efforts at political disengagement, her writing evinced a developing political consciousness much earlier, in concerns about an increasingly "permissive" culture that corrupted children's morals and undermined the influences of church and family: "For the sake of ourselves, our children, and our nation, we've got to return to the Bible," she argued as early as 1972.[40] The fact that Bryant's later political subjectivity was foreshadowed in even her earliest autobiographical writing may not be surprising, but it is significant. It exemplifies the ways in which the cultural and analytical roots of New Christian Right political engagement were present in conservative Christian communities well before the movement emerged as a visible political force in the late 1970s and even before individual members of these communities recognized the broader political consequence of these ideas.[41]

In particular, the understanding that the United States was undergoing acute moral decline was fundamental to the political reasoning of the New Christian Right, undergirding opposition to feminism, gay rights, and lenient obscenity laws, and imbuing these campaigns with a vital sense of urgency. During the 1960s and 1970s, rapid cultural change, the sexual revolution, and new Supreme Court decisions on the separation between church and state, along with domestic and global political unrest and economic instability, all converged to inform evangelical anxieties about impending disaster. Drawing on long-standing concerns about the impending end times in evangelical communities, the leading figures of the emerging New Christian Right spoke in apocalyptic language about the frightening decline of the American nation.[42] In the early 1980s, a fundraising pamphlet produced by the nascent Moral Majority asserted in no uncertain terms that the organization had to succeed in its "fight [against] pornography, homosexuality, obscene school textbooks[,]" and the expansion of the federal government "*if this nation is to survive.*"[43] Like Bryant, the leaders of the Moral Majority centrally believed that the United States was a fundamentally Christian nation. When they spoke about the survival of the nation, they were specifically concerned with preserving the union that they believed had always existed between conservative Christian values and American ideals.

These concerns dovetailed with a booming interest in apocalypticism in the 1970s that crossed over from evangelical communities into American popular culture. In 1970, the same year that Fleming H. Revell put out Anita Bryant's first book, the evangelical publisher Zondervan released Hal Lindsey's *The Late Great Planet Earth*, which became one of the bestselling books of the decade and one of the bestselling religious books of the century.[44] In it, Lindsey laid out evangelical ideas about the apocalypse in an accessible and urgent tone, connecting interpretations of biblical prophecy to contemporary global events, especially in the Middle East. In 1976, the *New York Times* reported based on a conversation with the president of the largely evangelical Christian Booksellers Association that the four bestselling genres in religious publishing were then "personal accounts of finding God, often by celebrities" along with "religious approaches to family problems such as sex, divorce, birth control and the like . . . family Bible study courses," and "'prophetic' or apocalyptic books such as those by Hal Lindsey."[45] None of these genres were overtly focused on political engagement, but each of them made specific contributions in laying the groundwork for the New Christian Right.

Assumptions about national moral declension were also embedded in Bryant's earliest books, in which a more pronounced sense of political awareness was conspicuously absent. Her reminiscences about her personal history expressed certain assumptions about secularization, moral decline, and the erosion of family roles, which would develop into a more explicit political philosophy both for Bryant and for a broader conservative Christian movement in the years to come. Just as Bryant's first book offered a particular picture of traditional gender roles, it also centered on a childhood steeped in patriotic nostalgia, against which she would always compare her adult experiences of Miami. In narrating her story as a fulfillment of the American Dream, Bryant recalled Oklahoma—the state in which she was born and raised—in terms of familiar tropes of a romanticized American past. She described a childhood centered on church and family, one that was materially poor but rich in love and adventure: in "a family as big as ours," she reminisced, "you knew you were loved."[46] In contrast, her third book—written four years before her self-described political awakening—focused on how to save this apparently disappearing ideal of Christian family life.[47] From the beginning, Bryant expressed particular anxiety about the prospect of raising children in Miami, which she saw as "too swinging a place, a good-time town for adults, with little of the old-fishing hole kind of fun for kids I remembered from my own childhood."[48] For Bryant, who moved to Florida as a twenty-year-old newlywed, her childhood memories would come to define an idealized vision of the recent American past, which became the backdrop for her growing concerns about a national culture that was becoming steadily more lascivious and less familiar. In keeping with her ideas about national moral declension, Bryant narrated this difference primarily as a function of change over time rather than regional difference, though both factors likely influenced her experiences of Miami.

Notably, Bryant's journey from the nation's rural center to a thriving coastal city was not merely an idiosyncratic experience. Rather, it resonated with larger national patterns of migration, such that many of Bryant's readers would have experienced—personally or through friends and relatives—similar migratory experiences that seemed to confirm contemporary conservative concerns about apparently growing dangers, especially in changing urban centers. During the postwar decades, thousands of families moved from states like Oklahoma, Arkansas, and Texas to the emerging flourishing Sunbelt, where they established new patterns of religious conservatism that incorporated traditions of southern evangelicalism with their experiences of Sunbelt prosperity.[49] Indeed, these migratory patterns were so widespread that they fundamentally changed the makeup of the Southern Baptist Convention, transforming it in the mid-twentieth century from a regional denomination into one of the largest and most influential denominations nationwide.[50]

The rhetoric of national moral declension that pervaded evangelical sub-culture during this period drew on American religious traditions as old as the Puritans but added new inflections that reflected concerns about the Cold War, the New Left, and other contemporary cultural changes. These concerns also carried racial undertones. Sunbelt migrants during in the mid-twentieth century typically moved from predominantly white rural areas to suburban homes in more racially diverse states. During this same period, suburban neighborhood covenants and federal lending policies made it virtually impos-sible for most nonwhite residents to migrate out of the cities, even as those cities lost most of their income from taxes and investment.[51] As these trends intensified, suburban homeowners developed a political language of "color-blind" meritocracy that blamed African American and Latino residents for the decline of the cities, without acknowledging the network of policies that had both contributed to this decline and ensured that its burdens would rest pri-marily on nonwhite Americans.[52]

Bryant's ideas about race reflected these developments, even though she rarely broached the subject. In all of the nine volumes that she published during the 1970s, Bryant alluded to race on fewer than ten pages. This does not mean that racial ideas were not influential in shaping Bryant's politics but rather reflects the fact that her politics developed in a context in which discussions of race were often coded, muted, or notable in their absence.[53]

Bryant mentioned African Americans almost exclusively in conjunction with a Sunday School class that she taught for eleven-year-old girls, which included African American children "from disadvantaged areas" who were brought in by the "church's bus ministry." It is telling that these children had to be brought by bus from neighborhoods that were otherwise alien to Bryant. At the same time that school districts across the country sought to fully inte-grate their schools by busing children from deeply segregated neighborhoods to other areas, these same patterns of residential segregation also made it possible for Bryant to avoid interacting with African Americans unless she chose to do so. This gave Bryant and others like her the privilege of thinking about race only rarely and without much complexity, using their minimal experiences to confirm broad generalizations based on stereotype. Bryant made this clear in her own description of the challenges she faced in teaching the class: "I had virtually no experience working with underprivileged chil-dren. Beyond that, I had almost no contact whatever with black people, and almost never dealt with kids who were neglected or untrained." Though she had many positive things to say about these children, she also pitied their poverty, characterized their neighborhoods as dangerous, and blamed their "unconcerned" or working parents that they were often unkempt and "undisciplined."[54] She also clearly equated blackness and poverty, using racial and class markers interchangeably to describe the half of the class that the bus ministry brought in.

In keeping with the overarching themes of her books, the declension narrative that Bryant expressed was most intimately tied to issues of family and gender. Her writing foreshadowed the gender politics of the New Christian Right as well as the stakes that conservative Christian women would have in the movement. "Never before have so many books and pamphlets been written concerning marriage and the family," Bryant's pastor wrote in the foreword to her third book in 1972, "yet our nation finds itself burdened as never before by the heavy load of broken homes."[55] In the same book, Bryant and Green argued that rising divorce rates had already initiated a disastrous cycle in which young men "refuse to be heads of their households" and young women—"even so-called 'nice girls' "—regarded premarital sex and mothers' workforce participation as acceptable and even unremarkable.[56] Nonetheless, Bryant's early work avoided direct political engagement in the same way that her friend Marabel Morgan did, pointedly emphasizing individual reform and not collective action as the solution to every problem that she raised.

Political Awakening in Dade County

Bryant typically began her narrative of politicization by recounting that she was shocked to learn in 1976 that her county commissioners were considering a gay-rights bill, and that she was staggered to find out that one of the bill's main sponsors was Ruth Shack, who was a friend of Bryant's and the wife of her booking agent. Bryant had publicly endorsed Shack's campaign as a personal favor, which made her feel particularly responsible for Shack's actions as commissioner. So Bryant's previously indeterminate concerns about the moral and spiritual condition of the nation's families transformed into an imperative to act: to step boldly and explicitly into the political sphere. She characterized her earlier endorsement of Shack as naïve, and she contrasted that experience with her new political awareness. "I'd never been politically oriented, nor really well informed about local or national issues," she said, adding that the news of the Dade County bill "began my awakening process. From that day forward, I knew I'd make every effort to become informed and stay current with the important issues of our day."[57]

After learning about the proposed antidiscrimination bill in Dade County, Bryant wrote a letter to the county commissioners asking them to reconsider their support for it. She later read that letter publicly on a local Christian radio show and she spoke at the commission's public hearing on the bill. She also founded the group Protect America's Children (PAC) to organize local supporters.[58] Initially staffed by volunteers from Bryant's church, the organization grew to include a diverse contingent of Miamians. When the bill passed despite their efforts in January 1977, Bryant gave a press conference outside the commission's offices, vowing: "We're not going to take this thing sitting down."[59] The group redoubled its efforts, sending out mailings, organizing phone trees, staging public rallies, speaking to the media, and mobilizing a get-out-the-vote campaign. On June 7, a countywide referendum decisively overturned the bill, with 69.3 percent of participants voting in favor of repeal.[60]

By the time of the referendum, Bryant's involvement had drawn national and international media attention to the Dade County fight.[61] Following the June repeal, Bryant expanded her campaign. She began to publish two semi-regular newsletters, which featured stories about ongoing struggles against the gay-rights movement nationwide. She also lent support to those struggles by making personal appearances at rallies across the United States and Canada and personally advocating against proposed gay-rights legislation in several states, including Kansas, Oregon, Minnesota, and California.[62]

In 1978, the singer founded Anita Bryant Ministries (ABM), which joined a nascent movement of Christian organizations focused on helping people "escape . . . from the homosexual life with the help of the Holy Spirit."[63] The organization relied on Bryant's established celebrity "as a mother—as an American—as a Christian," per one early fundraising letter.[64] Or, as a representative for the organization put it: "Anita Bryant is almost unique in America in terms of her ability to get press exposure."[65] According to a 1980 report in *Ladies Home Journal*, PAC and ABM together collected more than two million dollars from approximately 400,000 donors in their first eight months.[66]

Bryant's role in ABM further illustrates the ways in which the ideologies that undergirded the developing New Christian Right both necessitated and limited women's leadership within the movement. On one hand, Bryant's established celebrity made her an ideal representative of this movement. Her contributions to a growing evangelical women's subculture had helped to establish her as a leading voice in shaping popular conservative theologies of gender well before her explicit political activism in Dade County. Bryant's pastor, William Chapman, was instrumental in convincing her to take an active leadership role in the Dade County battle. Yet Chapman and others involved in the founding of Anita Bryant Ministries also insisted that the organization have an all-male board, which they argued was necessary to maintain divinely ordained systems of gender hierarchy.[67]

These same contradictions also played out in the national context. In 1977, the Southern Baptist Convention (SBC) adopted a resolution commending Bryant for her "courageous stand against the evils inherent in homosexuality."[68] The following year, a group of pastors campaigned for Bryant to be elected as the first female vice-president of the denomination. She was nominated, but soundly defeated by the Reverend A. Douglas Watterson, a Tennessee pastor whose victory rested on his "experience in church administration" positions that were notably closed to women.[69] Yet Watterson's election did not mark a straightforward rejection of women's leadership within the denomination. During this time, the SBC was embroiled in divisive political and theological battles, including a bitter fight over women's ordination. Watterson, who faced criticism for having personally ordained a woman, drew his support from the more liberal members of the SBC. Bryant's support came from conservatives, who opposed women's ordination but who saw no problem in electing a famous, socially conservative woman as vice-president—a secondary leadership role that would not require her to claim any kind of practical theological authority over men.

Leading female voices in evangelical women's culture helped to shape the priorities of the new religious right and to mobilize its female supporters. In turn, the grassroots activism of these supporters buttressed this growing movement in political battles across the country. Yet women's leadership in these contexts was never uncomplicated; the limits of traditionalist gender roles were constantly being negotiated and defined, in individual groups and churches as well as in national denominational bodies and internationally distributed books and newsletters.

The Politics of Women's Authority in the New Christian Right

Beginning with her first book, Bryant went to some lengths to insist that neither her work as an author nor her career as a performer had caused her to overstep her roles as a Christian wife and mother. As her political consciousness developed through the decade, the specifically gendered justifications that Bryant had used to rationalize her public career transitioned seamlessly into grounds for her political engagement. Her ambivalence about her political role offers insight into the limitations that women encountered in conservative Christian communities during this period, based on established theological and community conventions. However, her writing also reveals the strategies that evangelical women used to carve out more expansive roles for themselves within the framework of proper Christian womanhood. These justifications can be broken down into four major categories that reflect centuries of struggle on the part of American Protestant women, whose strategies for claiming authority in their communities gained new salience in the developing gender politics of a growing Christian conservative movement in the 1970s.

First, Bryant explicitly and emphatically constructed her authorial voice as an extension of her familial roles. In the introduction to 1972's *Bless This House*, Bryant stated plainly: "Writing this book, I'm much more Anita Green than Anita Bryant. Not that there's any role conflict. . . . The best role I could possibly play is Anita Green, Bob's wife and our children's mommy."[70] Of course Bryant, like many other conservative Christian women, strained these boundaries in practice, and her protestations suggest her own awareness of that fact. Her career as a performer demanded a great deal of her time and attention, and she often relied on domestic staff to assist her with housekeeping and parenting duties.[71] Through her writing, she also became a public adviser to her readers: on family, religious, and political matters. By insisting on the primacy of her domestic roles, however, Bryant disavowed any undue authority and justified the public career through which her authority on these subjects had been established.

Second, Bryant highlighted her husband's support for her projects, making it clear that her writing occurred within the context of Bryant's submission to Green's headship. Indeed, Bob Green appeared on the cover of six of Bryant's nine books and as coauthor of five, lending the seal of husbandly approval and involvement. In her third book, and the first coauthored by Green, Bryant interpolated Green into her earlier writing, asserting that both of her previous books "definitely had Bob's stamp on [them]. We are very married. There's just no way to separate our experiences."[72]

According to Bryant, it was also Green who pushed her to expand her public testimony and to embrace both writing and public speaking.[73] In their coauthored books, Green wrote in conversation with Bryant about family and Christian life, and together they outlined a conservative ideal of family based on fundamentalist Christian principles. Green emphasized the fatherly duty to discipline his children as well as the practical and emotional support that husbands ought to give their wives. He also divulged how he struggled to live up to his role as "spiritual head" of his family, a theme that mirrored Bryant's expressions of difficulty with the doctrine of submission, although the two resolutely promoted the system as a whole.[74]

Third, Bryant wrote primarily to other women, leaving Green to speak to the specific concerns of men, as husbands, fathers, and potential Christian leaders.[75] In doing so, Bryant situated herself firmly within the history of evangelical women's ministries, which conceded women's capacity to teach other women as long as they did not assert authority over adult men of comparable social standing.[76] Bryant demonstrated her experience with the more traditional forms of this practice when she discussed her regular participation in a Sunday School class for women and her leadership of another Sunday School class for girls.[77] As we have seen, the construction of national evangelical communities blossomed in the late 1960s and 1970s, and books like Bryant's translated the tradition of women's ministry into print culture and contributed to the development of national communities that spoke specifically to the needs and interests of evangelical women.

Fourth, just as female preachers had done for centuries, Bryant insisted that she only presumed to speak publicly out of a calling from and a duty to God. From Elleanor Knight in the early nineteenth century to Aimee Semple McPherson in the early twentieth, prominent female preachers have presented themselves as reluctant vessels, claiming that they faced divine rebuke in the forms of illness and personal harm when they failed to heed God's call.[78] Bryant, too, characterized herself as a shy public speaker and she detailed her struggles with witnessing directly to audiences and her efforts to build on her comfort with singing in order to be able to share her personal testimony.[79] The foreword to her second book applied these themes of reticence and divine calling to her work as a whole: "Anita Bryant never considered herself an author. In fact, she didn't even want to write her autobiography *Mine Eyes Have Seen the Glory*—until she realized that it was an opportunity to witness to thousands, through the written word, how the Lord has touched her life."[80] Bryant herself sometimes went further in renouncing her own authority and giving the glory to God. On behalf of herself and her husband, she wrote in her third book: "We're not experts on marriage and family life. Our home is not perfect. We don't have all the answers. *But the Bible does!*"[81] These kinds of statements served to emphasize not only her submission to her husband but also, and even more important, her submission to the authority of God and scripture.

As Bryant became more self-consciously political, she drew on these same ideas to justify her authority in the political realm. In 1976, she addressed herself in particular to other mothers, admonishing them to "Wake up!" and to protect their children not only from homosexuals and from myriad other threats including drugs, teen pregnancy, and youth violence, which seemed to her to pose an increasing danger in contemporary society.[82] She also strenuously insisted that both her husband and pastor shared her political concerns and approved of her involvement, though she ultimately represented the campaign as the result of a calling from God.

It was Bryant's pastor who first made her aware of the pending gay-rights legislation in Dade County and, according to Bryant's books, Bob Green was as convinced as his wife about the need to oppose it.[83] When Bryant began to write a letter to the county commission, which was her first act in opposition to the bill after an ultimately fruitless discussion with the bill's sponsor, Bryant sought the assistance of both Chapman and Green, but they were called away, to an "emergency situation" and jury duty, respectively. According to Bryant, she realized in that moment that "God didn't intend for me to rely on anyone else" and she turned for help to the ultimate authorities, God and the Bible. In her letter, Bryant presented herself as "the concerned mother of four children," and she argued that in choosing to amend the Dade County Code to protect homosexuals from discrimination, the commissioners would "be infringing upon my rights and discriminating against me as a citizen and a mother to teach my children and set examples and to point to others as examples of God's moral code as stated in the Holy Scriptures."[84] Throughout her narration of this story, Bryant drew on long-standing tropes to emphasize that her foray into politics was not a betrayal of her natural domestic role but rather an expression of it, and that it was undertaken with due deference to male and divine authority.

In the context of her new political role, Bryant also directly addressed the difficulty of her position as a female leader in a campaign that emphasized the importance of traditional gender roles. Writing in 1977 about the roots of the Protect America's Children campaign, Bryant recounted a conversation with Reverend Chapman following her testimony at the Metro Commission: "Why me?" she asked him, "I mean, I'm just a woman. I shouldn't be this involved. And it's not in the Bible!" Chapman countered, citing the biblical examples of Deborah and Esther to reassure her: "Yes, it is. . . . Anytime, throughout the Bible, when God's men didn't take their stand . . . He raised up a woman."[85] Expanding on Chapman's reasoning, Bryant chastised the men in her congregation, and Christian men in general, for their failure to act against the problems of national moral decline. She called on them to reclaim their proper roles as leaders of a movement that had so far—at least from Bryant's perspective—been driven primarily by women.

Bryant defended her position within a conservative theological framework, but she also challenged her fellow believers to expand their vision of women's potential contributions to public life, stating that "as Christians we have been quick to define our roles and criticize women who step out of what *we feel* are their proper roles."[86] She asserted that God had led her to see that such codes of conduct were often too narrow to suit divine purposes. Employing well-established models for claiming authority in evangelical contexts, Bryant drew on biblical precedence and her own personal experience of God's guidance to justify the position she held in this movement and to assert that the narrowest conceptions of proper gender roles might not themselves be biblically sound.

The New Christian Right: Politicization and Mobilization

Beginning in 1976, then, Bryant's writing became more self-consciously political. Her seventh book, which focused on the Dade County campaign, was evocatively titled *The Anita Bryant Story: The Survival of Our Nation's Families and the Threat of Militant Homosexuality*. A year later, *At Any Cost* took a more defensive tone, calling out media misrepresentations of PAC and detailing the stress and harassment that Bryant had faced as a result of her activism. The covers of these books featured a restyled Bryant, professionally attired in a collared shirt and blazer, speaking at a microphone on the cover of *The Anita Bryant Story*, and sitting next to her husband, apparently facing a press conference audience on the cover of *At Any Cost*. In these books, Bryant openly struggled with articulating a new political identity based on the concerns that had been developing in her writing over the past several years.

Previously the fresh-faced symbol of down-home comfort and American tradition, Bryant became their outspoken defender, forcefully articulating the political underpinnings of the ostensibly apolitical tropes that had made her such a successful evangelical celebrity. Though Bryant had previously noted troubling trends in American culture she had also consistently expressed her conviction that the United States was still essentially a Christian nation and that Americans overwhelmingly shared her basic beliefs and values. Bob Green wrote in their 1973 book: "America is still one nation under God. And no matter how we criticize our country—and we all do, if we love her—and no matter how much the world criticizes us, we still know we are God's people." Americans may have strayed from the righteous path, out of selfishness or ignorance or apathy, but "it's still a fact that God has sustained us through everything in our history. God is alive in America today."[87]

The idea of an "out" and "proud" homosexual movement challenged Bryant's unquestioned assumptions about American values and the bounds of propriety. Perhaps even more devastating, the fact that apparently "normal" Americans, including Bryant's own friend, would support such a movement defied her expectation that most Americans shared her values, based on a common biblical morality. In this way, the PAC campaign compelled Bryant to contend with beliefs that she had not previously understood to be controversial.

As she experienced it, the Dade County legislative fight forced her into an ide-ological position although she had never been politically minded before. "One day it dawned on me," she wrote in 1978, "I was 'out of the closet,' too." She continued: "When you make a deliberate choice and take a stand, it requires courage, and so in a sense I could identify with what the homosexual was saying. Once I had overcome my apathy I could not go back to the position of noninvolvement as before."[88] Having once considered herself quintessentially normative, Bryant began to understand herself as part of an embattled cohort whose values were under attack.

Bryant's reportedly sudden recognition of the political implications of her views occurred within a broader political and cultural context that similarly informed the rise of the New Christian Right. This iteration of conservative evangelicalism would not become a dominant force in national politics until the late 1970s, when flourishing evangelical visibility and political mobili-zation converged to form a recognizable, if nebulous, movement. The 1976 presidential election brought intensified media coverage to evangelical com-munities, due in large part to Democratic candidate Jimmy Carter's Southern Baptist roots. Interpreting contemporary polling data, George Gallup famously declared 1976 "The Year of the Evangelical."[89] Three years later, Jerry Falwell inaugurated the Moral Majority and Beverly LaHaye founded Concerned Women for America, both organizations that would become important hubs in a movement without a single official leader or organizational affiliation. Bryant's crusade was also at its height in 1979, having grown over the pre-ceding three years from a local campaign into a national tour de force.

Like Bryant, both Falwell and LaHaye narrated their political awakenings as sudden shifts in perspective, the result of realizing that their religious commitments required political action in response to an imminent threat. Falwell famously had to justify his newfound political engagement, particu-larly in light of his widely distributed 1965 sermon "Ministers and Marchers," which condemned the politicking of Christian ministers on behalf of African American civil rights movements. Falwell explained this change through shifting his interpretations of scripture. He even drew explicitly on the lan-guage of the civil rights movement to characterize conservative Christians as an embattled minority in a changing American culture.[90]

Women like LaHaye and Bryant faced an additional challenge in seeking to justify not only their political engagement but also their national leader-ship in the context of their commitment to traditional gender roles. LaHaye did so most often by positing feminism as a particular threat to Christian women and by insisting that women were uniquely positioned to oppose the feminist movement. Feminists claimed "to speak for all women of

America," LaHaye frequently argued, and only American women could effectively prove them wrong.[91] Bryant justified her own political leadership by drawing on the language of maternalism, underscoring her role as a mother and insisting that her political action was merely an extension of that role. Building on a long history of maternalist rhetoric in women's social movements across the political spectrum, Bryant added new iterations to that rhetoric, responding to the contemporary feminist movement and elaborating on an existing language of political ambivalence within conservative evangelical communities.

Personal Responsibility and Individual Selfishness

Bryant's political ideas were also based on a particular understanding of the relationships between individuality, selfishness, and personal responsibility that suffused New Christian Right rhetoric and that Bryant tacitly negotiated in both her earlier and later books. The developing religious right combined free market economics and moralistic social conservatism in a rhetoric that was highly individualistic in its approach to solving social and economic problems, but it was also deeply critical of perceived selfishness in certain political movements and cultural trends.

In her early writing, as Bryant began to connect her personal concerns about cultural declension to national trends ranging from unwed mothers and rising divorce rates to student protests and the feminist movement, she consistently sublimated any political inklings in favor of an overarching emphasis on individual Christian and family life. Even when she lauded the teenage organizers of the 1969 Miami Youth for Decency Rally—a notable exception in her early writing, which otherwise did not directly acknowledge the possibility of collective political action—she presented this story not as a call to action but rather as a heartwarming narrative that evidenced the continued influence of Christian values among some contemporary youth.[92] More typically, Bryant framed the issues that she raised as problems of personal character, rooted in widespread selfishness and lack of discipline, and she advocated solutions premised on individual recommitment to God and family rather than political action aimed at redressing systemic concerns, as in her 1973 assertion: "I've come to believe America ultimately will be endangered unless each of us endeavors to become a really, strong, godly man or woman."[93]

Bryant also drew a clear line between individuals taking responsibility for their lives on one hand and the problem of personal selfishness on the other, characterizing the latter as a major factor in American cultural decline.

She blamed mothers at large for buying into a self-centered culture, sold to them in the pages of women's magazines that drew their attention away from their families and caused them to fail their children and "their husbands even more."[94] Significantly, however, she asserted that family breakdown was also "the *man's* fault" for failing to follow "God's plan" establishing him as head of the household.[95] According to Bryant and other contemporary Christian conservatives, individuals could redress national declension by taking responsibility for themselves in the context of the family, while at the same time, selfish individualism threatened to tear Americans' attention away from the family and toward the superficial concerns of a secularizing world.

Bryant also situated this selfishness at the heart of contemporary rights-based movements, at first obliquely and then more overtly. She asserted in 1972, for example, that "an enormous problem in America today is our sinfulness against God as each of us individually persists in carving out his own personal set of rules, his own so-called rights."[96] She underscored this sentiment even more forcefully in 1977, arguing that the "idols of personal liberation, self-indulgence, so-called 'human rights,' or 'do your own thing'" were tools that the devil used to distract mothers from their duty to protect their children.[97] In her earlier writing, the promotion of individual rather than collective action served to distance Bryant from the political activists that she subtly dismissed. As she came to embrace her own political role and to engage in collective action herself, however, the charge of individual self-centeredness became an increasingly explicit way for Bryant to discredit her political opponents. Maintaining this tension between the individual and political realms, Bryant suggested that the only correct political action, especially for women, was that which was an extension of existing personal responsibilities to one's family and one's community, as understood through a conservative theological framework. By this logic, when women aimed their political activism at achieving rights for themselves, they acted out of selfishness and therefore inappropriately.

Before 1976, Bryant repudiated political engagement in part through oblique identification against the feminist movement, which she did not explicitly name. "Think of today's unhappy women who struggle to usurp men's authority," she wrote in 1972. "Though most of us women don't consider ourselves activists in that sort of struggle, we may actually end up in the same camp, if we nag, bicker, criticize, and undercut the man God gave us to love."[98] Such representations of feminists as unhappy women and incapable wives would become commonplace in the exhortations of the religious right's male leaders, perhaps most memorably in Pat Robertson's reported statement two decades later that feminist efforts in support of the Equal Rights Amendment were "about a socialist, anti-family, political movement that encourages women to leave their husbands, kill their children, practice witchcraft, destroy capitalism and become lesbians."[99] Women like Bryant, however, contributed a different inflection to statements of this kind, making it clear that conservative Christianity could not be dismissed as the rambling of nervous patriarchs and that feminism could not be assumed to speak for the interests all women. Rather, the reactions of conservative Christian women to the feminist movement in the 1970s demonstrate that women's participation was vital in structuring competing visions of womanhood on either side of the brewing culture wars.

"A Day without Sunshine"

Bryant's involvement in the Dade County campaign and in subsequent battles over gay-rights legislation also made her a powerful symbol for a developing gay liberation movement throughout and even outside the United States. The idea of organizing for the rights of sexual minorities was not new in the 1970s, but the founding of gay liberation groups in the late 1960s marked the development of a newly vocal and assertive movement. Abandoning the respectability politics of the older homophile movement, these new activists took their inspiration from Black Power activists and others involved in radical identity-based fights. They emphasized gay visibility and pride and insisted on social acceptance and legal protection.

In the midst of the battle in Dade County, protestors began to show up at Bryant's speaking and signing engagements across the country.[100] One protestor—who described himself as a "Groucho Marxist"—famously hurled a banana cream pie in Bryant's face as she gave a press conference in Des Moines in 1977.[101] That same year, the National Gay Task Force spearheaded a nationwide educational campaign entitled "We Are Your Children," with the stated aim of countering "the image of gays suggested by Anita Bryant's 'Save Our Children' slogan by providing people with opportunities to learn the truth about the gay lifestyle."[102] In Holland, an openly gay member of parliament staged a benefit concert in Amsterdam called "The Miami Nightmare" to raise money for full-page pro-gay-rights ads in American newspapers with headlines like "A Message from Holland" and "What's Going on in America?"[103] Across the country, gay liberation groups simultaneously castigated Bryant for her anti-gay-rights stance and credited her for drawing attention and support to their movement.[104]

Opposition to Bryant culminated in a national boycott of the brand most closely associated with the singer: Florida Orange Juice. Gay bars across the country replaced their "screwdriver" cocktails (traditionally made with vodka and orange juice) with "Anita Bryants" (substituting apple juice for orange).[105] Gay liberationists produced merchandise and protest signs that alluded to Bryant's connection with the brand, bearing slogans like "Squeeze a Fruit for Anita!" and "Anita Bryant Sucks Oranges!" They repurposed the company's slogan, "A Day without Orange Juice is Like a Day without Sunshine" to assert instead that: "A Day without *Human Rights* Is Like a Day without Sunshine."[106]

Almost immediately, Bryant began to report that her bookings were suffering as a result of the protests against her. In February 1977, she issued a press release stating that she had been "blacklisted" from various professional opportunities because of boycotts and protests orchestrated by what she alleged was a "small number of vocal homosexual activists."[107] Around the same time, Bryant lost the contract for a daytime television show when the program's main sponsor—Singer Sewing Machines—pulled its support. In a telegram to Bryant, the television production company cited "the extensive national publicity arising from the controversial political activities you have been engaged in in Dade County."[108] The Singer company faced some backlash for this decision, from Bryant's supporters and from those who did not necessarily agree with Bryant but who firmly disagreed with "her dismissal—solely for her political views rather than her ability to perform."[109]

Seven months later, the Florida Citrus Commission grasped at political neutrality in its decision to retain Bryant as a spokeswoman. In a resolution adopted on November 16, 1977, and later released to the media, members of the commission's advertising and merchandising committee stated that "we are proud to be associated with Anita Bryant, but also feel that threats to boycott the use of Florida orange juice by either her friends or opponents is making use of a product in a moral issue in which it does not deserve to be embroiled."[110] Internal records indicate that the commission worried about a potential boycott by Bryant's detractors, but that members were also concerned about the possibility of political fallout if they let Bryant go. In the weeks surrounding the Dade County referendum in June 1977, the Florida Citrus Commission began receiving large volumes of mail addressing Bryant's role in the controversy, but this correspondence did not suggest a clear path forward. "The latest letters received expressed endorsement of Anita Bryant's stand which was a reversal of the letter writing campaign in the earlier stages," reported one member to the public relations committee on July 20.[111]

To help sort things out, the commission ordered two separate studies to determine how and whether Bryant's campaigning would affect their brand. Both studies found "about two-thirds of the respondents to be aware of the controversy and Anita Bryant's involvement" but also concluded that "this awareness level was not converted into a strong feeling for or against Anita Bryant as an effective spokesperson for orange juice nor does it appear to have a significant bearing on projected purchasing patterns." At the same meeting in which they heard this report, the advertising and merchandising committee also listened to a statement from Florida citrus grower Frances W. McElhainey, who expressed her longtime loyalty to Florida citrus, her newfound respect for Anita Bryant, and her disappointment in the commission's neutrality in the controversy. "Neutral, on homosexuality?" she asked, plainly incredulous at the idea that the commission was "in a no win situation" when it came to this issue. "Surely there are more potential citrus customers who do not consider homosexual choice a normal, viable procedure than there are those who practice perversion," she argued.[112] No opposing opinion was apparently raised.

Nonetheless, stories about the orange juice boycott's success took on a life of their own in gay communities and among Christian conservatives. The idea that the boycott had successfully driven Anita Bryant to ruin was a powerful one because it simultaneously served the rhetoric of two oppositional movements. For gay-rights supporters, the boycott represented an important early victory and an indication that gay liberation might be able to garner public support. Whether or not the boycott really had succeeded in unseating Bryant, it is absolutely the case that this was a critical moment for gay liberation groups across the country and a catalyst in the formation of a truly national movement. For conservative Christians, the idea that "a small group of militant homosexuals" had been able to wield this kind of social and economic power was also deeply resonant. It added support to the notion of cultural declension that undergirded the rise of the New Christian Right and contributed to a rising sense of cultural alienation among conservative Christians that helped to draw them to this developing political movement.

By the early 1980s, Bryant was in dire financial straits and beginning to fade rapidly from the public eye. The controversy surrounding her anti-gay-rights crusade may have contributed to her declining popularity, but it was her divorce from Bob Green that depleted her support among the conservative evangelicals who had made up the majority of her fan base for over a decade. In August 1980, Bryant divorced Green against both his protestations and the advice of their pastor. She publicly stated that their marriage had been rocky for years and that the stress of the Protect America's Children campaign had brought her to the brink.[113] The board of Anita Bryant Ministries, which included Bob Green and Reverend Chapman, responded by canceling "all her engagements for Christian ministry including contracts for [a] TV special and radio ministry."[114]

In December 1981, Bryant wrote a letter to her supporters asking them to confirm that "you still love me and believe in the cause which in many ways cost me so dearly." She also asked for financial support for her friend, televangelist James Robison, who hoped to "continue the fight" with his television special "Attack on the Family." Ken Campbell, the head of a large Canadian ministry and previously one of Bryant's strongest supporters, responded to this fundraising effort with a letter to Bryant that castigated her for her "self-assertiveness" in pursuing the divorce. He also sent a letter to Robison, calling Bryant's appeal an "abomination" and excoriating Robison for having "persisted in providing Anita with the 'moral' support for her wicked rebellion against the Lord which destroyed a family and publicly disgraced our Saviour." In the letter, he reminded Robison that Jerry Falwell had also "warned" him to discontinue his association with Bryant.[115]

Bryant's political authority had rested in her credibility as an exemplar and defender of traditionalist gender roles. Though it was distinctly Bryant, and not her husband, who led the Protect America's Children campaign, her continued leadership in the New Christian Right quickly became untenable without his public support. Divorce unmoored Bryant from the normative family and from the maternal role upon which she based her public identity and her political authority.

Despite this, it is conceivable that Bryant might have been able to weather the divorce with a greater proportion of her fan base intact if she had been willing to play the part of a contrite and humbled divorcée. Instead, she publicly condemned both her ex-husband and her pastor for their behavior during the separation, telling Ladies Home Journal in 1980 that the two of them conspired with Christian marriage counselor B. Larry Coy to ruin her reputation and career if she ended the marriage. Together, she said, three men formed a "devil's triangle" in a "satanically self-righteous conspiracy" against her.[116] More even than the divorce itself, these choices signaled to Bryant's conservative Christian supporters that she was no longer acting under the headship of appropriate male authorities or—by extension—in obedience to God. In this way, Bryant's career exemplifies the significant roles that women played as national leaders of the New Christian Right, as well as the limited parameters of their authority within this movement.

Conclusion

For three years, between 1977 and 1980, the Protect America's Children campaign was a powerful national phenomenon. Anita Bryant's emergence as a national spokeswoman for a developing rhetoric of "family values" helped to mobilize a new contingent of evangelical activists and to galvanize a nascent gay liberation movement. Though Bryant lost her platform quickly thereafter, her influence would continue to resonate among activists in both movements for decades to come. In particular, Bryant's rhetoric of child protection, which elaborated earlier concerns in the context of a new and emotionally charged anti-gay-rights discourse, would continue to characterize conservative Christian arguments against "special rights" for sexual minorities into the twenty-first century.[117]

When Anita Bryant began writing the celebrity memoir that would be published in 1970, she could not have anticipated the changes in her public role and political engagement that would take place over the next ten years. Yet even her earliest writing provides glimpses into the beliefs that would come to undergird her political commitments and the strategies that she would use to justify her new, public, political role. Tracing Bryant's gradual politicization over this crucial decade reveals the ways in which pervasive understandings of moral declension and assumptions about shared American values predated and supported the rise of the New Christian Right, not only in earlier iterations of evangelical activism but also in the purportedly apolitical spaces of conservative evangelical subculture.

Bryant offers a representative example of women's leadership in this movement. Her writing offers new insights into the New Christian Right's ascendancy in the late 1970s, from its members' initial expressions of profound political ambivalence to its amalgamation of complex rhetorical influences from across the political spectrum. The example of her political career underscores the importance of analyzing the roles that women played in this movement and the ways in which they understood those roles, not only on the grassroots level but also as nationally prominent figures. Women's leadership in this movement was limited and fragile, but it was also essential in shaping the movement's rhetoric of gender and family and in making antifeminist activism attractive to a new contingent of evangelical supporters who were beginning to understand their religious and family commitments not only as private matters but also as the basis for public political engagement.

3

Beverly LaHaye Defies Feminism

IN 1979, BEVERLY LAHAYE, a pastor's wife, evangelical author, and newly minted political activist, founded Concerned Women for America (CWA) with the goal of forging "the largest women's lobbying group in the nation."[1] Directly pitting her group against the feminist National Organization for Women (NOW), LaHaye asserted that CWA presented a choice to the American woman: "She can join the feminists and spend her life with the family agitators who would destroy the 'patriarchal' system; or she can join those who are working to preserve Christian morality and the traditional family.'"[2] Four years later, LaHaye moved CWA from its early headquarters in San Diego to a new office in Washington, DC. At a press conference to mark the occasion, she announced that CWA "is here in Washington to end the monopoly of the feminists who claim to speak for all women."[3] At the same press conference, LaHaye claimed over 200,000 members for the four-year-old organization, approximately four times the number cited for Catholic activist Phyllis Schlafly's eleven-year-old Eagle Forum in the same year.[4]

Through her work with CWA, LaHaye became one of the most important national figures in the New Christian Right. Her career is also representative of the regional trends that influenced the national rise of postwar conservatism. LaHaye began her public career in San Diego, at a time when southern California churches populated by recent Sunbelt migrants were beginning to define the conservative theologies that would undergird national conservative Christian movements in the decades to come.[5] Beverly's husband, Tim LaHaye, was a megachurch pastor in this milieu who later became an early architect of the New Christian Right, helping to found many of the movement's most influential organizations, including the Moral Majority. Postwar southern California was also fertile ground for conservative women's organizing, producing a variety of interconnected women's groups that focused on issues ranging from communism to sex education.[6] Beverly LaHaye drew inspiration from her husband's work and from the rich tradition of conservative women's activism in the region. In founding CWA, she purposefully and successfully combined these precedents with the rhetoric and reach of evangelical women's culture to create a political organization that spoke directly to the concerns of evangelical women. At the same time, she also mobilized the language of sudden political awakening and newfound national danger to downplay these precedents and to portray her organization as wholly unique and sorely needed.

This strategy was in keeping with movement leaders' broader emphasis on sudden politicization in response to urgent threats. In LaHaye's case, it also reveals the tense negotiations surrounding ecumenical cooperation and denominational identity that characterized this newly expansive conservative Christian movement. In its focus on mobilizing conservative women against feminist causes, CWA often replicated the work of the Eagle Forum, a national conservative women's organization founded by Phyllis Schlafly in 1973. LaHaye was aware of the Eagle Forum before she founded CWA, and she often promoted Schlafly's work in CWA literature. Nonetheless, she also frequently referred to CWA as the "first" or "only" lobbying group for conservative Christian women, implying that she did not consider the Eagle Forum to be sufficiently focused on religious matters or that she did not consider Schlafly—who was Catholic—to be properly Christian. The relationship between CWA and the Eagle Forum exemplifies the strained ecumenism that characterized the development of the New Christian Right. On one hand, this movement thrived because of new efforts at political coalition building between previously adversarial religious groups, especially conservative Catholics and fundamentalist Protestants. On the other hand, Protestant leaders continued to frame their activism in theological terms that foregrounded evangelical beliefs and that often subtly disparaged Catholics, Mormons, and other newfound religious allies.

As the founder and head of CWA until she stepped down in 2006, LaHaye built an explicitly political career centered on women's issues and conservative evangelical theology. She worked to establish an expansive political program for CWA, asserting in 1984 that hers was not only "a defensive fight" against the forces of the contemporary left but also a broad platform of advocacy for "women's and families' rights" as she interpreted them.[7] Through her work with this organization, LaHaye strove to amplify the voices of conservative Christian women. She also focused on issues of central concern to the New Christian Right more broadly, including opposition to contemporary feminism, homosexuality, sex education, secular humanism, and the threat of government overreach both federally and in the global sphere. As a national organization, CWA acted as a clearinghouse for grassroots conservative Christian women's movements across the country and provided direction to conservative women interested in advocacy on local and national levels.

Finding a Voice

Beverly Jean Davenport was born at the dawn of the Great Depression in Southfield, Michigan, a working-class suburb of Detroit.[8] Though she is nearly a decade older than Marabel Morgan, the two women's childhoods bear striking similarities. Beverly's father left when she was two years old, resulting in economic distress that forced Beverly's mother, Elie, to take a job at the telephone company and to move with her two daughters into the home of a neighbor.[9] The family lived there until Elie Davenport remarried two years later. When a heart condition and nervous breakdown left Elie bedridden, Beverly had to take on adult economic and domestic responsibilities at an early age.

Morgan, Bryant, LaHaye, and Tammy Faye Bakker all came from families deeply marked by divorce and resulting hardship. Yet in their adulthoods, each would draw on declension narratives that spoke about family breakdown as a new and troubling phenomenon.[10] In the 1970s, as divorce rates rose, mass media outlets fretted over the state of the modern family, and feminists advocated new gender and family arrangements, these women likely understood the contemporary women's movement as unwittingly promoting the kinds of childhood experiences that had left each of them feeling isolated and precarious. Though no particular politics necessarily follows from any given childhood experience, the early experiences of these women, read in their particular religious and cultural contexts, do suggest one reason they were ultimately drawn to a political platform that emphasized family stability, men's responsibility, and feminine domesticity rather than one that centered on marriage reform, nontraditional family arrangements, and women's labor-force participation.

In 1946, at the age of seventeen, Beverly enrolled at the evangelical Bob Jones University in Greenville, South Carolina. It was there that she met Tim LaHaye, a twenty-one-year-old Air Force veteran, also from Detroit, who had been a gunner in Europe during the Second World War. The couple married within a year of meeting, forming a partnership that would last for nearly seventy years, until Tim's death in 2016. After graduating from college in 1948, Tim became a minister and the LaHayes spent eight years in small pastorates in Pumpkintown, South Carolina, and Minnetonka, Minnesota, before moving to Scott Memorial Baptist Church in San Diego in 1956. Under Tim's leadership, the already sizable three-hundred-congregant church transformed into an early megachurch with over two thousand members, three campuses, and an annual budget of over one million dollars. It also grew to include child-care and counseling centers, the Institute for Creation Research, and full-time Christian education programs ranging from kindergarten to college.[11] During this time, Tim and Beverly also raised four children: Linda, Larry, Lee, and Lori.

Throughout her career, Beverly LaHaye revealed much less about her personal biography than did most of the other women at the center of this study. Instead, she took a more distanced approach in both her political and non-political writing. Focusing on issues of gender, sexuality, and antifeminist politics, LaHaye frequently referenced scriptural, social scientific, and nonpersonal anecdotal sources, but she said very little about her own life. At least one writer has suggested that this is because LaHaye was ashamed about parts of her past.[12] In particular, she had to work full-time while her children were still young in order for the family to be comfortably supported. Arguments against young mothers' working outside of the home would later become central in LaHaye's and CWA's political work, and this biographical detail could have embarrassed LaHaye and weakened those arguments. This inconsistency may have motivated LaHaye's reserve, but it also would not have been difficult to frame this experience as a cautionary example in the language of evangelical testimony. Perhaps more significant, then, is the fact that LaHaye was painfully shy well into adulthood. Although she eventually overcame this trait, she never developed the penchant for personal sharing that typified evangelical subculture in general and evangelical women's literature in particular.

At the beginning of her husband's career, LaHaye approached her role in the ministry with as much reticence as possible. Rather than ministering alongside her husband, she initially worked in the background, organizing and speaking to ladies' groups and counseling other women.[13] In fact, LaHaye has reported that she was uncomfortable with even the most limited public and social duties that this role required of her: "I refused most invitations to speak to women's groups because I felt very inadequate and questioned if I really had anything to say to them," she wrote, describing herself as having been "a fearful, introverted person with a rather poor self-image."[14]

This changed in the mid-1960s, nearly two decades into her husband's career when a conversation with conservative self-help speaker Henry Brandt helped LaHaye to understand her introversion as fundamentally selfish.[15] Later, like other conservative Christian writers including Anita Bryant, LaHaye would talk about selfishness as a marker of inappropriate political activity as well as a motivator for inappropriate political *in*activity. "It appears that the lines are being drawn between traditionalists in the church and women who are leaning toward the feminist positions," she wrote in 1984, characterizing feminism and apathy as similarly self-serving. "The differences at first may be minimal, but the division widens as the emphasis shifts to more of the self and less of God."[16] In this way, LaHaye infused her story of political awakening with the language of religious devotion and she encouraged her readers to understand their own political engagement as a necessary component of a deeper commitment to God.

LaHaye became a more active partner in her husband's growing ministry beginning in the 1970s. In 1971, Tim and Beverly founded Family Life Seminars, which gave them a forum beyond Scott Memorial Baptist Church in which they could preach on topics related to the family, the Bible, and personal self-help.[17] What began as a local and then regional ministry quickly spread beyond southern California, in the form of nationally and internationally distributed cassette tapes, two-day seminars for Christian couples, a radio show, and books that sought to "restore Christ-centered family living to American life."[18] In keeping with their shared belief that mothers should focus on the domestic sphere, Beverly did not begin to lead the seminars with Tim until 1976, the year that their youngest child reached adulthood.[19] By 1980, Tim and Beverly LaHaye were both nationally known figures in the evangelical world.

The Spirit-Controlled Woman and The Act of Marriage

The LaHayes built their national ministry through the established and growing networks of evangelical subculture in the late 1970s, becoming well known as self-help authors and going on to forge explicitly political careers in the burgeoning New Christian Right. Though their projects were often deeply connected, most of their later endeavors were also clearly delineated along gendered lines, mirroring gendered divisions within the larger evangelical culture. Beverly LaHaye's activities represent the ways in which conservative evangelical subcultures during this period promoted and fundamentally relied on the work of prominent women, at the same time that the leading voices in this subculture—among them, those same women—sharply reinforced the boundaries of women's authority.

Beverly LaHaye's career as an author and public speaker began with her serving as a feminine counterpart in her husband's newly established brand of family and marital advice. She made her authorial debut in 1976 with the publication of *The Spirit-Controlled Woman*, a spin-off of Tim's 1966 advice manual *The Spirit-Controlled Temperament*. Also in 1976, the LaHayes coauthored the marital and sexual advice manual *The Act of Marriage*, which would go on to become one of the best known evangelical books of its kind. Their writing was deeply conversant with other evangelical authors and with the tropes of evangelical subculture more generally. Drawing on broader cultural fascinations with marital advice, personality testing, and self-improvement, they infused these genres with overarching messages about the fundamental importance of evangelical conversion and daily Christian devotion.

The development of women's authority in evangelical subculture made Beverly LaHaye's initial contributions to her husband's growing ministry permissible and even necessary. Beginning in the mid-1970s, Beverly began to speak alongside Tim at Family Life Seminars and to give solo lectures on marriage, motherhood, and "the Spirit-filled life" at evangelical women's conferences and events.[20] Her publication of *The Spirit-Controlled Woman* arose from this work. Building on the tradition of women's ministries in the context of a growing women's subculture in the evangelical world, Tim, Beverly, and their editor at the evangelical publisher Harvest House agreed that Beverly, and not Tim, should speak and write to female audiences. As Tim wrote in the foreword to this book, "For years I have been asked to write a book on temperament and the Spirit-filled life from the woman's point of view. I have recognized the need for such a work, but my problem is, I don't think like a woman."[21] The idea that men and women had fundamentally different ways of thinking was one core component of conservative gender theology that helped to establish the need for women's authorship in evangelical subculture. It also helped to undergird conservative women's resistance to the feminist movement, since many contemporary feminists directly opposed the notion that binary gender differences were innate or worth preserving.

At the same time, Beverly's prominence also required justification in the context of an insistent conservative emphasis on women's domestic roles. Even as evangelical women's culture flourished in the late 1970s and 1980s, evangelicals continued to struggle over setting the terms of women's cultural and political authority. In this, they relied on long-standing strategies to justify Christian women's public contributions including emphases on the husband's permission, the woman's initial reluctance, and God's firm insistence. The foreword to *The Spirit-Controlled Woman* highlighted Beverly's qualifications for writing the book, including her gender and her experience lecturing on the topic. Equally significant, Tim's authorship of this foreword made it clear that Beverly wrote the book with her husband's blessing and under his headship. His foreword to the coauthored *Act of Marriage* did similar work while also underscoring Beverly's hesitance to take on a public role until she felt an insistent divine calling. According to Tim, Beverly had been "reluctant to get heavily involved with the endeavor until the Lord gave her a specific sign" through a series of remarkable successes in her counseling of married women that "convinced her that God required her active participation in the project."[22] These were the same rhetorical devices that Anita Bryant used to account for her own emergence as an author and then as a political activist, because both women drew on the strategies of female evangelical leaders in the United States dating back to the seventeenth century.[23]

The development of women's authority in evangelical subculture also bore a complicated relationship to contemporary feminism. In her later political writing, Beverly LaHaye would often invoke feminism as the imminent threat that justified her own political career. If feminism purported to speak for all women, she reasoned, then only vocal conservative women could effectively counter feminists' claims. At the same time, the gains of contemporary feminist movements helped to draw attention to a widespread absence of women in leadership roles and to stoke demand for women's prominence, even in antifeminist spaces. "At first we weren't sure how the pastors and churches would receive a woman lecturer," Tim mused in 1978, "but in the providence of God, Bev's ministry has actually drawn a greater audience than we expected. Apparently, in this 'day of the woman,' it has helped to see a husband-and-wife team share in such a program."[24]

The evangelical publishing house Zondervan apparently agreed with this perspective. In 1974, just as rival publisher Fleming H. Revell was beginning to experience phenomenal success with Marabel Morgan's *The Total Woman*, an editor at Zondervan approached the LaHayes to write their own book about "sexual adjustment in marriage," saying that such a book written specifically "by a Christian couple" was "sorely needed."[25] Yet despite this emphasis on coauthorship in the foreword, Tim's authorial voice dominated this particular book. Most conspicuous in this regard is the frequent use of the first-person singular to refer almost exclusively to Tim's experience, whereas Beverly is almost always referred to in the third person. These stylistic choices make it all the more striking that both Zondervan and Tim LaHaye were so insistent on Beverly LaHaye's involvement, correctly predicting that a marital manual written by a Christian couple would be more successful in the contemporary Christian book market than one written by a solo male author.[26] As Tim wrote in the book's first paragraphs: "To keep the facts that every couple needs to know from being offensive, I am writing this book with the help of Beverly, my wife of twenty-eight years." For the LaHayes and their audience, a feminine perspective brought a "delicate sense of balance" to the book and safeguarded its sexual content from charges of vulgarity.[27]

The LaHayes' *Act of Marriage* was published in the same year that Morgan's second book *Total Joy* hit the shelves. In seeking out a well-known pastoral couple to write a book of sexually explicit marital advice, Zondervan sought to capitalize on the interest in this subject matter and to stake their own claim in this market by striking a different tone. Whereas Morgan's books were short, chatty, and euphemistic, *The Act of Marriage* was relatively dense, clinical, and graphic. For example, a relatively explicit passage in *Total Woman* read: "For super sex tonight, respond eagerly to your husband's advances. Don't just endure." Morgan continued, "He may enjoy making love even when you're a limp dishrag, but if you're eager, and love to make love, watch out! If you seduce him, there will be no words to describe his joy. Loving you will become sheer ecstasy."[28] By contrast, a typical passage in *The Act of Marriage* instructed readers that "the husband who would be a good lover will not advance too quickly but will learn to enjoy loveplay. He will not only wait until his wife is well-lubricated, but reserve his entrance until her inner lips are engorged with blood and swollen at least twice their normal size."[29] Morgan addressed her readers as if they were close friends. In contrast, the LaHayes frequently mentioned their experience counseling married couples in their congregation to establish their expertise and to set the stage for a more authoritative and distanced approach. As a pastoral couple, the LaHayes were able to address both men and women and to present their book as a complete guide on the topic of marital sexuality, whereas the gendered divisions of evangelical authority limited Morgan to addressing women only.

Despite these differences, many of the LaHayes' overarching messages about sexual relationships were very similar to Morgan's. Like Morgan, they decried "Victorian" attitudes about sex and encouraged couples to think about marital sexuality as a blessing from God. Morgan and the LaHayes encouraged couples to seek out information about sex before their wedding night in order to avoid a painful and potentially traumatic experience.[30] Because the LaHayes offered advice to men and women, they explored both partners' potential faults in fostering a bad relationship, but their general advice to women was very similar to the advice that Morgan gave. They emphasized the importance of the wife's mental attitude, encouraged her to "never nag, criticize, or ridicule" her husband, and even echoed Morgan's central home improvement metaphor in suggesting that "'clean up, paint up, fix up' is a good motto for every loving wife to remember just before the time of hubby's arrival."[31]

Beverly LaHaye's first solo-authored book also bore striking similarities to Morgan's work. The bulk of *The Spirit-Controlled Woman* (1976) was based on Tim's *The Spirit-Controlled Temperament* (1966), which combined neatly categorized personality testing with spiritual advice. Beverly's book followed this model and added advice to wives on dealing with their husbands. Her emphasis on submission and her instruction to "Understand Him," "Please Him," "Respect Him," and "Examine Yourself" closely followed Morgan's "four A's": "Accept Him," "Appreciate Him," "Admire Him," and "Adapt to Him."

These similarities were not accidental. At the beginning of the chapter "For Women Only" in *The Act of Marriage*, Tim mentioned reading *The Total Woman* and being pleasantly surprised to read Morgan's assertion "that the brain is the control center in women for making love."[32] He continued, "I had long been aware of that fact, but was astounded to find a woman who would admit it." The LaHayes drew some of their inspiration directly from Morgan; other similarities between the two books resulted from the authors' mutual immersion in a subculture that was connected nationally through books, tapes, conferences, and periodicals exploring similar themes in similar contexts. The short bibliographies included in *The Total Woman* and *The Act of Marriage* reveal that Morgan and the LaHayes relied on many of the same books in producing their work. On opposite coasts, in California and Florida, these authors were immersed in the same evangelical subculture and as a result, they both consumed and produced similar ideas about the Christian family and its place in a changing nation.[33]

Tim LaHaye's voice dominated *The Act of Marriage*, but it did not take long for Beverly LaHaye to develop her own public career and to become one of the best-known and most prolific authors in evangelical women's culture. Between 1976 and 2010, she authored or coauthored thirty-four books, ranging from domestic advice to straightforward polemics—and often blurring the lines between these genres.[34] She began with books like *The Spirit-Controlled Woman* (1976) and *How to Develop Your Child's Temperament* (1977), which built on her husband's self-help concept but focused on the concerns of women in general and mothers in particular.

Like other female writers of evangelical marital advice during this period, Beverly LaHaye also promoted the doctrine of wifely submission while emphasizing that it should be a "chosen, deliberate, voluntary response to a husband" rather than "a status of inferiority."[35] But while some readers interpreted antifeminist politics in Marabel Morgan's work, LaHaye made those connections explicit, asserting, for example, in *The Spirit-Controlled Woman*: "Regardless of what the current trend towards 'Women's Lib' advocates, anything which departs from God's design for women is not right."[36] With this book, LaHaye entered into a national conversation among evangelical women that, as previous chapters have discussed, both emphasized and renegotiated the doctrine of women's submission in terms of conservative theology and in response to the growing influence of the feminist movement. Immersed in the political climate of southern California and influenced by her husband's political commitments, she also stepped more decisively into the political sphere than

Morgan ever did, and she did so earlier in her career than Bryant had.[37] Yet what is equally striking about LaHaye's advice manuals is that in spite of these sometimes explicit political claims, her writing fits seamlessly within a broader culture of evangelical women's writing in which political engagement was not always declared, though significant political assumptions were always present.

In 1984, LaHaye published two different books with two different evangelical publishers, each covering similar subject matter but in starkly contrasting tones. Both books were more explicitly political than typical evangelical women's advice literature. In both, LaHaye made direct arguments against contemporary feminism, secular humanism, and the erosion of traditional family mores. In both, she promoted the work of CWA and encouraged readers to deepen their spiritual commitments in part through political action on behalf of the traditional family. Yet the books were clearly aimed at two different audiences, one already politically engaged and the other immersed in evangelical women's culture but not (yet) involved in political activism.

Who But a Woman? was the most direct, its subtitle a blunt appeal: "Concerned women can make a difference." It began with a story about the successes of anti-communist women in Brazil and then carried readers through the early history and ongoing work of CWA in the United States and abroad. In place of a more traditional altar call, the book ended with "God's Challenge to Women": to get "right with God" and then "join with us in one of the most important women's movements in the history of this nation—or for that matter—the entire world." As she would do throughout her career, LaHaye collapsed religious and political messages in order to advance a vision of conservative political activism as an essential component of Christian duty. The book ended with the clearest possible articulation of this idea. "If we are truly committed to Jesus Christ," she wrote, "we have no other alternative but to wage warfare against those who would destroy our children, our families, our religious liberties. There is no other option."[38]

The Restless Woman was more circumspect. Its cover, with a soft-focus portrait of a young white woman holding a rose, looked like the covers of countless other evangelical women's advice books. It combined biblical analysis with historical and global perspectives on women's history that placed the blame for women's oppression on communism and "uncivilized" cultures. It condemned feminism and sought to offer an alternative. Indeed, the "restless woman" to whom the was book addressed seemed afflicted with a malaise similar to the "problem that has no name" described in Betty Friedan's groundbreaking *The Feminine Mystique* (1963). But whereas Friedan presented liberal feminism as a panacea for unfulfilled housewives, LaHaye posited feminism itself as the problem; the restless woman was "a woman who has been 'liberated' from traditional moral standards, yet now finds herself feeling empty and without goals."[39]

Both books reached similar conclusions: women's fulfillment could come only from a deep relationship with God and a commitment to protecting traditional family values in both the personal and political spheres. The fact that LaHaye published both books almost simultaneously highlights an important aspect of her career and of the history of conservative evangelical women. Even as LaHaye stepped decisively into the realm of political advocacy, she recognized that this remained a fraught prospect for many evangelical women and she continued to try to reach those women through the venues and rhetoric of evangelical women's culture. Throughout her career, LaHaye's work combined these themes in varying concentrations as she sought to mobilize different audiences. Her work did not simply become more explicitly political as her career developed; instead, LaHaye continued to blur the lines between the explicit politics of the New Christian Right and the purportedly apolitical traditions of evangelical women's culture in order to reach evangelical women still deeply divided on the proper relationship between religious and political engagement.

Becoming Concerned

Beverly LaHaye's prolific writing constituted only one part of a career that intertwined evangelical women's culture and activism on behalf of the New Christian Right. She founded CWA in 1979, three years after she published her first books and in the same year that her husband joined with Jerry Falwell and Paul Weyrich to form the Moral Majority. Both LaHaye and her husband had been involved in the political development of the New Christian Right before this point, as evidenced in the implicit political claims present in their books and Family Life Seminars, in Tim's sermons and the ministries of Scott Memorial Baptist Church, and in their friendships with people like Falwell and Weyrich, who would also become some of the best-known figures in the developing movement.

LaHaye's political career was also a product of her location in southern California, the cradle of the New Right in the decades after the Second World War. Conservative women's groups were particularly active in postwar southern California, where housewives in the Sunbelt suburbs developed their social networks into political ones, hosting coffees and luncheons to inform friends and neighbors about pressing local issues. Often becoming politicized through single-issue campaigns, especially around issues related to their children's education, these women gradually developed broader political interests and activist networks.[40] CWA grew out of this same political climate, coming onto the scene at a time when conservative women's groups had already been active for decades.

In her account of CWA's beginnings, however, LaHaye downplayed these precedents. Instead, she relied on a narrative of sudden political awakening that mirrored the rhetoric of the broader religious right and that sought to appeal to women who were committed members of their churches but ambivalent about political activism. The organization's debut newsletter explained that CWA was "the outgrowth of a few San Diego area women who became aware of the growing number of legislations [*sic*] that involved women and families."[41] Like many conservative women's groups at the time, CWA started as a series of "informal coffees and dessert meetings" where women shared their concerns with each other and with members of their communities. According to the newsletter, "they found that thousands of other women in their community also had little or no knowledge of the changes and laws and 'rights' that were being effected" and they concluded that "action could be accomplished only through an officially incorporated organization." The story ended with a rallying cry that justified the new organization's existence and called on other women to join in the fight, celebrating the idea that "Concerned women increasingly have voiced their dissatisfactions with the goals of the vocal feminist movement and organizations who represent them." This front-page story of the organization's inaugural publication carefully presented CWA as a group of ordinary women working against a clear and present danger that affected women's proper spheres—home and family—and that threatened women themselves.

In her own writing and public speaking, Beverly LaHaye consistently told two different but intimately related origin stories to explain both her own politicization and the genesis of the organization. The first had to do with the audacious claims of feminist leader Betty Friedan, the other with the International Women's Year (IWY) Conference held in Houston in 1977. "I shall never forget the day when Tim (my husband) and I were watching Barbara Walters interview Betty Friedan on television," LaHaye wrote in a direct-mail appeal to supporters in the early 1980s, repeating a story that she also told in several other publications and interviews. "Something in me was stirred to action as I realized Betty Friedan thought she was speaking for the women of America. I found myself saying verbally to Tim, 'They don't speak for me!! And I don't think they speak for the vast majority of women in America.'"[42] Here again, LaHaye presented her political awakening as a response to an existing threat, which conservative women must address by speaking out against the misrepresentation of their particular views and interests in the public sphere.

Similar themes were at the heart of the story that LaHaye told about the 1977 IWY conference in Houston. Funded by the federal government and actualized by the work of feminist activists nationwide, this conference proved a significant force for mobilizing conservatives—and especially conservative women—who were horrified by the apparent government endorsement of an explicitly feminist agenda. Significantly, LaHaye did not attend that event. Instead, she was giving a talk on "the power of prayer" at a Christian women's convention in Anaheim when a friend told her about the goings-on in Houston.[43] Based on her friend's account, LaHaye painted a picture of the conference as inherently hostile to conservative women and to Christianity writ large. In her 1984 book *Who But a Woman?* LaHaye wrote that the conference was "not in any way an open forum for the honest exchange of ideas on women's issues."[44] Instead, she alleged that feminist organizers ignored "fairness or parliamentary procedures" in order to push through resolutions in favor of the Equal Rights Amendment, gay and lesbian rights, "federally funded abortion on demand," and "federal government involvement in twenty-four-hour-a-day child care centers."[45] She further alleged that organizers had refused to read a minority report prepared by conservative delegates and that they had tried to silence these women altogether by passing out their names on an "enemy list" that warned other delegates to "AVOID THESE WOMEN. DO NOT VOTE FOR THEM."[46]

According to this story, the impetus for CWA's incorporation came directly out of the Houston conference: "On the return drive to San Diego from the Anaheim convention, five friends and I talked non-stop about the Houston convention and the feminist movement." They decided that although they "had been trying to live as good Christian women, being decent mothers and citizens," they "had been completely ignorant of the social forces that threatened to destroy our families and our nation."[47] Determining to organize in opposition to the feminist movement "or any movement that purposed to destroy the sanctity of our homes," these six women gathered others and began to host informal coffee meetings to educate their peers.

Narrating the organization's growth over its first few years, LaHaye concluded: "We were filling a void that had existed far too long. Traditional Christian women desperately needed to have a voice in the affairs of this nation." She asserted that "radical feminists" had been gaining ground in government and mass media "by default," but told her readers that thanks to CWA, "No longer do the feminists have a monopoly. No longer can they claim to speak for *all* American women. We are here, hundreds of thousands now, telling the world that feminism is a false view of the world."[48]

Of course, this was not an entirely accurate retelling of the history of conservative women's activism, as LaHaye herself well knew. In this same book and in other publications produced during the same period, LaHaye lauded the work of women who were organizing on behalf of "traditional values," both outside the aegis of CWA and well before CWA was founded.[49]

Indeed, the success of CWA's initial rally likely had a great deal to do with the fact that it was held shortly after the November 1978 failure of California Proposition 6, which would have made it illegal for the state's public schools to employ gay men or lesbians. This ballot measure was the brainchild of Republican State Senator John V. Briggs, who visited with Bryant's team in Florida before announcing the plan, which he called his own "'Save Our Children' campaign." Back in California, Tim LaHaye openly supported the passage of the proposition that came to be known as the "Briggs Initiative." Its close defeat was a sharp disappointment for conservative activists. For evangelical women who had been mobilized by the Briggs fight, CWA offered opportunity and direction for continued activism beyond that single cause.[50]

By framing the origins of CWA in a narrative of sudden political awakening and by presenting the organization itself as wholly unique, LaHaye made a canny appeal to women immersed in the culture of conservative evangelicalism but who had not yet made the leap to active political engagement. Downplaying her earlier political awareness and her connections to other prominent figures in the New Christian Right, LaHaye identified herself with her intended audience, as a housewife who had been uncomfortable about contemporary political and social changes but who did not know what to do about it or even whether it was her place to do anything.

This strategy dovetailed with the initial political ambivalence of a developing religious right and paralleled similar narrative choices among women across the political spectrum. LaHaye's nemesis, Betty Friedan, had been a union organizer and journalist in the 1940s and 1950s, but excised these biographical details in her 1963 bestseller *The Feminine Mystique*, presenting herself instead an unfulfilled housewife eager to help herself and others to find fulfillment through working toward gender equality.[51] Friedan's choice was motivated in part by the legacies of McCarthyism and the Second Red Scare; she wanted to avoid being disparaged as a communist. This was not a concern that LaHaye shared in framing her own political work, but for both Friedan and LaHaye, these choices proved successful in reaching beyond audiences of already politically engaged women to mobilize new activists.

Concerned Women for America

From the beginning, Beverly LaHaye intended for CWA to take its place as one of the leading conservative Christian organizations in the nation. Even in the group's earliest days as a small activist association based in the San Diego suburb of El Cajon, LaHaye often styled herself as CWA's National Director, an ambitious title that indicated her vision for the organization. In January 1979, LaHaye incorporated CWA as a 501(c)(4) tax-exempt organization, and she put out the first *CWA Newsletter* in the spring of that year. Before CWA was even a year old, Beverly LaHaye was ready to expand across the country.

The third *CWA Newsletter*, published in September 1979, called on readers to consider joining or founding local chapters in their areas. "We need hundreds, even thousands, of concerned people to respond to our challenge to join one of our prayer chapters," LaHaye wrote. "Let us hear from you this week and be part of the effectual fervent prayer group that could make the difference in our future and that of our children's [sic]." [52] CWA relied on the members of these chapters to mobilize other women in their communities and to organize local campaigns against any threat to conservative values, from smutty movies to the Equal Rights Amendment. From its headquarters in California, CWA sent detailed instructions to chapter leaders about how to establish their groups through introductory "luncheons, teas, coffees, and brunches" and how to organize local prayer chains, letter-writing campaigns, and other actions in coordination with the organization's national efforts. [53] These chapters proliferated rapidly. By February 1980, just thirteen months after the organization's incorporation, local activists had established fifty-two prayer chapters in at least fourteen states. [54]

In 1983, the organization began to add state and regional supervisors who volunteered to receive special training from CWA in order to organize and expand on the activities of chapters in their regions. The same year, LaHaye hired Carol Hummer as the organization's first National Field Director, a full-time staff position dedicated to coordinating prayer chapter activity. She also tasked Hummer with establishing 50,000 active prayer chapters within two years. [55] This herculean goal sprang from LaHaye's ambition to build a CWA prayer chapter in every evangelical church in the country. The following year, she put her husband Tim in charge of an effort to identify "Bible-believing pastors" across the nation and to ask them to nominate women in their congregations who might become chapter leaders. Carol Hummer did not ultimately meet her goal of 50,000 chapters within the two-year timeframe, but CWA's growth during this period was nonetheless impressive. By 1986, only seven years after its founding, the organization had expanded to include more than a thousand local chapters, spread over forty-nine states.[56]

It was also during this time that LaHaye partnered with a young attorney named Michael Farris to establish CWA's Educational and Legal Defense Foundation (ELDF), which would pioneer new strategies in the judicial arena on behalf of the religious right.[57] As "legal counsel for CWA," Farris litigated high-profile cases that focused on a long-standing concern among American conservatives: the rights of parents to protect their children from progressive influences in public school curricula.[58] In particular, CWA represented conservative Christian parents in cases related to homeschooling and "anti-Christian" materials in public schools. Farris also made it part of CWA's modus operandi to file amicus briefs in higher-court cases related to the organization's core concerns, including education, gay rights, and obscenity. He presented these legal pursuits to CWA's grassroots base in accessibly written articles for the *CWA Newsletter* and in pamphlets dedicated to educating CWA members about the law, as it related to CWA interests. These activities also became central to the organization's fundraising campaigns, serving as concrete examples of CWA's work and of the need for donations to cover legal fees and associated costs.

In October 1983, the four-year-old organization accomplished what LaHaye referred to as a "long-term goal" by establishing a permanent presence in the nation's capital. Michael Farris and CWA staffer Barbara Gibbons ran the Capitol Hill office, which LaHaye hoped would give CWA a more "effective voice in Washington on the key family and moral issues of the day."[59] Just over a year later, in the months after the 1984 presidential election, Tim and Beverly LaHaye also relocated to Washington in order to "be more effective" in their respective efforts to "present . . . the Christian viewpoint at the federal level."[60] In March 1985, Beverly LaHaye shuttered the CWA headquarters in San Diego and made Washington, DC, the organization's sole base of operations.[61]

These moves reflected CWA's increasing focus on influencing federal policymaking through direct lobbying efforts. In April 1984, CWA introduced a volunteer lobbying project called the "535 Program," named for the combined number of senators (100) and congressmembers (435) on Capitol Hill. Through this program, CWA aimed to train 535 women from the DC area—each assigned to one legislator—who would act as volunteer lobbyists on the organization's behalf. In addition, CWA called on women across the country to volunteer as Home District Congressional Liaisons, who would coordinate with local prayer chapter leaders "to develop a strong base on whom we can depend for hundreds of responses to our calls for prayer and action."[62] Shortly afterward, CWA also published the first iteration of its perennially popular pamphlet "How to Lobby from Your Kitchen Table," which—in addition to encouraging women to join CWA and the 535 Program—included practical tips for writing effective letters to newspaper editors and legislators.[63]

This emphasis on lobbying through relationship building marked a subtle but significant shift in the organization's political identity and its posture toward state and federal governments. Early CWA newsletters spoke about government efforts in antagonistic and exasperated tones, urging CWA members to join local fights against the Equal Rights Amendment and other federal government initiatives—including the 1979 White House Conference on Families—but offering little in the way of organized structure or support. Gradually, as the organization grew, it became the locus for highly organized national campaigns that combined the efforts of professional lobbyists with the power of a substantial grassroots network. Newsletters also shifted during these years toward presenting the government not only as an adversary but also as a potential ally, praising and actively working toward the passage of socially conservative legislation and the election of conservative legislators. Beginning in the mid-1980s, CWA attorneys and representatives began to regularly give testimony at congressional hearings on issues related to religious freedom, lobbying regulations, and legislation that particularly affected women.[64] Between 1986 and 1991, Beverly LaHaye herself testified before Congress on behalf of the Supreme Court nominations of conservative jurists Antonin Scalia, Robert Bork, and Clarence Thomas.[65]

This does not mean, however, that CWA reversed its core position on the evils of government overreach. Instead, as the organization grew, it developed a nuanced approach to state and federal governments, which balanced antagonism and cooperation on an issue-by-issue basis. During the 1980s, the pages of the CWA News were full of praise for President Reagan and often castigated his critics, including the NOW and the American Civil Liberties Union (ACLU).[66] Yet, in the midst of the Reagan presidency, in October 1985, CWA declared that the government "has increasingly become an institution aligning itself in an anti-family position," particularly with regard to parents' rights to discipline and educate their children. At the same time, CWA's proposed solution to this problem—a constitutional amendment protecting parents' rights—indicated substantial faith in the government's potential to help realize the organization's goals.[67]

A similar paradox was at play in CWA's response to the 1985 Protection of Pupil Rights Amendment (PPRA), which limited the kinds of information that schools could request from students and which CWA heralded as a "victory in public education" for parents' rights.[68] In praising the law, CWA commended federal legislators as heroes in the fight against government overreach, represented in this case by local public school teachers and administrators. Scholars of the modern right have sometimes puzzled over social conservatives' willingness to work with government to effect legislation in certain areas while simultaneously decrying the evils of big government. However, for CWA as for other organizations across the political spectrum, this balancing act between cooperation with and criticism of government has marked a nuanced, necessary, and effective approach in the context of a political system that is itself complicated and often internally contradictory.

Ecumenism and the End of Days

When LaHaye introduced CWA as wholly unique at its foundation in 1979, she most glaringly elided the work of another prominent conservative woman, Phyllis Schlafly, whose Eagle Forum had been doing similar work since 1973. Each founded by a charismatic leader in response to an increasingly vocal feminist movement, CWA and the Eagle Forum were the two largest organizations representing conservative women by the early 1980s.

Schlafly first founded the Eagle Forum to mobilize conservative women's opposition to the ERA after its passage through Congress in 1972. Gradually, the organization's platform expanded to include opposition to abortion, gay rights, and feminism as a whole. These were also the central concerns driving CWA, and the two organizations often approached these issues in similar ways. For example, both organizations opposed the United Nations' International Year of the Child (IYC) in 1979 as a prime example of government overreach and antifamily policy, and they both encouraged their members to attend IYC planning meetings and to educate others in their communities about the potential consequences of the IYC's progressive values.[69]

But despite shared concerns and even shared rhetoric, there were also significant differences between the two women and their organizations. Compared to Schlafly, LaHaye got a late start in public and political life. In 1946, at the age of twenty-two, Schlafly began a job as a researcher at the conservative American Enterprise Institute. Six years later, she launched her first of two, ultimately unsuccessful bids for a congressional seat. She was a fervent supporter of Barry Goldwater's 1964 presidential campaign and first gained national recognition when her pro-Goldwater book *A Choice, Not an Echo* sold over three million copies.[70] By the time she became the face of conservative women's opposition to the ERA in the early 1970s, she was already well known and well connected, not in the evangelical world but among conservative Republicans and politically active right-wing women.[71]

Both women were Christian and used the language of "Christian values" in their political platforms, but religion was a dividing point as much as it was a unifying one between them. Schlafly's political life was not as structured by religion as was LaHaye's; she came to politics earlier and out of a direct interest in the political system, whereas LaHaye entered the political realm through a specifically religious community. As a Catholic, Schlafly also did not have the same cultural privilege that allowed LaHaye to make her religious values so central in her campaigns and that fueled LaHaye's unquestioned assumption that her specific religious values were—or had once been, or should be—the values of all moral Americans.

Indeed, in the years preceding the rise of the New Christian Right, virulent anti-Catholicism had been common among American Protestants, especially fundamentalists and conservative evangelicals.[72] As recently as 1960, the National Association of Evangelicals (NAE) had spearheaded a campaign urging pastors across the country to organize prayer meetings, distribute literature, and speak out to congregants against the election of John F. Kennedy. "If a Roman Catholic is elected President," one direct mail appeal warned, "the Church of Rome will have a new, great advantage and the United States will no longer be recognized as a Protestant nation in the eyes of the world." Its central plea asked plainly "Don't you agree that it is time for the Protestants of America to stand up and be counted?"[73]

Even as conservative Protestants began to form alliances with conservative Catholics in the 1970s, evangelicals still harbored anti-Catholic sentiments. In the LaHayes' 1976 The Act of Marriage, for example, the couple explicitly blamed "Roman theologians" for negative Christian attitudes toward sexuality, even accusing medieval Catholics of allowing pagan asceticism to take precedence over biblical celebrations of marital sex.[74] Accusations of anti-Catholicism as well as anti-Semitism dogged Tim LaHaye throughout his career, from questions about his hiring policies at Christian High School to his reluctant resignation from Jack Kemp's presidential campaign team after his earlier anti-Catholic remarks captured public attention in 1987.[75]

Given this history of animosity between evangelical Protestants and American Catholics, ecumenical cooperation within the New Christian Right was both remarkable and fraught. In the late 1970s, evangelical leader Francis Schaeffer adopted and promoted the concept of "co-belligerency" to encourage conservative Protestants to join the anti-abortion movement, which was then overwhelmingly Catholic.[76] Defining a "co-belligerent" as "a person with whom I do not agree on all sorts of vital issues, but who, for whatever reasons of their own, is on the same side in a fight for some specific issue of public justice," Schaeffer offered fellow evangelicals a way of conceptualizing ecumenical cooperation without doctrinal compromise.[77] This idea proved influential. In 1979, for example, Jerry Falwell cited Schaeffer's influence to explain his decision to work with Catholic conservative Paul Weyrich in founding the Moral Majority. But even as ecumenical cooperation became a feature of the modern religious right, denominational identities and religious differences prevailed. "Christians must realize that there is a difference between being a co-belligerent and being an ally," Schaeffer wrote in 1982; "we must never forget that this is only a passing cobelligerency and not an alliance."[78]

Beverly LaHaye's own explanation of her willingness to work alongside nonevangelical women reveals the broader sense of embattlement and cultural alienation that inspired these pragmatic alliances. "I sincerely believe that God is calling the Christian women of America to draw together in a spirit of unity and purpose to protect the rights of the family. I believe it is time for us to set aside our doctrinal differences to work for a spiritually renewed America," she wrote in 1984. "The women of this nation are at a crossroads of history. The battle lines are becoming more clearly drawn. The forces of darkness are becoming darker. There is no neutral ground in the battle to come."[79] In this view, religious divisions became less meaningful and contingent alliances more conceivable in the urgent fight against secular humanism and moral relativism.

Yet even as she made this call for ecumenism, LaHaye clarified the boundaries of inclusion. She addressed the statement specifically to "Christian women," which for many evangelicals would have implicitly excluded Catholics. Further, although she made a similar plea in the same book to "men and women of all faiths," atheists were clearly and consistently excluded.[80] The apocalyptic tone of her language would also have made clear to evangelical readers that ecumenical partnerships were provisional and contingent on the dire circumstances of the times.

LaHaye prominently worked with Phyllis Schlafly, frequently referencing Schlafly's work in her publications and often featuring Schlafly as a speaker at CWA conferences.[81] Yet this acknowledgment of Schlafly's work throughout the 1970s and 1980s makes LaHaye's comment about CWA being the first organization for "traditional Christian women" all the more meaningful, given the implication that Schlafly's organization did not count, whether because Schlafly was Catholic or because the Eagle Forum focused insufficiently on religious principles in LaHaye's view. Perhaps even more notable, LaHaye spoke approvingly of the work of a conservative Mormon woman in a 1984 book despite the widespread evangelical belief that Mormonism was a "cult."[82] Yet in the same book, she winked at evangelical women who may have been shocked by this approval. Immediately after her statement about allying with "men and women of all faiths," LaHaye wrote without elaboration that "Christians were even beginning to work with cult groups who shared the same concerns for religious freedom."[83]

By the late 1970s and early 1980s, as the New Christian Right grew into a nationally significant political force, it was not a single issue—not communism, or abortion, or even feminism writ large—that brought traditionalist Protestants into common cause with conservative Catholics as well as libertarians and others. Instead, it was a much broader sense of alienation and embattlement, combined with an apocalyptic urgency that brought these groups into uneasy cooperation. For LaHaye and CWA, affiliations with other conservative women were important but were always tempered by the very particular understanding of Christian morality and evangelical identity that rested at the heart of any political reasoning. In her writing, LaHaye vacillated between broad ecumenical language and statements that made clear, at least to incisive evangelical readers, that coalitions formed with nonevangelical groups were always pragmatic and provisional.

CWA and Evangelical Women's Culture

Even if she sometimes overestimated the breadth of the void that CWA filled, LaHaye was not wrong in asserting that the organization—as a national political group focused specifically on conservative evangelical women— mobilized a particular niche of traditionalist women in a new and significant way. Speaking in the language and forums of evangelical women's culture, CWA reached out to women who were already immersed in the political assumptions that undergirded the New Christian Right but who had not necessarily begun to think of themselves as potential political actors.

Beverly LaHaye launched her political career by reaching through the national networks of evangelical women in which she was already well known as an author and public speaker. She gave talks related to CWA at evangelical women's conferences, prayer breakfasts, and other events at churches across the nation.[84] In other words, she promoted CWA at the same kinds of events at which she was already a sought-after speaker on topics related to marital adjustment and the power of prayer. As she began to publish more explicitly political books, she relied on the same evangelical publishers and distribution networks that she and her husband had used for their earlier writing.

During CWA's early years in the late 1970s and early 1980s, LaHaye argued forcefully in favor of Christian women's political mobilization, but she also echoed sentiments about women's political organizing that were more typical of evangelical women's culture at the time. For example, even in her definite opposition to contemporary feminism, LaHaye's rhetoric paralleled some of the ambivalence toward the movement expressed by writers like Morgan and Bryant, including the assertion that she was certainly in favor of women's equality but that the feminist movement had gone much too far. Just as Morgan insisted in 1975 that she was in favor of equal pay—"everybody in their right mind would have to be for that"—but lamented that feminists' emphasis on paid work "made the woman at home feel like a dodo," LaHaye wrote in 1984: "I am not against equal rights for women. I am totally in favor of equal pay for equal work; I support a woman's right to be free from sexual harassment on the job."[85] But an immediate caveat, targeting the Equal Rights Amendment, was much more specific and direct than Morgan's earlier hedge: "What I am against," LaHaye wrote, "is an amendment to the constitution that is a cleverly disguised tool to invite total government control over our lives."[86]

The differences between the two statements reflect the two women's different dispositions and career goals, as well as the passage of time. At the beginning of Morgan's career, though Phyllis Schlafly had already launched her own campaign against the Equal Rights Amendment, the New Christian Right was still in its infancy. By contrast, LaHaye's public career began as the movement was beginning to flourish, and she developed her ideas in the political contexts of Sunbelt conservatism and her husband's involvement with nascent conservative Christian organizations. The similarities between the two statements are equally telling. Nearly a decade apart, and despite the intervening work of CWA, the Eagle Forum, and other conservative women's groups, both women found it necessary to clarify that in opposing the feminist movement, they did not mean to oppose women's equality or their basic rights. Through the 1970s and 1980s, as the New Christian Right sought to control the public meaning of words like "morality" and "family," the feminist movement was already widely understood to represent the politics of women writ large. Though LaHaye and CWA would struggle explicitly against this understanding, the conflation between "antifeminist" and "antiwoman" posed a public-relations problem for the organization and for other conservative women's groups.[87]

As LaHaye developed political arguments for evangelical audiences, she built on the foundations of her earlier work. The power of prayer, for example, remained a central theme in CWA materials and in its organizational structure. As the organization developed, it included prayer as one of many lobbying strategies recommended for members. From the beginning, CWA named its local affiliate groups "Prayer chapters." As the November 1979 newsletter put it: "Because of the critical hour that America is in, we feel more strongly than ever before that prayer is the answer—the supreme power to save our country and turn it back in the right direction."[88] The organization also encouraged more tangible forms of activism including letter-writing campaigns, rallies, and lobbying, but it consistently situated prayer among these as an equally effective and absolutely central political tool. "Prayer chains" were organized across the country like telephone trees, receiving "alert notices" from the national organization "whenever any new issues rise, so we can all hold up the needs of other states as well as national matters of concern."[89] This strategy indicates the theological foundations of CWA's principles and structure. It was also an effective organizing tool, allowing all members to feel needed and involved, even if they could not, or were not yet willing to, attend meetings or rallies, distribute literature, or write letters.

LaHaye also made sure to alert members when God seemed to answer their prayers. In the spring of 1982, she wrote an article for CWA's newsletter entitled "Effective Prayers of CWA Women." In it, she reminded readers that she had asked them to "pray (and fast if possible)" every Wednesday for the first half of the year in order to help defeat the Equal Rights Amendment. "The battle lines were drawn," she wrote, "the feminists on one side with their high-powered media support, 15-million dollar fund-raising effort, Hollywood stars, and backing by ex-Presidents and their wives."[90] But, "all the feminist strength and energy in America cannot compare with the powerful tool of thousands of Christian women praying and some fasting on the same day, calling on God to heal our land (II Chronicles 7:14) and to defeat the ERA.' "[91] Those prayers had been answered, LaHaye reported, as evidenced by eight state votes against the ERA and a Supreme Court decision against its extension, all passed on Wednesdays. This, LaHaye wrote, was "nothing more than God's providential answer to thousands of Christian women praying and some fasting."

The theme of prayer remained central in CWA literature, and in 1990, LaHaye made it the focus of her book *Prayer: God's Comfort for Today's Family*. In this book, LaHaye outlined various political battles in which CWA members had been involved, and she highlighted the role that prayer had played in each of them: as an expression of support to the people at the center of these controversies, as a tool for discerning God's guidance, and as a reminder of God's control over every situation. The book ended like most evangelical books, with a call to action. In the style of the altar call to Christian conversion, LaHaye called on Christian women not only to rededicate their lives to Jesus but also to get involved in political activism: "Many women say, 'But the job is so big, and I am so limited. What can I possibly do that will make a difference?' " To this imagined audience, she responded enthusiastically: "I'm glad you asked!"[92] LaHaye's answer emphasized the power of praying and of being an example to one's family, but it also mentioned the work of other women who had written letters, organized local groups, and sought help from CWA. Offering further encouragement—and practical tools—for getting involved, the book ended with bullet-point information about CWA and contact information for the organization.

Conclusion

Beverly LaHaye stepped down as president of CWA in 2006, after holding the office for twenty-seven years. In that time, she authored dozens of books as well as hundreds of pamphlets, newsletters, and speeches promoting a particular vision of traditional family values for the home and for the nation. Today, CWA is still the largest conservative women's lobbying group in the nation, with approximately half a million members and an annual budget of four million dollars. Its Educational and Legal Defense Foundation continues to operate alongside Prayer/Action Chapters across the country. Meanwhile, a subgroup called Young Women for America serves as an outreach on college campuses and CWA representatives make frequent appearances as policy experts on cable news programs.

Beverly LaHaye's influence on the organization remains readily apparent. The Beverly LaHaye Institute (BLI), founded in 1999, acts as the organization's research and policy arm. As "the 'think tank' for Concerned Women for America," BLI produces statistical and analytical reports "to inform and educate policymakers and opinion leaders, the media, and the general public" in an effort to "counter the prevailing ideologies and agendas of radical leftists and secular humanists."[93] LaHaye's original priorities and vision also guide CWA as a whole. On its current website, the organization's core concerns are defined in terms of a familiar declension narrative: "In recent times, Western Civilization has willingly chosen to exchange the faith and logic of a Biblical worldview for an unthinking and cruel relativism. This foolish exchange is at the root of the glaring injustices of modern American public policy."[94] CWA's seven core issues—"sanctity of life, defense of family, education, religious liberty, national sovereignty, sexual exploitation, and support for Israel"—reflect many of the concerns that inspired LaHaye to found the organization in 1979.

Beverly LaHaye's career demonstrates some of the ways in which the modern religious right has relied on women's leadership even as traditionalist gender ideologies would seem to limit women to the domestic sphere. LaHaye began her career as a leading voice in evangelical women's culture, a necessary feminine counterpart to her husband's ministry. In the context of rising feminist cultural critiques and the growth of evangelical women's subculture, Beverly added an authority and marketability to Tim's family-focused ministry, which he could not have achieved on his own. As she established herself as a cultural phenomenon and political leader in her own right, her concerns remained grounded in the realms of family, sexuality, and home. From these positions, LaHaye was able to make wide-ranging political contributions, and she was able to assert that her voice—and the voices of other conservative women—were uniquely necessary to counter the claims of the feminist movement. Combining explicit political rhetoric with the language and forums of evangelical women's culture, she was also able to mobilize already politically active women alongside women who were reluctant to think of themselves as political activists. She also helped to expand the terrain of ideal Christian womanhood, going beyond the assertion that political activism was permissible under certain circumstances to insist instead that political engagement was a necessary component of every woman's Christian duty.

FIGURE I Marabel Morgan, 1974 ©Bettman/Getty

FIGURE 2 Anita Bryant, 1978 ©Reg Innell/Getty

FIGURE 3 Beverly LaHaye with President Reagan, 1984. Courtesy of the Ronald Reagan Library.

FIGURE 4 Tammy Faye Bakker, 1987 ©Bettman/Getty

FIGURE 5 Sarah Palin, 2012 Courtesy of Gage Skidmore.

FIGURE 6 Michele Bachmann, 2012. Courtesy of Gage Skidmore.

Tammy Faye Bakker Responds to the AIDS Crisis

ON JUNE 18, 1987, Tammy Faye Bakker's life was in a shambles. The expansive televangelical ministry that she had built over the past two decades with her husband Jim was falling apart, hit by a sexual and financial scandal that would eventually end in jail time for Jim and the complete destruction of the ministry that they called PTL (Praise the Lord, or People that Love). On this summer day, Tammy Faye appeared in front of news cameras for what reporters described as a "rambling, teary-eyed press conference."[1] Jerry Falwell, rival celebrity preacher and one-time friend of the Bakkers, had taken over the PTL ministry, but Tammy vowed that she would not let him take her lavish South Carolina home.[2] Mascara streaming down her face, she wept: "I wake up in the morning just wishing they'd killed us, and Jim does too. It would have been better if they'd just put a bullet in us."[3]

For many observers, this would become the lasting image of Tammy Faye Bakker: a sobbing, disgraced, and melodramatic televangelist whose most salient features were her excessive emotionality and heavy makeup. For many scholars, Tammy Faye was beside the point, a trivial contributor to a ministry and a scandal that were primarily driven by her husband Jim.[4] But Tammy Faye Bakker is significant in her own right, and the 1987 scandal surrounding Jim's sexual and financial indiscretion is far from the most interesting thing about her. Though the weight of the scandal has sometimes obscured their contributions, Jim and Tammy Faye Bakker were important figures in building the televangelical empires that marked the American religious landscape of the 1980s. They helped to build the three largest Christian television ministries of the era, the Christian Broadcasting Network (CBN) and Trinity Broadcasting Network (TBN), in addition to their own PTL Network. At its height, PTL included not just an internationally broadcast television station but also a rambling campus in South Carolina that housed a counseling center, campgrounds, a water park, a shopping mall, permanent residences, and the third-most-visited theme park in the United States (after Disneyland and Disney World). Tammy Faye in particular pioneered new expansions of evangelical women's culture on television, drawing from existing models in both Christian and non-Christian media.

Tammy Faye Bakker also represents the ongoing negotiations surrounding Christian women's roles in the public and political spheres in the 1980s. The gradual politicization of evangelical subculture through the 1970s and 1980s made political engagement unavoidable for Bakker, who embraced many of the positions of the New Christian Right, including opposition to pornography, abortion, and contemporary feminism. But whereas Beverly LaHaye declared in 1979 that her religious commitments compelled her fully into conservative activism, Bakker perpetuated throughout the 1980s a more complex negotiation of the relationship between religion and politics, and of Christian women's roles as political actors.[5] Her career helps to demonstrate the range of political options still available to conservative Christians, and particularly conservative Christian women, even at the height of the New Christian Right ascendancy.

Bakker's career as a televangelist peaked during the fomenting culture wars, which defined the 1980s and 1990s in terms of an increasingly irreconcilable rift between family-values conservatives and socially progressive liberals, each typically represented by their most strident spokespeople.[6] During these decades, the political undercurrents of evangelical women's culture became even more pronounced, but not all conservative Christian women responded in the same ways. As we have seen, shifting evangelical ideas about what constituted political and apolitical space in the 1970s and 1980s had given some women the ability to enter the public sphere without overstepping their commitment to conservative gender roles. With the understanding that their visions for a Christian America represented normality rather than a political agenda, they argued that theirs was defensive fight against militants and deviants. Presenting themselves as primarily Christian wives and mothers, women like Anita Bryant argued that their activism aimed only at reclaiming the church and the home as spaces exempt from political encroachment. Others, like Beverly LaHaye, embraced the politicization of the family and promoted a fusion of religious and domestic duty with active political engagement. These same negotiations of political and apolitical space also allowed some women to continue to occupy each realm differently, sometimes ambivalently and even subversively. For Tammy Faye Bakker, the choice not to make political engagement a central feature of her career made it possible for her to push at the bounds of contemporary Christian conservatism, most notably in her surprising call for Christian communities to welcome homosexuals and people living with AIDS as early as 1985.

For Bakker, such political deviations came in part from theological commitments that differed from those of the other women at the center of this study. Brought up in the Pentecostal Holiness tradition, Bakker emphasized salvation and soul winning above all else.[7] She rejected the strict moralism of her childhood church while retaining its expressive emotionality and emphasis on God's healing grace. For example, her famously outlandish makeup and penchant for sequins marked a rejection of early Pentecostal moral regulations that prohibited cosmetics and flashy clothing, and—more significantly for Bakker—also drove church members to shun her mother for being a divorced woman. The emotional fervor with which Bakker and her husband conducted services was typical of their Pentecostal upbringings, and their emphasis on forgiveness rather than condemnation marked a particular but not altogether peculiar choice among revival preachers.

These deliberate theological choices also informed the Bakkers' politics, which tended away from the reproving tone more typical of conservative Christian leaders at the time. The Bakkers' ministry grew in the 1970s and 1980s, alongside the expansion of evangelical subculture, charismatic televangelical ministries, and the New Christian Right. This latter movement flourished in part through the development of new alliances between divergent Protestant denominations that occupied different spaces on the spectrum of evangelical and fundamentalist theologies. Yet even as these coalitions came together, denominational differences continued to matter as leaders and grassroots supporters sorted out the relationship between religious and political commitments for themselves. It is therefore impossible to understand this significant political movement without examining the theological tensions that helped to define it. For conservative Protestant women, who often identified their concerns as primarily religious and only secondarily political, these theological and denominational fissures may have been especially salient.

Bakker's career is instructive because it highlights how evangelical women's negotiations of political boundaries made room for prominent women to simultaneously embrace and reject political engagement even in highly politicized cultural contexts. In particular, it reveals how Christian women's equivocations about political engagement could also provide them with space to espouse sometimes surprising political commitments. Bakker is significant, then, not because her politics were typical but because they demonstrate the political leeway afforded to evangelical women by gender ideologies that simultaneously depended on and obscured their political leadership.

The "Can't Do" Church and a "Can Do" Faith

Tamara Faye La Valley was born on March 7, 1942, in International Falls, Minnesota, the oldest of eight children born to Rachel La Valley.[8] Tammy and her brother Donny were born before their parents' divorce when Tammy was three, and their six younger siblings were born after Rachel's remarriage to a man whom Tammy later described as "a wonderful man whom I love dearly and was to me my daddy."[9] The ten La Valleys lived in a four-bedroom house, heated by a woodstove and without indoor plumbing. Recounting her childhood later, Tammy Faye would say that her family was "almost poor" but not quite, because they "always had clothes and food."[10]

Tammy Faye's attitude toward her childhood differed sharply from her husband's accounts of his. Jim Bakker was one of four children, the son of a machinist. He grew up in Muskegon, Michigan, a Grand Rapids suburb then benefiting from the postwar economic and industrial boom. When Jim was a teenager, the family moved to a "lumber-era mansion" with a bedroom for each child.[11] In high school, he cruised around town in Cadillacs that he bought used. Nevertheless, Jim later wrote, "I thought we lived in poverty."[12] This framing allowed Jim to tell a story of rags-to-riches prosperity that fit within PTL's "health and wealth" gospel. It also reflected a pattern of lifelong dissatisfaction that plagued Jim and sometimes sent him into deep depressions. His parents were emotionally distant and Jim felt an abiding "resentment" against them for their inadequacy in meeting his needs.[13] He thought that his family was poor because at Christmas, "instead of getting an abundance of toys like most kids" he and his siblings "got clothes and maybe one or two toys."[14] Meanwhile, Tammy Faye wrote about her smaller home housing twice as many children: "I thought our house was huge until I got married and discovered how little the house really was. But to me it was the biggest house in the whole world."[15]

As was the case for most of the other woman at the center of this study, Tammy Faye's parents divorced when she was very young and their divorce was a formative experience for her. Like Morgan, Bryant, and LaHaye, she would later draw on this experience to underscore the importance of the intact nuclear family. In her 1980 book *Run to the Roar*, which focused on teaching readers to overcome their fears, Bakker traced her own history of anxiety to "her anguish and pain of a broken home," as another of her books put it.[16] "My mother and dad divorced when I was three years old, and that put a great fear in me. All my life I'd feared that the same thing would happen again and that I would be without a dad or a mother and be left alone like a lot of kids that

I knew," she wrote. In 1987, the serious legacy of anxiety in Bakker's life would be underscored by news of her addiction to anti-anxiety medication.[17]

However, Bakker did not explicitly draw the same political conclusions from this experience as other authors, who traced direct lines between a rising divorce rate and purportedly surging rates of juvenile delinquency, teen pregnancy, and crime. Instead, the central lesson that Bakker took from the experience of her parents' divorce led her in a political and theological direction centered on acceptance and inclusion rather than moral absolutes. After Rachel La Valley's divorce in 1945, the family's Assemblies of God church would no longer let her play the piano or take communion. "My mother was a fantastic pianist," Bakker recalled in 1976, "but the church would do without a pianist before they would let my mother play the piano because she was divorced. To the church, my mother was just a harlot."[18] Bakker traced many of her persistent emotional issues to this experience, but she also drew broader connections that compelled her to take her own ministry in a different direction. In particular, Bakker asserted that this condemning, rules-based theology led to unproductive splits within the church and inappropriate priorities among believers. "Our church fell apart twice and closed its doors," she recalled. "It seemed everybody in the church was vying for power."

Perhaps even more problematic for Bakker, the unforgiving unkindness of her childhood church seemed to be fundamentally detrimental to the project of evangelism: "The way the church treated my mother may have a bearing on why my brothers and sisters aren't Christians today," she wrote in 1978. "There were eight of us and most of them don't know the Lord and don't care about the church."[19] In adulthood, Bakker would help to build a ministry that was centrally focused on acceptance, forgiveness, and evangelism and that downplayed rhetoric about sin and condemnation, to the point that some critics would later accuse PTL of moral relativism, a cardinal sin in the eyes of many conservative Christians.

Bakker asserted that her childhood church's emphasis on condemnation also held her back from a full relationship with God until she "received the baptism of the Holy Spirit" when she was ten years old.[20] Although she later narrated this experience as a rejection of that church, her intensely personal conversion experience and her emphasis on the Holy Spirit—as opposed to God or Jesus—highlight the continued influence of her Pentecostal background. Before this experience, she said, "I would pray, but I never thought God would answer my prayers. I was afraid I wasn't good enough for Him to answer." Contrasting her new faith with her past experience of church, Bakker said: "I don't know why I even went back to the church" that treated her mother so poorly, "except that I loved the Lord so much. The baptism of the Holy Spirit is the only thing that allowed me to keep my sanity. Praise the Lord, He became more precious to Mom and I through it all."[21]

This experience also led Bakker to question the authority of the church more broadly, which in turn strengthened her emphasis on emotional knowing and on each believer's personal relationship with God, both central elements of evangelical theology that are paramount for Pentecostals. For Bakker, these tenets of the faith became a way to reject other aspects of her church's doctrine, especially those that emphasized the strict regulation of believers' behavior. Perhaps most apparent in this regard was her first experience trying on the makeup that would become her trademark. Here again she situated condemnation as the language of a wayward church and acceptance as God's primary mode: "I had been taught that if you put on lipstick you are going to hell. That was it! How thankful I was that by now I had learned that God really loved me."[22] She began to wear eye makeup regularly, and although "the kids on the church bus saw it and talked about my eyes," she did not let it bother her, reasoning: "I was very close to the Lord and felt that God would speak to me in my heart if I really shouldn't wear it. When I did wear make-up I didn't feel condemned," she went on; "I began to wonder if maybe there wasn't more to serving the Lord than I had thought."[23] Decades later, the Bakkers would use this same reasoning to build a ministry that—although it opposed abortion, alcoholism, and even feminism—lacked the same condemnatory fervor that characterized other ministries of the New Christian Right. Whereas many of their contemporaries—including Anita Bryant—argued that Christian love must be demonstrated through the condemnation of sin, the Bakkers would continue to emphasize love in the absence of condemnation.[24]

At mid-century, Holiness Pentecostal churches, like those that Jim and Tammy Faye were raised in and later led, were undergoing dramatic demographic and doctrinal changes. Along with other evangelical denominations, these churches grew expansively during the Great Depression and in the years following the Second World War. Particularly in the latter period, they welcomed a more economically diverse population than before. At the same time, many of the working-class white people who had traditionally populated many of these denominations benefited disproportionately from postwar industrialization and prosperity, such that previously working-class denominations began to move toward the middle class even without the benefit of new membership. During the second half of the twentieth century, many of these churches also began to soften or even eschew strictures that prohibited members from seeing doctors, taking medicine, watching movies, attending dances, drinking cola, wearing jewelry, or donning makeup.[25] Various churches, including PTL, participated in and interpreted these changes in varying ways. Building on her own experiences of rejection in the church and her subsequent rejection of the church's rules, Tammy Faye would help to build a ministry founded on the emotional expressiveness of Pentecostal religiosity even as it used that emphasis to reject traditions of asceticism and to indirectly challenge the moral strictures that characterized the ministries of fundamentalist leaders including Falwell and the LaHayes.

The Bakkers' ministry was also representative of the increasing popularity of "prosperity gospel" in many Christian ministries, especially Pentecostal ones, in the 1970s. This theology, sometimes derisively known as "health and wealth" or "name it and claim it" gospel, has roots in older American religious and cultural traditions. The Puritans, after all, were Calvinists who looked to their material successes and failures to determine whether they were among God's elect, predestined for eternal salvation. More recently, in the last decades of the nineteenth century, a variety of philosophies from inside and outside the aegis of Christianity promoted "mind-over-matter" approaches to spiritual well-being, physical healing, and material profit.

During the first half of the twentieth century, the link between these disparate categories of prosperity took firm root in Christian ministries ranging from mainline Protestantism, to charismatic Pentecostalism, and even some Catholic ministries. Ministers drew on new interpretations of familiar biblical passages to prove that material blessing was a permissible, desirable, and even laudable component of a full Christian life. They assured congregants that upward mobility was achievable and that, once achieved, it would not bar them from the kingdom of heaven. This theology also contributed to the rapid growth of many independent ministries that promoted it. Beginning in the 1960s, charismatic preachers propagated the notion that "seed money" donated to God's work would come back to the donor in the form of abundant blessing from God. The prosperity gospel had its detractors, not least among them Christians who saw this theological emphasis as a perversion of their faith, but its popularity grew throughout the 1970s and 1980s, resonating with congregants' hopes for better lives and afterlives, and propelling the growth of ministries like PTL.[26]

Also during the 1970s and 1980s, the already porous boundary between the designations "evangelical" and "fundamentalist" would begin to fall away, as both became shorthand terms for the movement of Protestant Christians that was becoming increasingly vocal in conservative politics across the nation. Scholars of the movement have tried to delimit the boundaries of each term, but two factors complicate this exercise. First, most who would best be described by these terms do not identify with either, preferring instead designations like "Bible-believing," "born again," or even simply "Christian." While the first term leans more fundamentalist (focused on Biblical literalism) and the second more evangelical, neither belongs exclusively to either group, and the insistence on a "just Christian" identity belongs firmly to both. Fundamentalists have tended to be more critical of prosperity gospel while evangelical churches have been more likely to embrace it, but even this distinction is not absolute. Second, while the movement that would become known as the New Christian Right was premised on both fundamentalist and evangelical priorities—concerned with moral absolutes and intent on sharing those beliefs—at least some supporters of the movement, particularly conservative Catholics, would likely have rejected either designation. At the same time, a vocal contingent of evangelical liberals directly challenged the conflation of evangelical Protestantism and conservative political values.[27]

Anita Bryant and Beverly LaHaye both came from Baptist backgrounds, and the relative fundamentalism of the denomination is apparent in their shared emphasis on Bible reading and scriptural proofs as well as their central concerns with naming and condemning sin as they saw it in contemporary American society. Bakker's roots in charismatic Pentecostalism fostered a greater emphasis on emotional ways of knowing, which prompted her very personal understandings of sin and forgiveness. At the same time, all three women shared a central belief in direct, two-way conversation with God, highlighting the significant overlaps that make clear-cut theological designations so difficult. Nonetheless, Bakker's dominant emphasis on emotion rather than scripture reflects her charismatic roots, and in her case fostered a theological emphasis on acceptance that affected the ways in which she chose to engage and not engage with politics later in life.

Building a Ministry

Like Morgan and LaHaye, Bakker left home as a young adult to attend one of the hundreds of Christian colleges proliferating across the country, and it was there that she met her future husband in 1960. Jim Bakker was two years older than Tammy, also a student at North Central Bible College in Minneapolis, and the "hall monitor" who warned Tammy not to go out with groups of boys even if she thought the outings were harmless. The two started dating shortly after this encounter and they began a whirlwind courtship. They kissed after their first date although Tammy would later assure readers that she "had never given a boy a kiss on the first date" before. On the second date Jim asked Tammy to go steady and on the third date he proposed. Though she seemed to acknowledge in her 1978 autobiography that things moved quickly between them, Bakker also said of the proposal: "I had no doubts. I never would have said that to any other guy I had ever dated."[28]

Faculty and mentors at the college, as well as Jim's own parents, disapproved of the pace of their relationship, expressing particular concern that the two would not finish college if they married right away. Tammy Faye later conceded that in the midst of their romance, the couple's "grades started to drop because all we could think about was each other." But she also emphasized her total confidence that marriage was the right decision, by drawing again on the language of personal assurance granted by God. She said of her response to Jim's proposal: "When you love the Lord there is something inside you that bears witness, and God can speak to you and there's no great big thing. Jim also had a call on his heart and wanted to be a minister. We shared that calling together. We were totally in love."[29] Here again, Bakker's emphasis on emotional knowing and personal guidance from the divine helped her to feel certain of her decision despite the misgivings of others around her. A cynical reading of this kind of belief might raise concerns about its potential use in rationalizing a person's own desires regardless of dogmatic or community pressures. However, it is important to recognize that this is not how most believers—who typically perceive personal condemnation as well as personal justification from God—experience their own faith.

The Bakkers were married in a small ceremony near North Central Bible College in 1961. They were surprised to learn shortly afterward that school rules would not permit married students to remain registered, and so neither graduated. Jim Bakker slipped into a depression and "refused to attend church because he resented the church for denying him and Tammy the opportunity to stay in school and still be together." Tammy continued to attend church regularly and she worried deeply about her new husband's newfound irreligion: "I thought, 'Oh no. What has happened? Jim is backsliding. Have I made a mistake?'"[30]

In Tammy's retelling, "God moved in a powerful way" to lead both her and Jim into the ministry, by first compelling her to begin leading the church's music service at the pastor's request. After a few weeks, "a concerned church member" called Jim to say "'if you don't get back to church and do what God wants you to do, your wife is going to be the minister. She's the one that God's going to be using and you are going to be left sitting home on the shelf." According to one writer, "That was all the encouragement Jim needed. He wasn't about to be left behind."[31] It is unclear from this telling whether the church member, Sister Fern, was primarily concerned about Jim's state of mind or about Tammy Faye's leadership in the church, unmoored from her husband's authority. The former interpretation seems more likely in this context, however, given a long history of women's ordination in the Assemblies of God, the long-standing (though not uncontested) history of charismatic women's itinerant preaching, and the fact that it was the male pastor who initially asked Tammy to take a public role.[32]

Jim rejoined the church and quickly became a frequent speaker at the pulpit, as Tammy Faye continued to lead the music ministry. A short time later, a visiting preacher invited them to lead a revival meeting at his church in North Carolina. The first meeting was a failure, and so was the second, and the third, and the fourth. Jim nearly gave up, but on the fifth night, according to Tammy Faye "ten people received the baptism of the Holy Spirit . . . and all heaven broke loose. . . . So we decided, 'Praise God, we're going to stay in the ministry after all.'"[33] They had originally planned to become missionaries in the Amazonian rain forest but after those plans fell through, they began to travel across the United States instead, staying with pastors of local churches and leading revivals wherever they were invited. They became especially well known for their children's ministry, which featured the homemade puppets Allie the Alligator and Susie Moppet. The latter was made from a Porky the Pig shampoo bottle, with ears removed and a curly blonde wig added. These homemade puppets continued to be a regular feature of the Bakkers' ministry even as they built a multimillion dollar television empire.[34]

The puppet ministry drew the attention of televangelist Pat Robertson, who had founded the first major Christian television station, Christian Broadcasting Network (CBN) in Portsmouth, Virginia, in 1960. Robertson made several requests to the Bakkers to appear on the network, but they were apparently uninterested until he suggested creating a children's program around the characters of Allie and Susie. In 1965, the Bakkers joined CBN as the hosts of a new children's program called *Come On Over*, later renamed the *Jim and Tammy Show* to reflect the Bakkers' growing popularity. That same year, Jim Bakker also contributed to the development of Robertson's flagship program, *The 700 Club*, the first to bring the late-night talk show format to Christian television.[35]

The Bakkers stayed at CBN for seven years, building a considerable following among viewers. By 1967, their children's show had its own fan club with over three thousand members.[36] It was also during their time at CBN that their first child, Tammy Sue, was born. Audience members sent so many baby gifts to the Bakkers that Tammy Faye reported: "I never had to buy one thing until she was two years old. She was 'their baby' because they had watched me on TV and shared my pregnancy."[37] This closeness with audience members would become a feature of the Bakkers' ministry, beginning at CBN and intensifying once they developed their own network. They ad libbed most of their programming, and Tammy especially presented with such candor that many viewers almost regarded the Bakkers as family or as intimate friends. As PTL grew in the following decades, the Bakkers spent hours every day producing live television programming. Like other popular televangelists of the time, they lived a substantial portion of their lives on TV, inviting viewers to share in their joys and struggles, and even to watch their children grow up with the ministry.

As the Bakkers continued with CBN through the late 1960s and early 1970s, however, they had frequent disagreements with other staff members over the Bakkers' requests for increased pay and additional sick leave as well as their blunt fundraising style. Ultimately, Tammy Faye related that it was again God's calling that led them to leave CBN in 1972. "The Lord spoke to us through the Word in Ezekiel 12:1–6," she wrote, referring to a passage that reads in part, "you live among rebels, who could know the truth if they wanted to, but they don't want to. . . . Pack whatever you can carry on your back and leave your home—go somewhere else."[38] She said of this experience: "It shocked us that God would speak harshly. But every Bible we had would fall open to this passage. So we knew it was God."[39] What Bakker describes here is a common evangelical method for divining God's will, by allowing a Bible to fall open and then seeking guidance from the first verses glanced on the open page. In this case, Bakker emphasized God's hand in the message in part to distance herself from its harshness; though reportedly "shocked" that God would condemn Robertson and the CBN staff as a band of ignorant "rebels," Bakker asserted that she had no choice but to follow God's lead. Robertson and his supporters had their own stories about these conflicts, that Jim wanted more control at the network than Robertson was willing to give him and that the Bakkers grew ever more demanding as their popularity increased.[40] But for those predisposed to side with the Bakkers, Tammy's story of biblical guidance added divine authority to their account.

From there, with no plan in mind according to Tammy Faye, the Bakkers resumed their itinerant ministry. This time, they did not go from church to church but rather visited small local Christian television stations across the country, helping these ministries to run fundraisers in order to stay on the air. Eventually, they landed in California. There, they met Paul and Jan Crouch and together the two couples founded the Trinity Broadcasting Network (TBN). Again, Tammy Faye told a story of providential blessing on TBN as evidenced by her own personal feelings as well as material outcomes: "Miracles of God began to happen. We knew God was confirming what He had allowed us to do," she wrote, relating that gifts of typewriters, desks, cameras, and other necessary items came to the station, along with "air-conditioning men and electricians just when we needed them. It was a miracle of Almighty God. The people would just walk in the door, not even knowing why they were coming."[41] What is important here is not the degree to which this account is accurate—it is entirely possible, for example, that appointments with contractors were made without Bakker's realizing it. Instead, this story is important for what it reveals about the Bakkers' worldview. Like other proponents of the prosperity gospel, the Bakkers believed that God's presence manifests in the lives of the faithful in the form of material blessings. They expressed this belief in part through a tendency to interpret every event, from the major to the mundane, as a meaningful sign from God.

The Bakkers stayed with TBN for less than a year; they were gone by the end of 1973.[42] The pastor of the California church that had been backing TBN disliked the Bakkers and their style of ministry. In particular, according to Tammy Faye, he accused Jim of being "too emotional" and insisted that Jim "shouldn't be praying for the sick, or talking about the baptism of the Holy Spirit on the air."[43] In other words, he disagreed with their Pentecostal version of prosperity theology. Eventually the Bakkers left over a question of ownership. Taking many of the station's staff with them, they returned to Charlotte, North Carolina to found the network that would become the base of their expansive PTL ministry.

During this time of transition the Bakkers also had their second child, Jamie Charles, who, like his sister, grew up in the spotlight. When Tammy Faye suspected she was pregnant, she did not immediately share this news with Jim. Instead, she went to the doctor to confirm, and when she returned from the appointment, "Jim was on TV and I walked in on the middle of a PTL Club program and whispered in his ear, 'We're going to have a baby.'" The PTL musician "started playing 'Rock-a-bye Baby' on the piano, and the whole world knew we were going to have a baby."[44] Even more than they had at CBN, on PTL the Bakkers lived their lives before the television audience, sharing their triumphs alongside their failings and cultivating a ministry that they often referred to as a kind of extended family.[45]

The Bakkers had started the PTL show at TBN, and this became both the flagship show of the new network as well as the name of the network itself. Initially it stood for "Praise the Lord," chosen, as Tammy Faye put it, because "we felt it was a code so that when Christians looked at the program they would automatically know what it meant."[46] Later, the Bakkers would also use the abbreviation to stand for "People that Love," employing this phrase interchangeably with "Praise the Lord" in their ministry. They also used "People that Love" as the name for many of their outreach ministries, including drug addiction and marriage counseling centers.[47] During the late 1970s, PTL took the theme further in *Action*, a glossy magazine sent to anyone who donated money to the ministry, with content organized under headings such as

"People that Love," "People that Laugh," "People that Listen," and "People that Learn."[48]

Over the next decade, PTL expanded its reach into every corner of Christian charity and merchandising. The Bakkers founded not only a drug rehabilitation center and marriage counseling program but also a maternity home for women in need as well as an adoption agency, both aimed at reducing abortion rates by providing pregnant women with other options.[49] In the late 1970s, the couple began producing books including Jim's *Move that Mountain!* in 1976; Tammy Faye's first autobiography *I Gotta Be Me* in 1978; and the coauthored *How We Lost Weight and Kept it Off!* in 1980.[50] Each of these books focused on faith and miracles, drawing on the couple's experiences of failure and success to illustrate the overarching message that God provides—materially and spiritually—to the faithful.

Tammy, who sang regularly on PTL's television programming, put out at least nine solo records between 1977 and 1986, while the ministry also produced records featuring the PTL band, songs from the ongoing children's ministry, and even an album by the Bakkers' sixteen-year-old daughter in 1986. In each of these arenas, the Bakkers marketed into and helped to expand the evangelical subculture that contributed to the rise of the New Christian Right. They were central figures in helping to build national networks of evangelicals and—even though they never made politics a central feature of their ministry—propagating many of the political assumptions of the religious right in ostensibly apolitical contexts.

Tammy Faye in particular helped to expand evangelical women's culture on television through a deliberate infusion of tropes from mainstream women's cultures into Christian broadcasting. Over the years, she developed several specific women's programs on PTL including the *Tammy Faye Show* and later *Tammy's House Party*. Using the established format of the daytime talk show, Tammy Faye broadcast from a set designed to make viewers feel at home. As on all PTL programming, interviews were conducted in a living-room like setting. But the set of *Tammy's House Party* also included a kitchen for recipe demonstrations, an indoor "backyard," and a dining room that symbolically extended to include the studio audience who were also seated at tables.

The show defined women's concerns as women's magazines and television programming had long defined them: in terms of women's consumer interests in personal and home improvement. "God has called me to the woman who can't have diamonds and furs and has to wear the fake ones," Bakker explained; "I'm called to the woman who doesn't have the money to buy new furniture for her home and who so desperately wants to make a nice home." Explaining how she would teach women to "rub peanut butter into certain furniture [so] you won't even see the scratch" or to "get good deals in the bargain rooms at stores where Jim and I buy most of our furniture" or to turn one simple dress into several nice outfits using scarves and costume jewelry, she concluded: "I'm doing this primarily for the woman who doesn't know Jesus and needs an answer."[51] For Tammy Faye, these borrowings from mainstream women's consumer culture were so intimately related to the project of evangelism that the jump from one to the other required no explanation or segue. In the context of an evangelical women's culture that had grown over the past decade to include books, conferences, classes, and even a dedicated glossy magazine, this connection made perfect sense, and its expansion into television was a significant step.

Makeup and fashion tips were a significant part of Tammy Faye Bakker's ministry. This is particularly worth noting since Bakker's own makeup and fashion choices have drawn such derision, allowing critics to dismiss her as quintessentially frivolous, silly, and inconsequential. But these choices were a meaningful part of her persona, giving permission to other Christian women from austere backgrounds to enjoy a little vanity in a Christian context. For his 1988 study of televangelical ministries, sociologist Stewart M. Hoover conducted interviews with PTL viewers before the 1987 scandal. He found that some viewers were attracted to Bakker because of her showy style, while those who were uncomfortable with it used the same language of emotional knowing that Bakker herself used to justify her choices: "I really believe she's a woman of God and a child of God, and gets the leadership from God," one informant told Hoover; "I've never *sensed* that she's out of the spirit in anything she's had to say, never, never. If she had, I would have sensed it."[52] Tammy's flashy clothes and heavy makeup also corresponded with the ministry's prosperity gospel, which framed material wealth as a sign of God's blessing. Indeed, Hoover argues that both Tammy's appeal and the appeal of Christian television more broadly sprang from their ability to connect with the attractive elements of the secular world while maintaining a believably "authentic core."[53] Bakker's apparent authenticity was foundational to her success as a televangelist. She was giggly, energetic, and seemingly guileless. She related to guests and audience members alike as if they were all her best friends. And just as these traits helped some viewers to rationalize her fashion choices, they also played a role in legitimating her political positions as well as her assertions of disinterest in politics.

Inside and Outside the New Christian Right

PTL was at its height in the late 1980s. It grew up in tandem with the New Christian Right, and benefited from the religious and cultural networks that sustained that movement. As Christian celebrities, Jim and Tammy Faye were involved in supporting various platforms of the religious right, though they did not make these political commitments central to their ministry in the ways that Falwell, the LaHayes, and others did.

For example, Jim Bakker was present at the 1980 Washington for Jesus rally, a major event in the development of the modern religious right, but his presence there does not necessarily demonstrate a commitment to political engagement on behalf of the movement. This rally attracted at least 200,000 attendees from across the country, who came together in support of a broad-based family-values platform. The event helped to cement alliances between disparate conservative Christians and to augment the national visibility of a burgeoning religious conservative movement.[54] Yet even this rally in the nation's capital underscored ongoing equivocations among conservative evangelicals over what did and did not constitute political engagement. While prominent participants including Pat Robertson and James Robison used the event as a platform for discussing their opposition to homosexuality, abortion, and other social ills, the event's main organizer, John Gimenez responded to criticism of the event by insisting that its focus was "spiritual, not political."[55] Gimenez argued that the rally aimed to "reverse the trend of the nation away from God" which had led Americans to believe that "to do wrong is normal and to do right is abnormal."[56] In other words, he relied on a long-standing rhetorical strategy among conservative Christians, attempting to render his event uncontroversial by expressing his goal as a return to normality rather than political or even social upheaval.

The Bakkers, too, walked the line between activism and disengagement. Though political themes never became a central focus of the PTL ministry, Jim did, for example, pen cover stories on the presidential candidate Ronald Reagan and the incumbent Jimmy Carter in separate 1980 issues of PTL's *Action* magazine.[57] Characteristically, Bakker had positive things to say about both men and he focused on their statements about their Christian faith rather than their policy positions. Bakker did not instruct his readers how to vote, but he did take the stance that "we, as Christians, not only have the right to exercise our voting power, we have an obligation—both as citizens of a country we love, and as Christians before the Almighty God."[58] In his particular religious and political context, this was a significant political statement in itself. Yet it was also the exception to the rule in an extensive ministry whose television programming, periodicals, books, and direct-mail appeals all tended to emphasize improving the self, reaching out to those in need, and focusing on God's love.

In an interview in early 1987, just before the scandal broke, Tammy Faye expressed serious reservations about direct political engagement: "You're damned if you do and damned if you don't," she said. "If you're a Republican, the Democrats are mad at you. If you're a Democrat, then the Republicans are mad at you. We have to minister to all the people."[59] The Bakkers were not alone in their political ambivalence, even in the 1980s. While Baptist leaders like the LaHayes and Falwell urged Christians to understand political activism as a fundamental component of their religious duty, many Pentecostal figures expressed sentiments closer to the Bakkers': "Jesus would never get into politics," Ohio-based televangelist and megachurch preacher Rex Humbard argued. "We preach love out of the corners of our mouths, and then jump on homosexuals or politicians. We should preach the Gospel to everybody."[60]

Yet despite a general evasion of explicit political statements, the Bakkers were prominent figures in a conservative Christian subculture that had gradually taken on political overtones over the same decades in which they built their ministry. As in other purportedly apolitical spaces within conservative evangelical culture, political ideas and assumptions were apparent throughout their ministry whether or not Jim and Tammy Faye identified active political involvement as a priority.

The Bakkers' opposition to abortion, for example, was evident in the language that they used to describe their maternity home for unmarried pregnant women as well as their adoption agency, called Tender Loving Care (TLC). On the back cover of a brochure for the TLC Agency, Jim Bakker was pictured holding a baby "saved from abortion through PTL's concern."[61] In letters to their supporters written after the scandal, Jim and Tammy wrote that they had founded the Heritage House Girls' Home "to address the needs brought about by wholesale abortion," and they included the "babies that were saved from abortion" among the ministry's successes.[62] But while Beverly LaHaye and others situated abortion at the center of a crusade against feminism, humanism, and pathological self-centeredness, the Bakkers—and especially Tammy Faye—said little about it beyond their promotion of these targeted outreach ministries.[63] Instead, the Bakkers took a pro-life stance but also maintained a close focus on individual failings rather than social ills, in keeping with the self-help focus of the prosperity gospel.

These elements of PTL's ministries represent the impossibility of avoiding political engagement in evangelical subcultural production in the thick of the late-twentieth-century culture wars. They also demonstrate the leeway that refusing an explicitly political identity could afford. In particular, the Bakkers' theological emphases on acceptance and love generated a different approach to the key concerns of the religious right, even as the Bakkers—like their activist counterparts—opposed abortion and pornography and preached a modified doctrine of wifely submission. These tensions were especially apparent in the Bakkers' response to the conversion of *Hustler* owner Larry Flynt to evangelical Christianity in 1977. While many prominent evangelists continued to denounce the outspoken pornographer, the Bakkers publicly supported him because they "felt he [Flynt] needed a friend." In language very similar to that which she used to describe the judgmental congregants at her childhood church, Bakker denounced Flynt's detractors, saying, "I put a question mark behind the word 'Christian' because the Bible says the reason that you know you've passed through death into life is because you have to love one another." Insisting that "there is almost nothing in the world that Jim and I hate more than pornography," she nonetheless concluded: "The issue wasn't pronography [*sic*], it was that a man had been born again."[64] As with the issue of abortion, however, the Bakkers wrote little about pornography outside of this specific circumstance.

Even if the Bakkers spent relatively little time on explicitly political issues, their central emphasis on prosperity theology itself held political significance in the context of a Christian conservative movement centered not only on social issues but also on an economic philosophy that opposed state welfare in favor of individual striving and a firm belief in meritocracy. Their emphasis on God's provision and their own rags-to-riches narratives subtly reinscribed conservative understandings about the deserving and undeserving poor, while adding a potential basis for spiritual judgment against those who were not materially blessed. If their descriptions of their own experiences of childhood hardship and their admonitions to give generously to the needy worked toward destigmatizing poverty, these same discourses also upheld contemporary conservative emphases on self-reliance and private charity.[65]

Tammy Faye's particular contributions to evangelical women's subculture also coincided with contemporary conservative rejections of the women's liberation movement although Bakker was typically circumspect on this issue as well. In particular, her uncritical emphases on beauty, home, and family as quintessentially feminine concerns overlooked prevailing feminist critiques that sought to highlight women's interests and capabilities outside of these spheres. Indeed, cultural theorist Lawrence Grossberg named Tammy Faye Bakker as one of the "best images" of conservative "attempts to rearticulate the trajectory of the women's movements" through a "pernicious . . . ironic reversal . . . which locates people's freedom in their ability to choose to reject change."[66] And while Bakker obviously got a great deal of personal joy out of her makeup and clothing, she also echoed Marabel Morgan and others in reminding women that their beauty routines should be considered marital obligations: "I don't care how old you get," she said in 1987, at the age of forty-five, "I think a woman should stay sexy for her husband. She ought to dress sexy and keep herself exciting."[67]

Bakker also supported the basic premises of submission doctrine, including a firm belief in binary gender and family roles. "I think one of the most important things in the world is to allow a man to be a man, to feel like a man," she said. "Be supportive of him, encourage him. I believe in keeping the male ego intact."[68] This idea closely mirrored statements that Marabel Morgan and Anita Bryant had made over a decade earlier, in which each expressed her own concerns about changing gender roles and the fragile male ego. Indeed, Bakker's relationship to contemporary feminism corresponded much more neatly with the subtler political negotiations engaged by these women than with Beverly LaHaye's more contemporary crusade against the feminist movement, which LaHaye connected to concurrent threats including secular humanism, lingering communism, and selfish liberalism. Asked in early 1987 what she thought about the women's liberation movement, Bakker responded, "I think Christian women are the most liberated women in the whole world. . . . I love being under submission to my husband. That, to me, is not a lack of liberation."[69] Reclaiming the idea of liberation within the framework of Christian salvation, Bakker expressed her commitment to conservative gender ideologies and rejected the contemporary women's movement without substantively engaging with either feminist or antifeminist critiques.

Yet Bakker also endorsed women's career choices across the board: "I say if a woman wants to work, let her do that. If she wants to stay at home and be a housewife, do that. But she shouldn't be at home and be a housewife . . . and hating her children for keeping her there."[70] Like Marabel Morgan had done fourteen years earlier, Bakker attempted to downplay her political engagement through an emphasis on the self and an interpretation of family as a still apolitical realm. But whereas Morgan had been able to plausibly express surprise in the early 1970s that her work would ever be considered political, by the late 1980s evangelical Protestantism and conservative politics were becoming discursively linked. Even as they insisted on their political disinterest, it was obvious that the Bakkers would not be able to avoid political questions altogether.

"That's How Jesus Loves"

Tammy Faye's sharpest divergence from the politics of her religious right contemporaries came in November 1985. Four years after the human immunodeficiency virus (HIV) had first been observed by physicians in the United States, two years after the designation acquired immune deficiency syndrome (AIDS) had been coined, and only months after news media had begun to cover the intensifying epidemic as a serious event, Tammy Faye Bakker invited an HIV-positive gay minister to appear on *Tammy's House Party*. Steve Pieters, a clergyman at the gay-affirming Metropolitan Community Church in Los Angeles, was too sick to travel but the interview was conducted via satellite, with Pieters appearing on a television set inside the living room setting of the show.

At this time, very little was known about HIV or AIDS. Public understandings were often built on rumor and speculation in the absence of medical facts or reliable public health campaigns. Even among physicians, the pathology was firmly linked with homosexuality, at least at first. Before "HIV," the disease was officially called GRID (gay-related immune deficiency) and unofficially "the Four-H disease," because it disproportionately affected homosexuals, hemophiliacs, Haitians, and either heroin users or "hookers," depending on the source of the information.[71]

Prominent figures in the New Christian Right were quick to contribute to the stigma surrounding the epidemic, characterizing it as evidence of God's judgment against homosexuals and against the United States more generally. Pat Robertson's inflammatory, though not unique, rhetoric on the AIDS epidemic became a central feature of his (unsuccessful) bid for the Republican nomination in the presidential election of 1988. Late in 1987, for example, he publicly disputed new research findings. In spite of medical evidence, he insisted against that AIDS could be transmitted through the air and he reiterated his position that quarantine should be considered as a possible response to the AIDS epidemic.[72]

In 1985, a month before Bakker's interview with Pieters, a reporter on Robertson's *700 Club* spoke about actor Rock Hudson's struggle with AIDS in a more empathetic tone than was typical of Robertson's own public statements. Nonetheless, this reporter focused on the notion of homosexuality as a sin and the necessity that homosexuals repent. "Perhaps this [diagnosis] would be an opportunity for Rock to be exposed to the things of the Lord Jesus," the reporter, Scott Ross, said. "If God moved within the homosexual community and granted grace to a lot of those people to turn from their wicked ways, to turn from their sin and turn to the Lord Jesus Christ and there would be an outpouring of his grace . . . there could be a revival there."[73]

By contrast, the interview on *Tammy's House Party* in November 1985 was marked by an overwhelming admonition to Christian congregations to welcome and support homosexuals and people with AIDS, collapsing the imagined boundary in Ross's statement between the "here" of the churches and the "there" of the gay community. "How sad," Tammy Faye wept, "that we as Christians, who are supposed to be the salt of the earth are afraid so badly of an AIDS patient that we will not go up and put our arm around them and tell them that we care."[74] Reframing homophobia rather than homosexuality as the real threat to Christian families, she used the model of Pieters's accepting parents to enjoin other Christians in her audience to embrace their gay children. "They're still your boy. They're still your girl. No matter what happens in their life, and I think it's so important that we as mom and dad love through anything," she said, as she began to sob again, "and that's the way with Jesus, you know. He just loves us. Through anything. And that's the wonderful thing about Jesus."[75]

Bakker was not, however, wholly affirming of Pieter's homosexuality and she evinced a powerful commitment to heteronormativity throughout the interview. Early on, she asked Pieters about his sexual experience with women, and when he said that he had only ever "necked" with a girl, Bakker laughingly responded: "Do you think maybe you just haven't given women a fair try?"[76] She also made statements that reaffirmed ideas about homosexual deviance, particularly the association between male homosexuality and femininity: "What made you think that you were homosexual, Steve?" Bakker asked Pieters. "Did you feel feminine inside?" Pieters responded firmly, "No, my orientation is toward men." But he also cooperated in this rhetoric by constructing his own identity in terms of stereotypical gender difference, foregrounding his aversion to sports and his affinity for Peter Pan and "musical comedy albums."[77]

Yet Bakker's approach to homosexuality and AIDS in 1985 need not have been completely affirming to constitute a radical departure from the panic of her religious and nonreligious contemporaries.[78] Bakker's insistence on a framework of acceptance and her demonstration of empathy with Pieters resisted early media narratives that constructed the person with AIDS as an exceedingly monstrous other. By establishing AIDS as a disease that only people unlike "us" could contract, pundits imaginatively protected themselves and their cohorts from the epidemic. Thus, Jerry Falwell's assertion in 1986 that AIDS represented "God's judgment against America, for endorsing immorality, even embracing it," was not only an implicit condemnation of homosexuality but also a rhetorical intimation of immunity for anyone who did not "endorse" the kind of "immorality" that Falwell himself opposed.[79] Bakker resisted this formulation and instead relied on her characteristic self-focus to make sense of Pieters's experience: "My body did something to me once and I got very, very sick. And my body rebelled on me, but the whole time I thought—I'm going to beat this thing," she related. "Well, my sickness did go away and God touched me and I did beat it."[80] This reflection facilitated Pieters's own narrative of God's healing power. Relating his experience of being diagnosed HIV-positive, Pieters framed God's presence as healing in itself, whether or not he would ever experience a physical cure: "God touched me and I realized that my life was not yet over. That I still had time. That God was with me against this disease, *not* having given me this disease—but was with me against this disease."[81]

Pieters also used the opportunity of the interview to take the message of gay affirmation further than Bakker would. Responding to Bakker's declaration of Jesus's unconditional love, Pieters pronounced: "Absolutely. Jesus loves me. Just the way I am. I really believe that. Jesus loves the way I love."[82] By asserting that Jesus loved not only homosexuals but also homosexuality itself, this statement went far beyond the equivocal notion of tolerance that counsels evangelicals to "hate the sin, but love the sinner."[83] Bakker did not directly challenge Pieters on this point, though she was visibly flustered before changing the subject: "Listen, um, listen, um, Steve," she paused, "this is an emotional interview for me. I just met Steve and it's like meeting him in person right here. I just want to put my arm around him."[84]

Pieters's identity as a gay Christian—indeed, a gay minister—also challenged the pronouncements of New Christian Right leaders who understood homosexuality and Christianity as mutually opposed. Both Pieters and Bakker repeated throughout the interview that Pieters came from a loving "ministry family" and that he was actively involved in the church, chipping away at common linkages among evangelicals between homosexuality and bad parenting, or the purported secularization of American society.[85] Pieters also emphasized his experience in the Metropolitan Community Church (MCC), a Protestant denomination founded in 1968 by and for gay men and women. In doing so, he introduced Bakker's audience to the idea of Christian communities that truly affirmed gay congregants. "I finally found God when I met my gay brothers and lesbian sisters at MCC and I knew that I finally was home," Pieters said, "and it was through meeting other gay people who were happy with themselves—who were leading productive, active lives— who were in sacred, loving relationships with each other, that I realized that that was a possibility for me, too."[86] Thus Pieters subverted the notion, which was gaining attention through the emergent ex-gay movement, that gay people must be converted not only to Christianity but also to heterosexuality in order to become fully acceptable members of the church body.[87]

Finally, the interview also called into question the idea that had been the central organizing force of Anita Bryant's campaigns a decade earlier, namely, the notion that homosexual men necessarily constitute a threat to children. Bakker asked Pieters whether he would ever consider heterosexual marriage in order to experience fatherhood. Explicitly subverting the construction of gay men as child molesters, Bakker asserted: "I know a lot of homosexual men really love children, you know. And they've got the heart of a daddy, of course."[88] This assertion is particularly interesting given the Bakkers' early support for Anita Bryant's anti-gay-rights campaign in 1976. Bryant had centrally emphasized the notion that gay men were prone to molest little boys in order to "recruit" them to homosexuality, but this message did not seem to have stuck with Bakker nearly a decade later.[89] This association with Bryant offers another example of the range of political messages that appeared on PTL over the years, in part as a result of the Bakkers' ambivalence about most political issues. It is also worth noting that in 1976, the network was only two years old and the Bakkers were likely eager for guests with Bryant's star power.

Through this line of questioning, although Bakker implicitly refuted the notion of gay men as always dangerous to children, she did posit homosexuality as a barrier to family life. Pieters, however, turned the question into an opportunity to discuss gay rights by raising the issue of gay parenting through adoption. Bakker initially recoiled at the suggestion, asking: "Say a gay couple would be able to adopt children, you know. Would that automatically, do you think, cause the children to lead the same kind of lifestyle?"[90] But Pieters rebuffed her suggestion, arguing, "It's not a matter of what your parents do in the bedroom as to how you turn out."[91]

This interview is significant not because it was typical, but because it demonstrates the extent to which divergent religious and political frameworks coexisted within the nebulous movement that became known as the New Christian Right. Scholars have long situated opposition to homosexuality as one of the foundational issues of this movement, and for many of the movement's leaders and grassroots supporters it was absolutely central. But in 1985 Tammy Faye Bakker, co-leader of one of the biggest evangelical ministries in the nation, who counted Ronald Reagan, Pat Robertson, and Jerry Falwell among her friends and colleagues, conducted this interview using language of acceptance and empathy that was radical compared to even the mainstream press at the time.[92] The Bakkers' theological emphasis on inclusion, along with their efforts to avoid political controversy made this interview possible. So, too, did Tammy Faye's particular subjectivity as a Christian woman in a conservative evangelical ministry. It is significant that the interview took place on *Tammy's House Party* and not on the ministry's flagship program. In the first place, this may have been a calculated decision aimed at minimizing any fallout from the interview given that Tammy's niche program attracted a smaller audience than PTL's eponymous show. Second, it may have been a reflection of Tammy Faye's willingness to take risks that Jim's dogged pursuit of fundraising prevented him from considering.[93] Third, it reflects a persistent assumption within evangelical communities that women's ministries were less serious (in every sense of the word) than were the ministries typically led by men for mixed-gender congregations. Tammy Faye's theological choices, her negotiations of the boundaries between political and nonpolitical discourse, and—perhaps most important—her position as a prominent woman in a cultural context that downplayed her contributions made it possible for her to push at the theological and political boundaries of the New Christian Right.

Even as evangelical subcultures gradually politicized over the 1970s and 1980s such that political discourses were eventually inextricable from religious ones in these contexts, not all prominent figures and likely not all congregants chose to become centrally involved in political battles or to engage in these battles in the same ways. At the same time that Beverly LaHaye insisted that Christian doctrine left devoted women "no other option" than to become politically engaged in a very specific program of explicit opposition to feminism, secular humanism, and homosexuality, Bakker demonstrated that even within conservative evangelical subcultures, different religious and political priorities were possible. While both Jim and Tammy Faye Bakker continued to rely on shifting negotiations of the relationship between religion and politics in order to situate themselves outside of the political sphere in most cases, Tammy Faye was also able to mobilize the presumed inconsequentiality and disinterest in politics that attached to her gender in order to step outside the bounds of the New Christian Right agenda and introduce new perspectives to her viewers without sparking an immediate political controversy.

Yet, although it was not specifically mentioned during the 1987 scandal, it is possible that the Pieters interview—along with the Bakkers' other divergences from the politics of the New Christian Right—contributed to the collapse of their ministry at that time. Most prominent ministers turned against the Bakkers and publicly condemned them; but some, including Jerry Falwell, also accused Jim Bakker of homosexual acts with staff members at PTL, which Jim Bakker categorically denied.[94] As scholar Susan Wise Bauer has argued, this accusation went further than appending another sexual sin to the list of Jim's transgressions: "In the rhetoric of the new evangelical alliance, homosexuality was much more than a sexual orientation. It was a sign of the decadence of modern American culture. Public acceptance of homosexuality represented the relinquishing of absolute moral standards."[95] Whether or not the accusations were true, the Bakkers' emphasis on acceptance—along with their emotional excess and material extravagance—became another feature of their ministry that detractors turned against them in the context of the 1987 scandal.

Telescandal

In March 1987, the news broke that would spell the beginning of the end for PTL. A young woman named Jessica Hahn claimed that Jim Bakker had drugged and sexually assaulted her in a Charlotte hotel room in 1980 when she was twenty-one years old.[96] In the intervening years, she said, PTL executives had paid her $279,000 in church funds to keep her silent. Jim Bakker admitted that he had had sex with Hahn but claimed that it was consensual, denied any involvement in the payoffs, and later alleged that the whole affair was a setup by Satan—in league with Bakker's earthly rivals—to destroy the PTL ministry.[97] This narrative of persecution was bolstered in Jim and Tammy Faye's perception by the reactions of other prominent ministers as well as the many PTL staff who began to add their own charges of impropriety against the couple and the ministry. The Reverend Jerry Falwell, whom the Bakkers had regarded as a colleague and sometime friend, staged a hostile takeover of PTL and Heritage Village ministries between 1987 and 1989, initially promising to help protect the Bakkers' reputations and later going to the press with his own allegations of the Bakkers' selfishness, opulence, and greed.[98]

The Bakkers had weathered small scandals over the preceding decade, with the *Charlotte Observer* being especially diligent in reporting their indulgent lifestyle and fundraising irregularities.[99] In 1978, the Federal Communications Commission (FCC) began to investigate PTL for failing to provide promised funds to ministries in Asia and Latin America. Compounding the problem, Jim Bakker and others at PTL had continued to promote these endeavors, especially in fundraising appeals that strongly implied that PTL had provided generously to its international partners. In the meantime, PTL was deeply in debt, struggling to complete construction projects and to meet its promises, even as Jim Bakker continually looked toward expansion. The FCC investigation encouraged some restructuring, but Bakker was largely uncooperative, and he insisted to his viewers and to the press that the investigation was nothing less than religious persecution.[100] This narrative appealed to the ministry's largely conservative Christian audience in large part because it resonated with a broader sense of cultural alienation and embattlement in these years.

The Bakkers also weathered earlier scandals because they consistently asked for forgiveness and received it from their viewers. In fact, they made their failings an integral part of their ministry, presenting these faults as evidence that no one was perfect and that the devil was actively working against believers using the tools of temptation and personal conflict. Most important, the Bakkers used these incidents as opportunities to underscore their overriding message of God's forgiving grace. In publications, in interviews, and on television, Jim and Tammy Faye made continual public admissions of personal shortcomings, openly discussing their crises of faith and their personal challenges both as essential elements of their unreserved and accessible personas and as platforms from which to affirm the healing power of a personal God.[101]

Writing in 1978, for example, Tammy related an episode in which Jim's ill health and the stress of their ministry left her literally crying over spilled milk. In that moment, she said, God spoke to her, saying: "Tammy, just be glad you have milk to spill and be thankful you have a husband to take it to."[102] She used this anecdote to highlight God's powerful presence in her life: "As I began to clean up the mess, God began to pour his strength into me and I became as strong as a rock." When she struggled with depression and anxiety, she said, "the Lord spoke to me and said, 'Tammy, let me be your psychiatrist.'" And Tammy reported that God healed her.[103]

Of course, as one scholarly examination of the Bakkers' lives notes, Tammy Faye regularly "supplemented her prayers . . . with Valium" but even her problems with prescription drugs became an opportunity for Tammy to talk about divine healing and the importance of the "PTL Family." In the Bakkers' first broadcast about Tammy's addiction, Tammy reported that "it was like Satan was trying to kill me" but the "outpouring of love" and prayers from supporters, along with medical care, had helped her to get well.[104] In a letter on the subject sent out to PTL supporters, Jim underscored God's healing power as well as the ministry's overarching messages of love and redemption: "God loves Tammy and me, and God loves you. He is always faithful and he will see us through this battle!"[105]

Jim's sexual scandal was different, however, in part because Jim had not followed the appropriate script. He did not confess until Hahn had already made her story public. Instead, he actively took steps to conceal the incident.[106] In addition, this scandal was much harder to blame on errors in calculation or on errant junior employees than were rumors about financial indiscretion. It was also literally sexier than any of the earlier accusations made against the Bakkers.[107] As media outlets across the country ran with the story, television talk show host Phil Donahue explained the attraction succinctly. In response to a caller who asked why "everybody is making such a big deal of this man's sex life," Donahue laughed. "It's fun to talk about it. We're all voyeurs, aren't we? I mean, it's the one thing we didn't get with Watergate—no sex!"[108] At the same time, the allegations of blackmail illustrated broader accusations of financial misallocation in a way that was easily understood and difficult to justify.

The Bakkers' extravagance soon hit the news both nationally and internationally.[109] Their lifestyle had never been a secret; in fact, it was a cornerstone of
their ministry, evidence of God's blessing in the logic of the prosperity gospel.
In the context of the explosive 1987 scandal, however, reporters represented
the Bakkers as exemplars of the excesses and hypocrisy of television ministers.
In response, other prominent preachers quickly and decisively renounced the
couple. Jerry Falwell mused in a 1987 press conference that Jim Bakker was
either "very dishonest or . . . emotionally ill," and fellow televangelist Jimmy
Swaggart—beset by his own sexual scandal—called Bakker "a 'cancer' that
needed to be excised from the body of Christ."[110] If these men had less to say
about Tammy Faye, it was not because they disliked her less but because they
did not understand her as a force to be reckoned with.

The fact that a preponderance of prominent ministers turned against the
Bakkers was one reason they were not immediately able to recover from this
scandal; the concurrent culmination of a second federal investigation against
the ministry was another. In August 1987, a federal grand jury began to hear the
case against Jim Bakker and other members of the PTL ministry (though not
Tammy Faye), brought by the Federal Communications Commission (FCC) and
the Internal Revenue Service (IRS). Among other things, Jim Bakker and his
colleagues were accused of selling more "lifetime partnerships" in PTL—which
included free hotel stays at Heritage USA—than their plans could actually ac-
commodate. If every one of the ministry's "lifetime partners" tried to redeem
their vouchers, the property's hotels would be overbooked every day of every
year, and no rooms would ever be available for paying guests. Meanwhile, the
ministry also raised more than twice the amount of money needed to build the
promised hotels and never finished building them. In October 1989, a federal
jury found Jim Bakker guilty on eight counts of mail fraud, fifteen counts of
wire fraud, and one count of conspiracy.[111] He was sentenced to forty-five years,
but he remained in jail only five, being paroled in 1994.[112] In the meantime,
PTL and Heritage Village declared bankruptcy in 1989 and Jerry Falwell sold
off the crumbling ministry in Charlotte. In 1992, citing hardships resulting
from the scandal and Jim's prison sentence, Tammy Faye initiated a divorce.[113]

Conclusion

After the 1987 scandal and her husband's imprisonment in 1989, Tammy Faye
Bakker tried to reestablish the ministry on her own. For a short time, she led a
small but growing congregation of former PTL members and new supporters
near her new home in Florida, but the stress of the ministry overcame her
and she quit in 1991, shortly before her divorce from Jim.[114] In the mid-1990s,

shortly after remarrying, she tried to restart her career in Christian television but was rebuffed by everyone that she called, including her old friends Pat Robertson at CBN and Paul and Jan Crouch at TBN.[115]

In 1996, the Fox Television Network offered Tammy Faye—now Messner— a secular talk show, which she co-hosted with gay actor Jim J. Bullock. At the same time, Messner discovered that she was becoming a kind of icon among gay men. Her flamboyant style, including a penchant for wigs and costume jewelry, was ripe for drag caricature but Messner largely missed the biting irony in these performances. Her simultaneous rejection from a church community that she had always criticized as too exclusionary and this attention from a community whose support she did not expect proved transformative for Messner. In 2006, she explained on *Larry King Live*: "When we lost everything, it was the gay people that came to my rescue, and I will always love them for that."[116] She expressed that love by embracing this new audience, emceeing drag bingo and look-a-like contests to raise funds for AIDS research, and attending a book signing for gay fans that was captured in her 2004 appearance on VH1's reality show *The Surreal Life*. She also briefly penned an advice column for the queer youth magazine *XY* in 2002.[117] In 1999, directors Fenton Bailey and Ryan Barbato chronicled and fomented this transformation in their documentary *The Eyes of Tammy Faye*.[118] With narration by superstar drag performer RuPaul, the documentary resurrected the Pieters interview and cemented Messner's image as a tragic diva. When she died from cancer in 2007, the national gay magazine *The Advocate* eulogized Messner fondly as "one of the few Christian conservatives to openly support us."[119]

This kind of relationship with the gay community would likely not have been possible—or indeed necessary—if Messner had not gone through the 1987 scandal and broken ties with the prominent figures in the New Christian Right whom she had counted among her friends. While it is true that the New Christian Right was always a nebulous coalition with room for some significant political and religious divergence, there were also limits. The reactions of other prominent figures to the Bakker scandal suggest that PTL overstepped those limits politically or theologically, and probably both.

Yet the fact that Jim Bakker was always the focus of the scandal, and Tammy Faye typically an addendum, highlights another significant feature of women's involvement in the religious right. Scholars have tended to underestimate the leadership of women like Morgan, Bryant, LaHaye, and Bakker, because— with the exception of LaHaye—these women tended to downplay their own significance as leaders. Each of them, including LaHaye, built her career in the context of an expanding evangelical community that was beginning to afford women more opportunities for cultural and political prominence but at the same time tended to assume that women's contributions were secondary and that they lacked the gravity of men's ministries and activism. For Tammy Faye, this assumption of insignificance afforded her the opportunity to take a remarkable theological and political approach when compared to many of her contemporaries.

5

Sarah Palin and Michele Bachmann Vie for the White House

THE 2008 AND 2012 presidential elections made two conservative evangelical women into new household names. When Sarah Palin emerged as John McCain's choice of running mate in 2008, observers variously extolled the Alaska governor's outspoken charisma and castigated her backwoods persona and lack of national political experience. Many observers found her positions on women's issues particularly confounding, puzzling over her simultaneous commitment to traditionalist family values and her selective identification with something that she called "conservative feminism." When Minnesota congresswoman Michele Bachmann declared her own candidacy in the following presidential race, her religious and political commitments provoked similar alarm among observers unfamiliar with the conservative evangelical world that had produced these women and many of their supporters. In 2012, Bachmann's stated commitment to the doctrine of wifely submission became a major talking point, raising questions about whether a submissive wife could or should be a head of state.

These women and their political positions should not have caused so much consternation. As we have seen, conservative evangelical women had long been vocal proponents of socially, economically, and religiously conservative causes, both as grassroots activists and as nationally prominent figures. In the 1980s and 1990s, the previous decades' battles between the New Left and the New Christian Right developed into an ongoing culture war centered on issues of family, sexuality, and national identity. During these years conservative women, including Beverly LaHaye and Phyllis Schlafly, continued to be some of the most prominent defenders of what they called traditional family values.

Culture wars do not foster nuanced understandings; instead, they operate on a field of stark divisions and clearly drawn lines. During these decades, feminists faced their own internal struggles but they also largely succeeded in positioning feminism as the natural voice for women's issues and characterizing antifeminist positions as necessarily antiwoman. Books like Susan Faludi's influential *Backlash: The Undeclared War against American Women* contributed to this narrative, in which women like LaHaye and Schlafly appeared not as representatives of a broader constituency of conservative women but as cynical or deluded handmaidens of the patriarchy.[1] Even as conservative women remained prominent figures, the idea of a conservative woman became harder to fathom.

Palin, Bachmann, and the reactions to them highlight important legacies of the culture wars and of the earlier history that this book traces. Both women grew up immersed in an evangelical subculture that deftly wove together religious and political concerns, and that insisted on traditional gender roles while also affirming that women could and even should take on political leadership in defense of conservative Christian values. These women's rhetoric and ideals demonstrate the influence of women like Morgan, Bryant, LaHaye, and Bakker while also underscoring important shifts in conservative evangelical gender ideology over the intervening decades.

At the same time, the wider reception of their candidacies demonstrates that even as evangelical subculture has grown into a multimillion-dollar industry with significant political impact, its language and ideas remain unfamiliar or inscrutable to many Americans. Scholarly analyses of these women have so far tended to treat them as either something new in the context of American politics or something understandable in the history of American evangelicalism. This chapter argues that they are both. Contextualizing them in broader political and religious histories offers a better understanding not only of their careers but also of the lasting legacies of the late twentieth-century culture wars and the continuing importance of women's leadership in conservative evangelical community life and political activism.

Palin and Bachmann were not the first conservative women to run for elected office, but they were among the first to make bids for the highest elected offices in the United States from within the Republican Party.[2] Their particular political emphases, their deep ambivalence toward the legacies of the feminist movement, and their negotiations of traditionalist gender ideologies all demonstrate the influence of the religious and political communities that produced them. This chapter examines Palin's and Bachmann's political careers, with particular attention to Palin's vice-presidential candidacy in 2008 and Bachmann's presidential bid in 2012. Analyzing their political rhetoric and cultural reception, it emphasizes the continued significance of the legacies of women like Morgan, Bryant, LaHaye, and Bakker. It also offers an opportunity to trace important shifts in conservative Christian rhetoric about gender over the past forty years, including a new willingness among conservative women to claim the mantle of "feminism" for themselves. This development in particular offers new insight into the ongoing legacies of the late twentieth-century culture wars by demonstrating the ways in which opposing factions have won, lost, and continue to fight over ownership of concepts like "morality," "family," and "women's issues." In short, this chapter offers a new historical framework for understanding women like Palin and Bachman within the context of a movement that has always relied on women's leadership.

Sarah Palin and the Culture Wars

Republican presidential candidate John McCain announced his choice of running mate in Dayton, Ohio, on August 29, 2008. Speaking to an enthusiastic crowd just days before the Republican National Convention in Minneapolis, McCain introduced Sarah Palin as a perfect fit for his "maverick" campaign.[3] "I found someone with an outstanding reputation for standing up to special interests and entrenched bureaucracies; someone who has fought against corruption and the failed policies of the past; someone who stopped government from wasting taxpayers' money on things they don't want or need, and put it back to work for the people," he proclaimed. "She's exactly who I need, she's exactly who this country needs to help me fight the same old Washington politics of me-first and country second."[4] As a Republican presidential candidate hoping to succeed an unpopular incumbent in his own party, McCain leaned on his reputation as an iconoclast who valued principle over the party line.[5] The choice of Palin—a true Washington outsider and a governor frequently at odds with the GOP establishment in her own state—underscored these themes as central priorities of the campaign.

At the same time, Palin's presence on the ticket was designed to reassure the party's right wing amid concerns that McCain-the-maverick was not a true conservative.[6] For these voters, McCain's tendency to buck the party line was as often troubling as it was charming. Many were openly critical of McCain's positions on issues ranging from immigration to climate change to campaign reform.[7] Evangelical conservatives in particular did not see McCain as a natural ally. In 2004, he voted against a constitutional amendment to block same-sex marriage, calling the federal legislation of this issue "antithetical in every way to the core philosophy of Republicans."[8] During his bid for the Republican presidential nomination in 2000, he denounced Christian Right luminaries Pat

Robertson and Jerry Falwell as "agents of intolerance" whose tactics "shame our faith, our party, and our country."[9]

A lack of support from evangelicals cost McCain in 2000, when he lost in the Republican primaries after a bitter fight against George W. Bush. Almost as soon as he began to eye a 2008 run, McCain worked to repair his relationship with this critical voting bloc. In 2006, he gave the commencement address at Jerry Falwell's Liberty University, where he emphasized his commitment to the Iraq War and to the principle of freedom.[10] At public speeches in a variety of venues, he took pains to highlight his support for President Bush, spoke frequently about his opposition to abortion, and once asserted that "the Constitution established the United States of America as a Christian nation."[11] But conservative Christian voters remained wary. In October 2007, McCain placed last in a straw poll of nine potential presidential nominees at the Values Voter Summit hosted by the evangelical Family Research Council (FRC).[12] James Dobson, founder of FRC and Focus on the Family, publicly stated in January of that year that he "would not vote for John McCain under any circumstances."[13]

In Palin, McCain found a running mate who could rally evangelical voters, deeply anxious about a Barack Obama presidency but unimpressed with the presumptive Republican nominee.[14] For these conservatives, Palin's evangelical background and her record of social and fiscal conservatism made her the ideal pick.[15] Wendy Wright, president of Concerned Women for America, praised McCain's choice, calling Palin "a woman of substance and character." James Dobson effectively overrode his earlier misgivings about McCain in asserting that Palin represented "an outstanding choice that should be extremely reassuring to the conservative base" of the party. Richard Land, president of the Southern Baptist Convention's Ethics and Religious Liberty Commission, went even further in his response saying, "I think ecstatic would be an understatement."[16]

Nonetheless, most observers were blindsided by McCain's choice. Palin was a one-term governor with little presence outside of Alaska. Her name was rarely raised in the speculation leading up to McCain's announcement. Instead, most reports focused on three men as McCain's most likely choices: former Massachusetts governor Mitt Romney, Connecticut senator Joe Lieberman, and Minnesota governor Tim Pawlenty.[17] Romney—a Mormon—bore his own difficulties with evangelical voters, as his 2012 presidential bid would clearly show.[18] Lieberman, a former Democratic vice-presidential candidate, lacked the conservative credentials that McCain needed. Tim Pawlenty offered a strong conservative record and an outspoken evangelical faith, but as a woman Sarah Palin brought something else to the table that Pawlenty could not.

The 2008 Democratic primaries were a hard-fought battle between Barack Obama and Hillary Clinton. The possibility of electing either the first African American or the first woman president was a source of excitement for many voters and political commentators.[19] Whereas Barack Obama faced pressure to name a white man as his running mate in order to "balance" the Democratic ticket, the McCain camp worried that a campaign led by two white men might send the wrong message in this electoral climate.

McCain's campaign organizers also hoped that a female vice-presidential nominee might turn disaffected Clinton supporters into McCain voters. Clinton had garnered a great deal of support from women, especially older white women, who were deeply disappointed when Clinton conceded to Obama in June 2008, and again when Obama named Joe Biden and not Clinton as his running mate on August 28.[20] Many perceived sexism in the criticism that Clinton faced from some party officials and pundits for not bowing out of the race earlier. Cynthia Ruccia, a Clinton supporter from Ohio, expressed these sentiments concisely: "Women who have been the backbone of the Democratic Party feel our party has betrayed us—this was our time."[21]

The McCain campaign hoped to capitalize on that disappointment.[22] When Clinton conceded the Democratic nomination to Barack Obama on June 7, she likened the votes that she had received during the primaries to "eighteen million cracks" in the "highest, hardest glass ceiling."[23] When Palin accepted the vice-presidential nomination on August 29, she referenced that already-famous line, though she avoided direct credit to Clinton for coining it. "It was rightly noted in Denver this week that Hillary left eighteen million cracks in the highest, hardest glass ceiling in America," she proclaimed, "but it turns out the women of America aren't finished yet, and we can shatter that glass ceiling once and for all."[24] The audience erupted in enthusiastic cheering.

Many on the left were immediately critical of this strategy. *New York Times* columnist Gail Collins described herself as "kind of ticked off" that Republicans seemed to assume "that women are going to race to vote for any candidate with the same internal plumbing."[25] Feminist activist and Clinton supporter Gloria Steinem asserted that Palin was antithetical to "pretty much everything Clinton's candidacy stood for." For disappointed Clinton supporters to "vote in protest for McCain/Palin, would be like saying, 'Somebody stole my shoes, so I'll amputate my legs,'" Steinem wrote in an opinion piece for the *Los Angeles Times*.[26]

The notion that some Clinton supporters might transfer their loyalty to McCain was not so far-fetched. Both candidates were political moderates whose policy positions and voting records often overlapped, even as they also clashed on several key issues.[27] On the other hand, the hope that Sarah

Palin might shore up the votes of erstwhile Clinton supporters—simply by virtue of being a woman—relied on an overly simplistic understanding of female voters and ignored the chasm that existed between Clinton and Palin in terms of both policy positions and rhetorical style. Palin's staunch conservatism contrasted sharply with Clinton's center-left approach on issues ranging from crime to environment to economics. Abortion and health care were focal issues for both women, who stood on opposites side of debates over *Roe v. Wade*, embryonic stem cell research, and public health care provision. Whereas Hilary Clinton was reserved, methodical, and experienced, Palin was outspoken and charismatic, heralding her lack of national government experience as a promise of "no more politics as usual." Even on the issue of gender in the campaign itself, Clinton and Palin were more divided than they were unified. Clinton's comment about cracking the glass ceiling was atypical of a campaign that pointedly downplayed the significance of the candidate's gender. Indeed, Clinton routinely emphasized that voters should *not* choose her because she was a woman but rather because she was the most qualified person to do the job.[28] Palin, on the other hand, drew on maternalist rhetoric from the very beginning, leaning on her personas of "mama grizzly" and "hockey mom" as frequently as she did on her experience as governor.

Yet if Republicans relied on overly simplistic gender analyses in this instance, so did some Democrats. In particular, the assumption that female voters would naturally support Clinton and the Democratic Party also relied on imperfect assumptions about women's political commitments. Clinton campaigners made the same mistake as McCain strategists in assuming that women would naturally hew to a female candidate. When it became clear that younger women favored Obama, many of Clinton's supporters expressed a profound sense of betrayal. In February 2008, feminist author Robin Morgan reprised her famous 1970 essay "Goodbye to All That" in support of Clinton's candidacy. In the updated version, Morgan excoriated sexist media coverage of the campaign and rebuked the women who did not support Clinton: "Goodbye to some women letting history pass by while wringing their hands, because Hillary isn't as 'likeable' as they've been told they must be," Morgan wrote. "Goodbye to some young women eager to win male approval by showing they're not feminists (or at least not the kind who actually threaten the status quo), who can't identify with a woman candidate because she's not afraid of *eeueweeeu* yucky *power*."[29] For women like Robin Morgan, who had helped to organize feminism's second wave in the 1960s and 1970s, feminist solidarity required that women vote for this female candidate. Anything else represented treason to the movement.

For many Clinton supporters, the notion that women might vote Republican was also unthinkable. Following a common pattern in contemporary political thinking, they relied on the notion that feminism is the natural standard-bearer of women's issues writ large. Thus, when they spoke about women's interests, it was with the assumption that these interests aligned with the major platforms of the modern feminist movement: pro-choice, pro-diversity, and left-leaning. Of course, this assumption requires that conservative women and their long history of active political engagement either be passively ignored or actively dismissed as illegitimate. Both responses were evident in feminists' reactions to Sarah Palin's candidacy.

Gloria Steinem elided conservative women's longtime activism on behalf of the Republican Party when she credited the feminist movement alone for the fact that "even the anti-feminist right wing—the folks with a headlock on the Republican Party—are trying to appease the gender gap with a first-ever female vice president." Feminist gains over the past half century undoubtedly influenced conservative communities' increasing willingness to expand their understandings of acceptable female leadership, but by 2008, women had been leading conservative movements in their communities and on the national stage for several decades. Steinem underscored her erasure of this history with the assertion that Palin "opposes everything most other women want and need."[30]

Others went even further, excluding Palin not only from the big tent of feminism but from womanhood itself. Feminist culture critic Cintra Wilson—in a column that began: "She may be a lady, but she ain't no woman"—called Palin an "opportunistic anti-female" and asserted that the "throat she's so hot to cut is that of *all* American women."[31] Wendy Doniger, a professor at the University of Chicago Divinity School, drew criticism from conservatives for her own assertion that Palin's "greatest hypocrisy is in her pretense that she's a woman."[32]

These responses highlight an important legacy of the ongoing culture wars that came into maturation during the late twentieth century. Culture wars—like cold wars—are long and nebulous. It is unclear when they begin and when they end, if they ever do. Indeed, many scholars have questioned whether the metaphor of culture war is useful at all—asking whether this phrase describes a noteworthy phenomenon or simply the ongoing disagreement necessary to political debate.[33] But the notion of culture war denotes something deeper than this—not simply disagreement over policy or ideas, but an almost unbridgeable divide in the fundamental assumptions that form the basis of each side's political philosophy. In this sense, the divide between the New Left, the New Christian Right, and the political heirs of each is rightly described as a culture war. The two sides are so deeply divided over so many basic assumptions—the righteousness of Christianity versus the value of religious diversity, the emphasis on individual responsibility versus a focus on systemic inequality, the question of whether attention to diversity exacerbates division or facilitates reconciliation—that these groups more often speak past each other than truly engaging in what might be called political debate.

The politics of gender and family constitute one of the most hotly contested battlegrounds in these culture wars and offer essential insight into their continued legacies as well as important shifts that have taken place over the past forty years. In particular, the question of defining "women's issues" illustrates a crucial point: although it can be easy to miss, battles in culture wars can be won. They are won—and lost—in the same way that they are fought: in the arena of language. Victories can be discerned in the naturalization of associations between particular groups and ideas. For example, the frequently assumed synchrony between "women's issues" and "feminism" illustrates that despite the best efforts of women like Beverly LaHaye, the feminist movement has largely succeeded in making the claim to speak for most, if not all, women. On the other hand, the notion that "values voters" belong firmly to the conservative wing of the Republican Party demonstrates the New Christian Right's success in claiming the concept of "values"—and "morality"—for its side, even if it is obvious upon reflection that virtually every political position is founded on a set of values and moral convictions.

It was these inheritances from the culture wars that made Palin so difficult to understand for many contemporary observers. The widespread conflation of "women's issues" with feminism erases the concerns of conservative women, making their political commitments seem impossible or ironic despite a long history of conservative women's activism. It is naturalized assumptions like these that undergird the wide discursive divides described by the concept of culture war. As we build a more robust history of American political movements across the ideological spectrum, it is also necessary that we recognize, historicize, and develop analytical frameworks for understanding the inherited assumptions that often go unnoticed in our daily political discourse.

Palin vs. Couric

In late September 2008, just over a month before the general election, Sarah Palin gave a series of interviews to CBS anchor Katie Couric that would in many ways come to define Palin's candidacy and national image. In the first month after being named McCain's running mate in late August, Palin gave only three interviews to national media outlets. She spoke to ABC's Charlie

Gibson in Alaska on September 11, to Fox News's Sean Hannity on September 18, and to Couric over the course of several days beginning on September 24. These interviews were largely unsuccessful for Palin, who struggled to answer several questions and whose gaffes were endlessly analyzed and replayed by virtually every major news outlet. Yet Palin's treatment by the media also galvanized her supporters and underscored the ideological gap between her conservative evangelical base and other American voters.

The McCain campaign faced serious criticism for its restrictive media policy, which aimed at giving the campaign maximum narrative control as Palin was introduced to a national audience. In most senses, the strategy was a failure. Lacking direct access, media outlets eager for information about the vice-presidential nominee had to lean more heavily on their own investigations and speculation. At the same time, this strategy seemed to indicate that Palin was unprepared to face the media or that the McCain campaign did not trust her to do so.[34] The few interviews that Palin gave also had an outsized role in shaping public perceptions of her, and the mistakes that she made during these interviews were endlessly discussed in the media but rarely addressed by the candidate herself.

The impact of the Couric interviews was bolstered by the fact that CBS divided them into segments and released them over the course of several days on various platforms and programs. For CBS, this strategy was designed to extend the ratings impact of this exclusive. For the McCain campaign, it was intended to keep Palin in the public eye even as she took a break from public engagements to prepare for the vice-presidential debate on October 2. The campaign would come to regret this choice, as the Couric-Palin encounter became the source of several high-profile blunders that would haunt Palin through the rest of the campaign.

Palin struggled throughout the interview to articulate clear positions on the economic bailout, foreign policy, and John McCain's senatorial record, often falling back on jumbled talking points as specifics eluded her. Perhaps the most famous of these moments came in response to Couric's question about what newspapers and magazines Palin regularly read during her time as governor. "I've read most of them, again with a great appreciation for the press, for the media," Palin began. Couric cut in: "But which ones specifically?" Palin reprised her initial response: "All of them, any of them that have been in front of me over all these years." Unsatisfied and visibly frustrated, Couric pressed: "Can you name a few?" Finally, Palin answered: "I have a vast variety of sources where we get our news too. Alaska isn't a foreign country, where, it's kind of suggested and it seems like 'Wow, how could you keep in touch with what the rest of Washington, D.C. may be thinking and doing when you live up there in Alaska?' Believe me, Alaska is like a microcosm of America."[35]

Reactions to this interview underscored the divide between Palin's base—comprised primarily of conservative Protestant voters—and the rest of the American polity. To those already wary of Palin, this interview confirmed that she was unfit to serve as vice-president. *New York Times* columnist Maureen Dowd described the interview as "stunningly junior varsity" and asserted that once "people realized that Palin had a few key lacunae in her understanding of the globe and even of her running mate's record, the myth of the Alaska superwoman continued to unravel."[36] Dowd's colleague, Bob Herbert, wrote that it "is not just painful, but terrifying, to watch someone who could become vice president stumble around like this in an interview." He described Palin's responses as "infantile" and the governor herself as "an embarrassment." These characterizations contrasted sharply with his description of Couric "gently interrupting" to press Palin on key issues.[37] Some conservatives agreed with these portrayals. *Washington Post* columnist Kathleen Parker initially supported Palin's candidacy but then turned against the vice-presidential nominee in the wake of the Couric interview. Parker described Palin as "a problem" for the McCain campaign who was so "Clearly Out of Her League" that she should "bow out" of the race to "save McCain, her party, and the country that she loves."[38] For Parker, and for some other Republicans, the Couric interview revealed that Palin's candidacy lacked substance and that Palin herself was unqualified for the second-highest office in the land.

By contrast, for Palin and her staunch supporters, the Couric interview became the basis of a front-and-center critique of the "lamestream media," with its anticonservative bias and "gotcha" questions. If this seemed like whining to her opponents, for many Palin supporters it captured a broader sense of disaffection from mainstream US culture and values. As we have seen, this alienation had roots in the rise of the New Left and the counterculture of the 1960s, which brought with them the apparently sudden political critique of ideals and values that had once seemed as American as apple pie. It intensified with the development of the culture wars over the following decades, and it was nurtured in an eventually all-encompassing evangelical subculture infused with politically conservative values and a deep-seated ambivalence toward mainstream American popular culture and politics.

Sarah Palin grew up in an evangelical world in which this subculture was already well developed. Born in 1964, she was a child when Morgan, Bryant, and LaHaye published their first books. As she came of age, she would have had access to a fully immersive evangelical subculture that seamlessly mixed conservative theology with American patriotism and free-market economics. Growing up in this environment, Palin's brand of religiously infused American patriotism—along with her distrust of big government and the "lamestream media"—came naturally, but they were not uniquely hers. Instead, they had developed in a broader cultural context unfamiliar to most Americans yet still deeply important in the nation's political culture.

Palin later explained her response to Couric's question about her media consumption as a matter of defensiveness. In a 2009 interview with Oprah Winfrey, Palin explained that if she had given a weak answer to the question, it was only because she was annoyed at being asked: "It was more like, 'Are you kidding me? Are you really asking me?'" Palin told Oprah, "It seemed like she was discovering this nomadic tribe . . . asking me, 'How do you stay in touch with the real world?'"[39] This annoyance had to do with regional identity but also with a sense that conservative Christians like Palin were frequently misunderstood in American media. In her memoir, published the same year, Palin took a direct swipe at Couric, saying: "Maybe I should have asked her what *she* reads. She didn't sound very informed on our energy issues."[40] In Palin's populist rhetoric, she and McCain represented the "real world" of America against the out-of-touch elites in media and government.[41] What seemed to be gaffes to some Americans appeared to others as evidence of Palin's mistreatment by the media, as well as the broader failure of coastal elites to understand their experiences, perspectives, and needs.

In certain cases, this defensiveness was merited. Particularly on the social issues most closely associated with the religious right, Couric clearly expected hardline responses from Palin and she treated Palin's more nuanced answers as equivocations. On the issue of abortion, for example, Couric began by framing her question in the most controversial of terms: "If a 15-year-old is raped by her father, you believe it should be illegal for her to get an abortion. Why?" Palin responded, "I am pro-life. And I'm unapologetic about my position there on pro-life" but she did not concede that she would criminalize abortion. Instead, she laid out a much less radical position than Couric attributed to her, saying: "I would counsel to choose life. I would like to see a culture of life in this country. But I would like to see taking it one step further. . . . I want . . . those women who find themselves in circumstances that are absolutely less than ideal, for them to be supported, for adoptions to be made easier. For more support given to foster parents and adoptive families." In this, she focused on a potential shared goal of pro-life and pro-choice camps: reducing the number of abortions not through criminalization but by making alternatives more easily available to all women. Couric did not accept this approach. "But ideally you think it should be illegal . . ." she pressed twice more, before turning to the question of the morning-after pill. In each case, Palin emphasized that she would choose life herself and would counsel others to choose life, but she framed her agenda as one of cultural rather than legislative change. Finally, she countered: "Let's be practical about it and let's be realistic about a vice-president's role in this debate. . . . [A] vice-president does not make law. And a vice-president does not interpret the law either." Pressed one more time, she again reiterated that she would like to see the culture change but that she would not seek to change the law.[42]

Couric pivoted to the question of evolution in public school curricula, and then to the issue of homosexuality.[43] She began this latter line of questioning with: "Your church sponsored a conference that claimed to be able to convert gays into heterosexuals through prayer. Do you think that gays can be converted, governor?" Palin corrected Couric, asserting that this was not her home church and that she was not in fact a member of any church (she said later in the interview that she wished she had the "time and consistency to be a more regular attendee of church"). Pressed on her position on church-sponsored reparative therapy—sometimes called "pray the gay away" ministries—Palin responded that she did not "know what prayers are worthy of being prayed. And I don't know what prayers are going to be answered or not answered. But as for homosexuality, I am not going to judge Americans and the decisions that they make in their adult personal relationships." For Palin, this answer was judicious; it did not commit her to any moral judgment on homosexuality but it also fit squarely into the evangelical understanding that God would deal with individuals on the basis of their own sins.

Couric's frustration with Palin's answers was palpable, and it was predicated on two things. First, Couric clearly expected Palin to take extreme hardline positions on these issues based on her association with the conservative Christian wing of the GOP base. Second, Palin had already established a pattern of evasive and unsatisfying answers to questions on foreign policy, global warming, and even her own running mate's political record. Given these contexts, Palin's attempts at nuancing her answers on abortion and homosexuality could easily be interpreted as more hedging. But these questions were squarely in Palin's wheelhouse and her answers reflect an attempt to maintain her appeal to conservative evangelical voters without alienating more moderate Republicans. For Palin's supporters, it was Couric who seemed deliberately obtuse in these moments. And what Bob Herbert had characterized as gentle interrupting appeared instead as an aggressive attack, consistent with a pattern that these audiences perceived as the mainstream media's broader failure to understand conservative Christian perspectives.[44]

The sense that the media treated Palin unfairly—and that she was misunderstood by the "liberal elite"—was exacerbated by *Saturday Night Live* parodies, which were often remembered as real Palin gaffes. This was at least in part because the late-night comedy sketches often did quote Palin directly, using her own missteps—but also her accent and her personality—against her. On the weekend after the first Couric-Palin interview segments aired, Tina Fey (as Palin) and Amy Poehler (as Couric) parodied the conversation in SNL's cold open.[45] The segment comprised primarily original jokes; Fey-as-Palin discussed her recent visit to New York, recounting that she had had "fifteen to twenty false alarms where I thought I saw Osama bin Laden drivin' a taxi" and that she was "disheartened" that most of the people she met at the United Nations were "foreigners," promising that "when Senator McCain and I are elected, we're going to get those jobs back in American hands." Poehler played the straight man in the sketch and acted as a surrogate for audience members confounded by Palin, blinking incredulously at each of Fey's goofy responses.

Portions of the sketch used Palin's real words, particularly her tortuous response to a question about the economic bailout: "Ultimately, what the bailout does is help those who are concerned about the health care reform that is needed to help shore up our economy, helping those—it's got to be all about job creation, too, though." CNN aired this clip of the sketch alongside a clip of the original interview, as anchors Wolf Blitzer and John King laughed over the comparison.[46] The *Huffington Post* also reported on this bit, saying that "Fey's mockery is more-or-less safe for broadcast even in the event of another writers' strike, as all it takes is Palin's own words to make the comedy work."[47] The comedic potential of Palin's own words may have been worth comment, but this reporting overplayed the extent to which the SNL portrayals were accurate depictions of Palin's responses.

During the 2008 election, perhaps the most famous quotation associated with Palin was, "I can see Russia from my house." But Palin never said this. Instead, it originated with another *Saturday Night Live* sketch, first aired on September 13, in which Fey (as Palin) and Poehler (as Hillary Clinton) appeared together to give a "nonpartisan message" about sexism in the media. The sketch emphasized the differences between the two political figures, portraying Clinton as a hardworking, if bitter, career politician and Palin as a charming idiot. When Poehler-as-Clinton asserted, "I believe that diplomacy should be the cornerstone of any foreign policy," Fey-as-Palin interjected: "And I can see Russia from my house!"[48] The joke was not cut from whole cloth. On September 11 and 12, 2008, Palin gave her first interview as vice-presidential candidate to ABC's Charlie Gibson. Early in the first interview, Gibson questioned Palin on her readiness to serve in federal politics: "When I asked John McCain about your national security credentials, he cited the fact that you have commanded the Alaska National Guard and that Alaska is close to Russia. Are those sufficient credentials?" Palin did not answer the question directly, but pivoted instead to talk about energy independence. Gibson reprised the question later in the conversation, asking Palin: "What insight into Russian actions, particularly in the last couple of weeks [in terms of recent Russian military action in Georgia], does the proximity of the state [of Alaska] give you?" Palin answered: "They're our next door neighbors and you can actually see Russia from land here in Alaska, from an island in Alaska." She went on to talk about "how small our world is and how important it is that we work with our allies to keep good relations with all of these countries, especially Russia."[49] Two weeks later, Couric brought up this question again: "You've cited Alaska's proximity to Russia as part of your foreign-policy experience. What did you mean by that?" Palin responded by emphasizing Alaska's "narrow maritime border" with Russia and expressing frustration with the media, that "a comment like that was—kind of made to—I don't know. You know. Reporters!" For many, this answer was just as unsatisfying as if Palin had responded that she could see Russia from her house, but for Palin's supporters the persistent mischaracterization of Palin's actual words offered proof that they and their candidate were misunderstood and unfairly treated.

Palin's early media appearances—particularly her interviews with Charlie Gibson and Katie Couric—revealed points of real weakness for Palin. At the same time, these interviews and the reactions to them underscored fundamental political divisions. For Palin's detractors, the Couric interview in particular furnished an ample selection of gaffes that clearly illustrated the vice-presidential candidate's inexperience and unfitness for the second highest office in the land. For Palin's supporters, these same moments became emblematic of unfair media treatment of their candidate and of their own mistreatment by mainstream American media, even as they identified themselves as the real representatives of American culture and their political opponents as elitist usurpers. Every failure of Palin's opponents to understand her appeal and every suggestion that she and her supporters were unintelligent or ridiculous simply fueled this narrative.

McCain and Palin lost the 2008 presidential contest but Palin remained in the national spotlight for several years. She continued to promote her personal brand of rugged femininity and became one of the leading figures in the Tea Party movement that helped to inaugurate a new iteration of conservative populism within the Republican Party. Very soon after the election, she became a regular presence on Fox News, first as a guest commentator on a variety of programs, then as a full-time analyst, and for a brief period as the host of her own show *Real American Stories*. In March 2010, she signed with the TLC network to make a reality program called *Sarah Palin's Alaska*, which would focus on the Palin family and life in their home state. The premiere, on November 14, 2010, attracted five million viewers, which was a record for the network. The show ran for nine episodes but was not renewed for a second season, which some observers regarded as a sign that Palin was eyeing a 2012 presidential bid.[50]

Palin also published two memoirs in quick succession after the 2008 election. *Going Rogue: An American Life* (2009) focused on telling the story of the campaign from Palin's perspective, with particular emphasis on responding to her critics in the "lamestream media" and within the McCain campaign. *America by Heart: Reflections on Faith, Family, and Flag* (2010), hewed more closely to the established conventions of evangelical women's writing, with its entwined emphases on family life and moral resolve embedded an over-arching narrative of national decline. Her later books further aligned her with the traditions of evangelical women's culture. *Good Tidings, Great Joy*, published in 2013, focused on "protecting the heart of Christmas" from liberal political correctness, while 2015's *Sweet Freedom* offered daily Christian devotionals. Traditionally, devotional books highlight one passage of scripture per day and offer the reader guidance for reflecting or acting on some key lesson. In Palin's *Sweet Freedom*, these lessons emphasized both personal spiritual development and political mobilization. As Palin built an ongoing media presence in the wake of electoral defeat, she pursued mainstream popular cultural forums, while at the same time making choices that revealed her familiarity and comfort with the traditional genres of evangelical women's writing.[51]

Palin resigned from the Alaska governorship in July 2009, two-and-a-half years into her first four-year term. Critics accused Palin of putting her new media career ahead of her responsibilities to Alaskan voters and pointed to her resignation as proof that she had never been fit to govern. Palin contended that her resignation had been necessary because of "frivolous" ethics complaints and Freedom of Information requests from political opponents, which were costing the state hundreds of thousands of dollars and making it impossible for Palin to do her job effectively. Jay Newton-Small, a political correspondent for *Time* magazine, pointed out that Palin's newfound affiliation with the right-wing of the national Republican Party had also contributed to her inefficacy, by alienating former Democratic allies in the Alaska statehouse.[52] The resignation fueled speculation that Palin intended to run for the presidency in 2012, since her departure from the governorship would give her greater leeway to maintain her national public presence.

Palin did not ultimately seek the presidency in 2012, but she did maintain a national presence well beyond the 2008 election. Her political endorsements in the 2010 midterm elections garnered a great deal of media attention and fostered further speculation about her 2012 intentions. Some media outlets referred to Palin as the "de facto leader" of the Tea Party movement, and most of her endorsements went to social conservatives with Tea Party connections.[53] Between 2009 and 2016, Palin was also a regular speaker at the Conservative Political Action Committee (CPAC), the largest annual gathering of conservative politicians, activists, and organizations in the United States. In January 2016, she endorsed Donald Trump for the Republican presidential nomination, appearing beside him at a rally in Ames, Iowa, to give a speech that characteristically excited her base and confounded outside observers.[54]

Palin and Conservative Feminism

In May 2010—around the same time that she began endorsing candidates for that year's midterm elections—Palin set off a media firestorm with her speech at the conservative Susan B. Anthony List's "Celebration of Life" breakfast. The issue at the heart of the controversy was Palin's identification with something that she described as "conservative feminism."

This was not the first time that Palin had identified as a feminist, despite her commitment to conservative values that many in the feminist movement's left-leaning mainstream saw as antithetical to their cause. In 2008, Katie Couric asked Palin: "Do you consider yourself a feminist?" and Palin responded in the affirmative: "I do. I'm a feminist who believes in equal rights and I believe that women certainly today have every opportunity that a man has to succeed and to try to do it all anyway." She went on to describe her rugged upbringing in Alaska and the "expectation that the boys and girls in my community were expected to do the same and accomplish the same." She made similar claims in her memoirs, in which she also highlighted her gratitude for Title IX of the Education Amendments Act of 1972, which had made it possible for her to participate in school sports at the secondary and post-secondary levels.[55]

Of course, Palin's contention that women "today have every opportunity that a man has to succeed" would have frustrated most feminists, who tend to emphasize that there is still work to be done in terms of the gender pay gap, rape culture, and other forms of structural misogyny. For example, Palin opposed the passage of the Lilly Ledbetter Fair Pay Act of 2009, which extended the statute of limitations for filing an equal-pay discrimination lawsuit. Just as CWA would later argue that the Ledbetter Act could allow "women to sue for workplace discrimination, even years after widespread workplace discrimination," Palin told Couric that the Act would "turn into a boon for trial lawyers who, I believe could have taken advantage of women who were many, many years ago—who would allege some kind of discrimination."[56]

Palin's identification with feminism in 2008 was equivocal. Though she identified as a feminist when Couric asked her in September, she gave a different answer to ABC's Brian Williams the following month: "I'm not going to label myself anything, Brian. And I think that's what annoys a lot of Americans, especially in a political campaign, is to start trying to label different parts of America, different backgrounds, different—I'm not going to put a label on myself."[57] To many, this inconsistency encapsulated Palin's hypocrisy, since it seemed that she was willing to identify as a feminist when speaking to a woman whom she perceived as feminist but then demurred when speaking to a man.[58]

By contrast, two years later Palin identified strongly not only as a "conservative feminist" but as part of "a new conservative feminist movement." "It's an emerging identity," she asserted. "For far too long when people heard the word feminist, they thought of the faculty lounge at some East Coast women's college, am I right? And no offense to them; they have their opinions and their voice and God bless them, they're just great. But that's not the only voice of women in America." Palin went on to argue that her feminist politics drew on "that tough, gun-toting pioneer feminism of women like Annie Oakley" and merged seamlessly with the pro-family, "small town values" of the social conservative movement that she represented.[59]

Drawing on the founding argument of the Susan B. Anthony List, Palin argued that first-wave "feminist foremothers" were pro-life and that conservative feminists represented the rightful heirs to their legacy.[60] She acknowledged that in the abortion debate, feminism had typically been associated with the pro-choice side, but she argued that this kind of thinking had it backward. "Together, our pro-woman sisterhood is telling these young women that they are strong enough and they are smart enough, they are capable to be able to handle an unintended pregnancy and to be able—in less than ideal circumstances, no doubt—but still be able to handle that, give their child life, in addition to pursuing career and pursuing education, pursuing avocations." By contrast, she accused feminists of hypocrisy for telling women: "You can't give your child life and still pursue education. You're not strong enough; you're not capable."

Across the internet, feminist writers responded swiftly and vocally to Palin's claims. *LA Times* columnist Meghan Daum rebuffed the idea that "supporting the right to choose represents a no-confidence vote for the idea of mothers leading fulfilling professional lives."[61] Jessica Valenti, cofounder of the popular blog and news website *Feministing.com*, argued in an opinion piece for the *Washington Post* that Palin's brand of conservative feminism represented nothing more than an appropriation of feminist language in an attempt "to sell anti-women policies shrouded in pro-woman rhetoric."[62] But whereas Daum asserted that she felt "a feminist duty" to accept Palin into the movement "if she has the guts to call herself a feminist," Valenti argued that if "anyone—even someone who actively fights against women's rights—can call herself a feminist, the word and the movement lose all meaning." Acknowledging the importance of "intellectual diversity" within feminism, Valenti insisted that "certain things are inarguable," including the under-standing that feminism is "a social justice movement with values and goals that benefit women. It's a structural analysis of a world that oppresses women, an ideology based on the notion that patriarchy exists and that it needs to end." For Valenti, Palin's feminism—premised on the notion that women had already achieved equality—could therefore be safely excluded even from feminism's biggest tent.

For the purposes of this analysis, the question of conservative feminist le-gitimacy is less important than the fact that a woman like Palin would want to claim a feminist identity at all. Palin's rhetoric on feminism bears the in-fluence of women like Beverly LaHaye and Phyllis Schlafly, particularly in her simultaneous emphasis on the importance of equality, her implications that the work of achieving equality is done, and her understanding that post-suffrage feminists have taken a good idea much too far. Yet Palin's willingness to identify with the feminist label marks a sharp departure from the explicitly antifeminist rhetoric of LaHaye and Schlafly, and even from the dismissive ambivalence of women like Morgan, Bryant, and Bakker. For conservative women finding their political voices in the 1970s, second-wave feminism was something new, a disruptive force associated with a host of unwanted social, cultural, and political challenges. Feminist critiques of mainstream family norms, from Betty Friedan's emphasis on housewives' malaise to more radical critiques of marriage as a whole, seemed to challenge their basic values, their religious beliefs, and even their core identities. For women like Morgan and Bryant, these critiques also threatened to shake the foundations on which they had built their careers as exemplars of ideal Christian womanhood. LaHaye more explicitly defined her political contributions in opposition to feminism through the argument that only conservative women could effectively counter feminist claims to represent women's issues writ large. For this reason, "fem-inism" was always the enemy against which LaHaye struggled; to identify as feminist would be unthinkable and it would cede too much ground to the other side.

Yet by the early twenty-first century, antifeminist women had largely lost the battle over defining "women's issues" in the public sphere. Indeed, the assumed equivalency between antifeminist and antiwoman is precisely what made Palin's gender politics seem "ironic" to many observers when she first rose to national prominence. At the same time, many ideas that were once revolutionary feminist claims—that women should have equal access to education and employment opportunities, that they should receive equal pay for equal work, and that partners should share household and parenting duties—have become mainstream assumptions, even if full equality is not yet a reality. In this context, the wholesale rejection of feminism sets conservative women up for mockery and reinforces the notion that these women are simply deluded into voting against their own interests. By identifying as conservative feminists, women like Palin attempt to carve out space for themselves as women committed to certain traditionalist politics of gender and family.

In 2012, the battle over defining "feminism" was neatly expressed in warring viral memes. The "Who Needs Feminism" project, originally started as part of a class assignment at Duke University, featured women and men holding handwritten signs inscribed with personalized resolutions to the prompt: "I need feminism because . . ." The project drew national and international media attention, and within a month of its inception the group's Tumblr page had received over eighty thousand visits.[63] Eight months later, an opposing Tumblr page titled WomenAgainstFeminism was founded, featuring women holding similar signs, this time with various statements beginning "I don't need feminism because . . ." Together, the pages and the reaction to them underscored the fundamental split between those who understood feminism as a voice for all women, and those who saw feminism as manhating, antifamily, and obsolete. Feminist writers responded with frustration. Jessica Valenti wrote for the *Guardian* that WomenAgainstFeminism demonstrated a "baffling level of ignorance about what feminism actually is."[64] She also suggested that supporters of the project had worked to misrepresent its popularity among women, writing: "I'm skeptical of how many 'women's' Twitter accounts suddenly popped up in the days surrounding the meme's creation." In other words, Valenti reiterated the understanding that antifeminism is primarily the purview of men, not only by rejecting prominent conservative women as unrepresentative but by suggesting that the apparently female supporters of this particular meme might be impostors.[65]

The notion of conservative feminism predated these memes, but this conversation is representative of the gap that it seeks to fill. If antifeminist women are subject to ridicule, then conservative feminists have eschewed direct opposition to feminism and instead try to claim the movement for their own. In certain ways, their language mirrors that of antifeminist women like Beverly LaHaye. Just as LaHaye centrally insisted that "feminism does not speak for all American women," Palin asserted that left-wing academic feminism is "not the only voice of women in America." Palin's 2012 argument that feminism limits women by underestimating their abilities also closely mirrored LaHaye's 1987 argument that feminism "is a message of confusion" because "they [feminists] say that women are superior to men, and yet, that you are handicapped if you are born a woman."[66]

Yet this particular notion of conservative feminism also marks an important break from LaHaye and her contemporaries. In identifying as feminist, these conservative women concede the equation of feminism with women's issues, but they assert that they—rather than the leftist mainstream of the feminist movement—are the proper heirs of feminism's legacy. Their emphasis on suffragist "foremothers" comprises a rejection of the feminist movements that developed after 1920, along with the assertion that feminists' work toward gender equality is complete. Even as these conservative women sometimes praise achievements made by second-wave feminists—including the Equal Pay Act of 1963 and Title IX of the Education Amendments Act of 1972—they situate these battles firmly in the past. The wage gap, according to conservative feminists, is a function of women's choices to forgo certain career aspirations in favor of focusing on family. Interpreting third-wave feminist priorities through the logic of free-market individualism, they argue that if feminism is about choice, then women should be free to make these political choices without being derided by feminists. For American women to continue to focus on gender inequality in the twenty-first century, they argue, is to insist on women's victimhood rather than their empowerment. To continue to fight for women's rights in this context is to move past equality in favor of misandry and female supremacy.

In one sense, the rise of conservative feminism represents an important victory for feminists in the culture wars. These are conservative women who would have proudly identified as antifeminist a generation ago. Their desire to repurpose the term rather than reject it marks feminists' success in propagating the notion that feminism is quintessentially prowoman such that antifeminist positions must also be antiwoman. However, this movement is also a legacy of the antifeminist work of women like Beverly LaHaye, Phyllis Schlafly, and the other women examined in the earlier chapters of this book. Their critiques of the mainstream feminist movement and their fundamental differences on key issues including equal pay, marriage equality, and abortion indicate the deep political divides that continue to exist among American women. They also underscore the folly in assuming that women's political commitments can ever be defined by gender alone.

Submissive Wife and Commander in Chief

In August 2011, Minnesota congresswoman Michele Bachmann emerged as the frontrunner for the Republican presidential nomination according to the Iowa Straw Poll, which was then the first official barometer in the GOP primaries. Against nine other major contenders, Bachmann received 28.6 percent of the nearly 17,000 votes.[67] Sarah Palin was also present at the Iowa State Fair where the poll was held, as part of her "One Nation" bus tour, but she had not yet announced whether she would run for the 2012 nomination and was therefore not on the ballot.

Bachmann campaigned on a socially and fiscally conservative platform that situated her to the right of most of the other contenders for the GOP nomination. She was an early favorite of Tea Party activists, who criticized establishment candidates in both parties for supporting government interests over the interests of the people.[68] Bachmann embraced this association, writing in her 2011 book *Core of Conviction* that the Tea Party represents "100 percent" of Americans because "I believe that nearly all Americans retain faith in the ordered liberty that the Constitution offers." Having positioned herself against President Barack Obama's health care reforms and his handling of the contemporary economic crisis, Bachmann went on: "Americans have rebelled against autocrats in the past; today they have no wish to see czars reigning on imperial thrones."[69] Like Palin, Bachmann drew on the language of conservative populism to present herself as an advocate of everyday Americans against the excesses of a bloated government. Drawing explicitly on the evangelical language of "servant leadership," which promotes humility and submission to God as a path to worldly and otherworldy success, Bachmann also portrayed herself as a humble representative running against a power-hungry tyrant.[70]

Even more than Palin, Bachmann was an heir to the traditions of conservative women's organizing in the second half of the twentieth century. Seven years older than Palin, she was sixteen years old when the Supreme Court ruled on *Roe v. Wade* in 1973 and she claims to have joined the pro-life movement in the 1980s.[71] During her campaign, she emphasized these credentials as well as her commitment to "profamily education policy." Following in the footsteps of the women who organized against sex education and progressive school reforms in the decades following the Second World War, Bachmann led the fight in Minnesota against what she saw as "a liberal, paternalistic, secular education agenda" in the late 1990s and early 2000s.[72] In the years before she was elected to the Minnesota House of Representatives, she toured the state speaking out against a new set of graduation standards called the Minnesota Profile of Learning, widely opposed by conservative groups as an example of unnecessary government intervention.[73] Echoing long-standing concerns among conservative education activists, Bachmann also asserted that progressive influences in school policy would promote "a socialist, globalist worldview" including "loyalty to all government and not America." Career aptitude testing, she said, could contribute to a "new restructuring of American society" by turning children into "human resources for a centrally planned economy."[74] Like postwar suburban activists, Bachman cut her political teeth on issues related to childhood education, which she interpreted through a now well-developed framework of anticommunist, pronationalist, and small-government conservatism.

Bachmann also made more frequent and more specific references to her Christian beliefs than Palin did. After outlining her core political principles in her 2011 memoir, she asserted: "I believe we must remember the work of the biblical Nehemiah, who rebuilt the sturdy walls of Jerusalem. That is, today we must reinforce the sort of ethical framework—for most of us, the framework provided by the Judeo-Christian tradition—that protects liberty from anarchy."[75]

As a conservative woman running for the 2012 Republican presidential nomination, Bachmann faced many of the same criticisms that hounded Palin during her 2008 vice-presidential campaign. But although commentators sometimes referred to Bachmann's policy positions as "antiwoman"—a charge that Bachmann explicitly rebuffed—commentators in general seemed less perplexed by the presence of a socially conservative female candidate than they had been four years earlier. In this sense, Palin's 2008 bid for the vice-presidency directly paved the way for Bachmann's presidential campaign.

However, one comment plagued Bachmann throughout her campaign. In July 2011, a five-year-old video surfaced that showed Bachmann giving a speech at the Living Word Christian Center during her first campaign for national office in 2006. In it, Bachmann described her decision to study tax law despite her own reluctance. She said that God had called her to go to law school and that her husband Marcus insisted that she return for a post-doctorate degree in tax law: "Why should I go and do something like that?" she initially thought, before remembering: "The Lord says, 'Be submissive wives. You are to be submissive to your husbands.'"[76] Bachmann's invocation of submission doctrine sparked a heated response in the context of her presidential bid. At the GOP debate in Ames, Iowa, two days before the straw poll, debate moderator and conservative journalist Byron York asked Bachmann to clarify her comments, specifically pressing: "As president, would you be submissive to your husband?" The crowd erupted into boos at the question, and shifted to laughter as Bachmann thanked York for asking it. She responded by saying that for her and her husband, "submission means respect." The following week, Bachmann reiterated this position to CBS News' Norah O'Donnell and clarified that submission is not about "subservience."[77]

This perspective on submission was not new. It echoed Marabel Morgan's own efforts to distinguish between submission and subservience in 1973.[78] Bachmann's emphasis on mutual respect within marriage also reflects a shift among conservative evangelicals since the 1980s away from an emphasis on women's submission to their husbands and toward a doctrine of complementarianism—emphasizing husbands' and wives' mutual submission under God.[79] For those immersed in the culture of conservative Christianity, Bachmann's perspective made perfect sense. Journalist Roland Martin sharply criticized York for his decision to question Bachmann on submission. In an opinion piece for CNN, he called the question "offensive" and "sexist." In keeping with mainstream evangelical interpretations of submission doctrine, Martin implicitly understood Bachmann's stance on submission as a private issue related to household decision making and entirely unrelated to her potential job as president.[80] As Morgan had emphasized in 1973's *Total Woman*: "I did not say that a woman is inferior to man, or even that a woman should be subservient to all men, but that a wife should be under her own husband's leadership."[81]

For those unfamiliar with the intricate history of submission doctrine, Bachmann's response seemed ludicrous and shocking. Several commentators suggested that Bachmann would do well to look up the word "submissive" in a dictionary. Journalist Leslie Bennetts responded to Bachmann's contention that "submission means respect" in no uncertain terms: "No, Congresswoman, in fact, it doesn't. Words have specific meanings, and your definition is incorrect, just as your answer to the question was disingenuous and obfuscatory."[82] Bennetts may have been right that Bachmann's definition of submission differed from its most common meaning, but she was wrong in asserting that Bachmann's response was disingenuous. Though words have specific meanings, those meanings are subject to change over time and to varying interpretations in particular cultural and subcultural contexts. Bachmann's understanding of submission reflects her immersion in conservative evangelical subculture and in evangelical women's culture. It also demonstrates the ways in which women's reinterpretations of submission doctrine in the 1970s still influence conservative Christian conversations about gender. The critical responses to Bachmann's speech underscore the fact that despite the size and influence of evangelical subculture in the United States, aspects of its core ideas remain opaque to many Americans.

If Palin's embrace of "conservative feminism" highlights the ways in which battles in the culture wars are won and lost, Bachmann's experience with the submission question demonstrates how culture wars are perpetuated. For conservative evangelicals, Bachmann's belief in submission was a nonissue. These audiences implicitly understood the nuances that had been infused into submission doctrine over the past forty years. For them, the focus on this issue provided further evidence of the mainstream media's fundamental failure to understand conservative evangelical communities. For audiences unfamiliar with this subculture, "submission" seemed to be a straightforward word with a clear dictionary definition; Bachmann's explanations contributed to perceptions that she was stupid, dishonest, or both. Despite a shared national context, these audiences did not come to this question from a shared cultural context. Rather than bridging this cultural gap, their reactions therefore served primarily to confirm their worst suspicions about one another.

Conclusion

Sarah Palin and Michele Bachmann were among the first women to run for the highest and second-highest offices in the United States. The fact that they were both conservative evangelical women highlights the powerful legacy of women's leadership in conservative evangelical communities. As women committed to traditionalist interpretations of gender and family roles, both women faced challenges in explaining their leadership and their policy positions to the public. However, it was primarily liberal and moderate commentators who balked at this apparent paradox. For most conservative evangelicals, women's political leadership in defense of traditional gender and family roles was a nonissue by the early twenty-first century, and the treatment of Palin and Bachmann as incomprehensible curiosities exacerbated a sense of cultural alienation and disaffection for many of their conservative Christian supporters.

In this sense, Palin's and Bachmann's campaigns mark the legacies of the women whose lives and careers are the focus of this book's earlier chapters. The fact that their political leadership was permissible and actively supported by many in the Republican Party's religious right wing is a direct result of the normalization of women's cultural and political leadership in conservative evangelical communities since the 1970s. In both cases, these candidates' rhetoric, priorities, and media strategies also bore the influence of conservative evangelical women's culture as it has developed over the past half century.

At the same time, their experiences highlight important shifts since the 1970s in conservative evangelical subcultures and their broader cultural contexts. Palin's choice to identify as a "conservative feminist" represents a kind of feminist victory in the culture wars; the feminist movement has become so firmly associated with "women's interests" that direct opposition to feminism is now a less viable strategy than the acceptance and reinterpretation of the feminist label. On the other hand, the response to Bachmann's affirmation of submission doctrine demonstrates that despite the continued growth of evangelical subculture and the political influence of conservative evangelicals within the Republican Party, many of the basic ideas embraced by this subculture have not permeated into mainstream cultural consciousness.

The divisions between conservative evangelicals and the broader culture are perhaps starkest on issues related to gender and family, precisely because these have been the primary battlegrounds of the culture wars for decades. Understanding conservative evangelical gender ideologies—and the significant roles of female leaders in shaping these ideologies—is therefore essential to understanding contemporary conservatism and fully grasping modern political battles over these still-central issues.

Conclusion

SARAH PALIN, MICHELE BACHMANN, and other politicians like them are not the only inheritors of the history that this book traces. Evangelical women's culture is still thriving. Fiction and nonfiction by and for Christian women crowds the shelves of Christian bookstores nationwide. Leslie Ludy's best-selling 2008 advice manual *Set-Apart Femininity*, for example, offers a contemporary take on complementarianism that emphasizes separate and divinely appointed roles for men and women while also condemning popular cultural emphases on women's appearance rather than their personalities or spiritual lives.[1] Ludy is also a popular speaker at Christian women's conferences and the director of *Set Apart Girl*, an online teen magazine with a conservative Christian bent, featuring articles such as "Responding to the Immodest Pressure" and "Reaching Young Women for Christ: Giving Them Vision for More."[2] Christian romance literature also constitutes a growing segment of evangelical women's culture that is often no less prescriptive than nonfiction like Ludy's. Characters in these novels model conservative piety, premarital chastity, and the expectation that romance will culminate in a divinely blessed marriage. Headstrong female characters push at the boundaries of gendered expectations and ultimately challenge some aspects of conservative gender theology while still reaffirming the system as a whole.[3]

At the same time, proliferating Christian women's conferences and retreats with names like Women of Faith, Girlfriends in God, and Pursuit 31 (named for the "ideal woman" described in Psalm 31) draw attendees from across the nation and sometimes from around the globe. In 2009, *Christianity Today*, one of the oldest and most widely read Christian magazines in the United States, added a section called "her.meneutics" to its website and print versions, in which women write to other women on a wide range of issues including "church life, marriage, parenting, discipleship, media, life ethics, relationships, health and food."[4] The past two decades have also witnessed the emergence and explosive growth of a Christian women's blogosphere, which has provided a new kind of space for geographically far-flung women to garner household and parenting tips, to share their experiences, and to discuss their perspectives on complementarianism, submission, and other tenets of conservative gender theologies.[5] In this blogging community, at inspirational conferences and retreats, in Christian fiction and nonfiction, and in other cultural forums, evangelical women continue to negotiate and redefine—both implicitly and explicitly—the roles that conservative Christian women should properly play in their homes, in their churches, and in political affairs.

While this book helps to explain the emergence of women like Palin and Bachmann, it is not only a preface to the stories of conservative evangelical women who have taken on (or run for) formal political leadership roles in elected office. It is also a story of the rich proliferation of conservative Christian women's political and cultural authority within a still-growing subculture of evangelicals that now reaches into almost every niche of American cultural life. In the first decades of the twenty-first century, women like Palin and Bachmann have been two of the most visible manifestations of women's political engagement within these communities, but they are not the only examples. Indeed, their careers flourished within the context of conservative evangelical subcultures in which women have played increasingly important roles as authors, activists, celebrities, and speakers over the past fifty years.

These precedents can be traced back to the second half of the twentieth century, and particularly the 1970s, when specific evangelical women's cultures blossomed in the context of growing national evangelical subcultures. Building on a tradition of gender-segregated evangelical ministries and adapting cultural forms from mainstream women's cultures, conservative Christian women established new national prominence and authority as authors, speakers, and conference organizers. In keeping with traditionalist understandings of women's appropriate spheres, these groups and media focused almost exclusively on themes related to womanhood, family, and marital sexuality. These emphases served to reinforce traditionalist gender ideologies. But women's new prominence as authors and speakers also meant that women were increasingly directing and nuancing these conversations. The growth of evangelical women's subcultures in the 1970s also helped to shape the political priorities of the emerging New Christian Right by contributing to a sustained emphasis on issues related to family, gender, and sexuality among conservative evangelicals.

In the late twentieth century, these issues became focal subjects of contention in the developing culture wars in part because of developments within evangelical women's cultures. As the New Left and ensuing identity-based movements developed through the last half of this century, conservative evangelicals were particularly well poised to react against challenges to traditionalist family and gender ideologies because of the conversations that had been ongoing in conservative Christian communities, and especially in conservative evangelical women's cultures, during the decades preceding the New Christian Right's ascendancy.

The movement's emphasis on traditionalist gender roles, however, also facilitated a widespread understanding that the whole movement could be accurately characterized by its vociferous male leaders and distinctly antifeminist positions. As a consequence, the significance of women's voices in building and sustaining the movement was overshadowed. The historical invisibility of women as prominent figures in this movement was also a function of the ambivalence of many of these women toward explicitly claiming leadership roles or political interest. These choices often expanded their impact, allowing them to reach audiences outside of explicitly political spaces and sometimes even allowing them to take a surprising range of political positions. At the same time, their refusal to explicitly and unambiguously claim political leadership meant that even as these women claimed new prominence within their communities, their progress and their significance were often unseen outside of those communities. Beside the male leaders of their own movement and in comparison to the feminist leaders that they opposed, these women and their contributions were frequently eclipsed. The continued legacy of their relative invisibility is apparent in the perplexity expressed over Palin's and Bachmann's political positions, even as these two women also exemplify the significant political work of conservative evangelical women over the past four decades. In the late twentieth and early twenty-first centuries, conservative Christian women were—and continue to be—essential in shaping the rhetoric of the modern religious right, in supporting the movement, and in building up the subcultures that undergird it.

Where Are They Now?

The first four chapters of this book focused on the lives and careers of four prominent women who helped to build evangelical women's cultures and to shape conservative Christian women's political roles. Each of these women made very different contributions to their communities and to national political discourse, and each has left a legacy that continues to resonate among conservative evangelicals and outside of these communities.

Marabel Morgan still lives in a suburb of Miami with her husband Charles. Her two daughters have both started families of their own, and both have followed in their parents' footsteps: one is a full-time homemaker like her mother and the other is a lawyer like her father. Morgan has not published anything since she put out *The Electric Woman* in 1985, but a new generation of conservative evangelical women has begun to take up her ideas in new ways. Her influence is apparent in work like Leslie Ludy's and in the dozens of other books on gender and marriage that are put out by evangelical publishers every year. In particular, the writing of Sheila Wray Gregoire, a well-known Christian blogger, speaker, and author whose humorous writing focuses on issues related to family, gender, and sexuality, closely mirrors the intellectual and stylistic trends that Morgan set in her pioneering work.[6] A recent article in the national Canadian newspaper the *Globe and Mail* rightly represented Morgan as an early pioneer of the still-ongoing trend toward erotically charged and relatively sex-positive evangelical marital manuals.[7] But all of this "sex talk" is not her only legacy. Morgan was also at the forefront of a new openness and levity in Christian writing about the family and gender more broadly, and she was among the first authors to prove the importance of including women's voices prominently in these conversations.

Anita Bryant was never able to fully rebuild her career after her disastrous divorce from Bob Green in 1980. Nearly a decade later, in 1988, she released an album titled *Anita, with Love*, which she described as "a mix of religious songs and old standards."[8] She also began appearing with some regularity as a guest host on Pat Robertson's *700 Club* television program. In 1990, she was remarried to her "childhood sweetheart" and former astronaut test crewman Charlie Day, with whom she tried to stage several show-business comebacks. In the year after their marriage, the two opened the "Anita Bryant Show" in Eureka Springs, Arkansas, only to discover that the town was—as one newspaper later put it—"the gay capital of the Ozarks."[9] In 1994, the couple moved the show to nearby Branson, Missouri, where they opened the Anita Bryant Theatre amid a growing local industry of Christian tourism.[10] Within a few years, however, the show flopped, and the couple declared bankruptcy in 1997. Subsequent attempts to establish similar productions were also unsuccessful. Currently, Anita Bryant Ministries maintains an incompletely constructed and infrequently updated website as well as an Oklahoma City office, though it is not clear what the ministry's current activities are.[11] Bryant and Day live together in a suburb of Oklahoma City.

More pronounced than her legacy in Christian or popular music, however, is Bryant's continued resonance as a symbol for gay-rights activists across the country. She appears frequently in journalists' overviews of the gay-rights movement, most often portrayed as a powerful adversary of gay rights who inadvertently mobilized the modern LGBTQ (lesbian, gay, bisexual, transgender, queer) movement.[12] A recent article in the *New York Times* credited Bryant with the "decline and fall" of the word "homosexual," which the Associate Press now discourages in favor of terms like "gay" or "lesbian."[13] In 2008, Bryant filled the role of the villain in director Gus Van Sant's biopic of openly gay San Francisco city councilman Harvey Milk.[14] Bryant appeared in the film via interspliced archival footage from her campaign in support of the 1978 Briggs Amendment in California.

In contrast, Beverly LaHaye's notoriety has always been primarily located within conservative evangelical circles, where she is still well known both as a significant political figure in her own right and as the wife of Tim LaHaye, who at his death in 2016, was best known for his involvement in producing the apocalyptic fiction series *Left Behind*. In addition to leading Concerned Women for America, Beverly LaHaye has served on the boards of several leading conservative Christian organizations including the Council for Biblical Manhood and Womanhood, Jerry Falwell's Liberty University, and the pro-life pregnancy crisis center network Care Net, among others. In 1991, the Southern Baptist Convention presented LaHaye with its Religious Freedom Award, and in the following year, Liberty University granted her an Honorary Doctorate of Humanities "for her lifetime achievements in protecting the rights of the family."[15] During this same decade, LaHaye launched a monthly newsletter and a nationally syndicated radio show, which won the National Religious Broadcasters award for "Talk Show of the Year" in 1993.[16] LaHaye stepped down as acting president of CWA in 2006, at the age of seventy-seven. The organization maintains a forceful presence in national politics, however, with active lobbying, research, and media arms in Washington, DC, as well as several energetic state offices involved in local and national activism across the country. The organization also offers important opportunities for conservative women interested in political careers, through internships and paid employment as well as public endorsements of conservative candidates. In 2011, Michele Bachmann directly credited LaHaye with inspiring her to embark on a political career.[17]

Tammy Faye Bakker Messner remarried in 1993. Her second husband, Roe Messner, was a church builder who had been involved with PTL but who did not have a close relationship with the Bakkers during that time. He would later say that he had admired Tammy Faye from afar but that she "was the queen" of PTL and he didn't feel like he could talk to her.[18] Through the 1990s and 2000s, Bakker cultivated her newfound celebrity within the gay community, as a vocal advocate for Christian tolerance and an active fundraiser for AIDS research. In 2004, she appeared on the second season of the VH1 reality television series *The Surreal Life* alongside rapper Vanilla Ice, adult-film actor

Ron Jeremy, *Playboy* model Trishelle Cannatella, and actors Traci Bingham and Erik Estrada (best known for their roles on *Baywatch* and *CHiPs*, respectively). Her outsized personality and cult following made her a natural fit for the show. She died three years later, in July 2007, after an eleven-year battle with cancer.

Jim Bakker remarried in 1998 and began a new daily television ministry in 2003. His Morningside Church complex in Branson, Missouri, is reminiscent of the now-decrepit Heritage USA property in Fort Mill, South Carolina. Though it does not include a theme park, it does house restaurants, shops, condos, a campground, and a studio where Bakker's television programs, including the live *Jim Bakker Show* are produced.[19] The Bakkers' daughter, Tammy Sue Chapman, makes regular appearances on these shows, which focus largely on fundraising, apocalypticism, and prophecy. The Bakkers' son, Jay, heads his own ministry, which has had churches in the hipster neighborhoods of Williamsburg, Brooklyn, and Uptown, Minneapolis, and which is currently focused on producing a weekly sermon via podcast. Jay's Revolution Church emphasizes inclusiveness and diversity, with a particular focus on advocating for the LGBTQ community. In 2012, he won the PFLAG (Parents and Friends of Lesbians and Gays) "Straight to Equality in Faith Communities" award. Revolution Church largely attracts young, urban professionals who have been disaffected by their experiences in more traditional evangelical ministries. In contrast to the large congregations, upbeat music, and moral absolutes found in those churches, Revolution attracted a small group to its in-person weekly meetings. Its services—and now podcast—consist solely of a sermon, often centered on themes of diversity and spiritual doubt.

Together, Morgan, Bryant, LaHaye, and Bakker represent the significant range of prominent women's contributions to the ascendant New Christian Right during the 1970s and 1980s. Their work and their legacies also continue to impact women's roles in modern Christian conservatism. Marabel Morgan's refusal to engage directly or explicitly with political debates did not prevent her from having a tremendous impact on contemporary debates over women's roles in their families, in their faith communities, and in political affairs. Her bestselling marital manual *Total Woman* emerged in the early 1970s during a historical moment in which the American political landscape was in serious flux and contested understandings of gender and family were moving to the center of national political debate. Morgan's writing helped to popularize and update conservative theologies of gender and family and to connect these perspectives to broader political issues including rising divorce rates, drug use, and juvenile delinquency, even as Morgan rejected any explicit political interest. Through her complex negotiation of ideas about traditional gender roles and the limits of the political sphere, Morgan helped to set the stage for critical and ongoing debates within conservative Christian communities about the relationship between family life and politics.

Morgan's friend Anita Bryant, by contrast, used her celebrity as a spokeswoman, singer, and evangelical author to raise awareness and support for her campaign against gay rights beginning in the late 1970s. Bryant popularized many of the religious right's most tenacious arguments against homosexuality including the ideas that gay men "recruit" children through molestation, that homosexuality is incompatible with family life, and that homosexuality is not a legitimate minority status in part because it is allegedly a preference that can be "cured." Bryant arguably set herself up for political failure by engaging in such a focused single-issue campaign and by promoting standards of family life that she herself could not live up to. Her impact is still felt in gay communities across the country, where the sardonically named "Saint Anita" is often evoked as a decisive galvanizing force for the modern gay-rights movement.

A popular narrative among gay-rights supporters is that Bryant's campaign failed because she was on the wrong side of history, a throwback to a bygone era whose reactionary bigotry was roundly defeated by the forces of progress. But political opposition to gay rights, often drawing on the very same arguments that Bryant engaged in the late 1970s, is still a powerful platform for many conservative Christian groups from the National Organization for Marriage to more broadly focused institutions like Focus on the Family and Concerned Women for America. Indeed, CWA recently named the "defense of family," including an understanding that "God made marriage between a man and a woman," as one of its seven core issues, alongside "sanctity of life, education, religious liberty, national sovereignty, [opposition to] sexual exploitation, and support for Israel."[20]

But this is not simply a story of conservative women's gradual politicization, from the era of women like Morgan to the era of CWA. Conservative Christian women continue to negotiate the boundaries of the political realm and the propriety of their engagement with formal political activism. Even at the height of the New Christian Right's ascendancy in the 1980s, prominent figures like Tammy Faye Bakker—who vocally opposed abortion, showed compassion in the midst of the early AIDS crisis, and counted President Ronald Reagan among her acquaintances—refused to identify as politically engaged. The relationship between religion and politics is still a hotly debated topic in conservative Christian communities, and the mixture of the two continues to be an especially fraught prospect for conservative Christian women struggling to maintain a commitment to traditionalist gender ideologies. Thus, many forums of evangelical women's culture—including fiction and nonfiction, conferences and retreats, periodicals and blogs—in which family roles are openly discussed and gender ideologies are openly debated continue to avoid identifying these issues as predominantly political in nature.

Christian conservatives continue to be a powerful force in American politics on the local, state, and national levels. The rhetoric of "family values" and "traditional gender roles" continues to resonate at the heart of this movement. Observers unfamiliar with this movement frequently dismiss these ideologies as cynical, insincere, or over-simplistic but these critiques fail to engage the complex and deeply held belief systems at the core of the modern religious right. Similarly, to dismiss this movement as simply patriarchal or anti-woman is to ignore the millions of women who attend conservative Christian churches, who support conservative Christian organizations, and who vote for conservative Christian candidates. Only by attempting to fully understand conservative Christian gender and family politics, and by recognizing the essential roles that women play in supporting this movement, can we hope to truly comprehend this pivotal historical and political force.

Notes

INTRODUCTION

1. Beverly LaHaye, *Who but a Woman?* (Nashville, TN: Thomas Nelson, 1984), 121–122.

2. See especially Lisa McGirr, *Suburban Warriors: The Origins of the New American Right* (Princeton, NJ: Princeton University Press, 2001); Michelle Nickerson, *Mothers of Conservatism: Women and the Postwar Right* (Princeton, NJ: Princeton University Press, 2012); June Melby Benowitz, *Challenge and Change: Right-Wing Women, Grassroots Activism, and the Baby Boom Generation* (Gainesville: University Press of Florida, 2015).

3. Many of the best works in this field are local studies, which offer in-depth examinations of these phenomena in cities across the country. See Arnold R. Hirsch, *Making the Second Ghetto: Race and Housing in Chicago, 1940–1960* (Chicago: University of Chicago Press, 1998); Kevin M. Kruse, *White Flight: Atlanta and the Making of Modern Conservatism* (Princeton, NJ: Princeton University Press, 2005); Robert O. Self, *American Babylon: Race and the Struggle for Postwar Oakland* (Princeton, NJ: Princeton University Press, 2003); Thomas J. Sugrue, *The Origins of the Urban Crisis: Race and Inequality in Postwar Detroit* (Princeton, NJ: Princeton University Press, 1996).

4. Matthew D. Lassiter, *The Silent Majority: Suburban Politics in the Sunbelt South* (Princeton, NJ: Princeton University Press, 2006), 1–2, 16.

5. McGirr, *Suburban Warriors*, 225–226, 266.

6. Seth Dowland, *Family Values and the Rise of the New Christian Right* (Philadelphia: University of Pennsylvania Press, 2015); Robert O. Self, *All in the Family: The Realignment of American Democracy since the 1960s* (New York: Hill and Wang, 2012); Natasha Zaretsky, *No Direction Home: The American Family and Fear of National Decline, 1968–1980* (Chapel Hill: University of North Carolina Press, 2007).

7. Throughout this book, I use the terms fundamentalist, conservative evangelical, and conservative Christian to describe the subjects of this study. The terms "evangelical" and "fundamentalist" describe often overlapping but not identical priorities within certain Protestant churches. Each term is associated with particular denominations and traditions (sometimes overlapping and sometimes oppositional), but the application of these terms is especially complicated because believers do not tend to identify consistently with either term, often preferring designations like "Bible-believing," "born again," or simply "Christian." Therefore, it is most useful to think of these terms as connotative and not as descriptors of clearly delineated denominational boundaries. In this sense, "evangelical" connotes an emphasis on sharing the gospel, whereas "fundamentalist" connotes a commitment to the idea of biblical literalism. Historically speaking, evangelicalism has deep roots in the United States, dating back nearly three centuries, whereas fundamentalism (as a recognizable subset of Protestantism) arose in the context of the profound religious and political rivalries of the 1920s (known as the fundamentalist-modernist debates). Politically, when fundamentalist believers align themselves with political positions, they tend to emphasize social and fiscal conservatism. Since the 1980s, evangelical Christianity has also become synonymous with conservative politics for many Americans, although evangelical churches are located across the political spectrum. My choice to use the terms fundamentalist, conservative evangelical, and conservative Christian throughout this study represents the alignment of the study's subjects with historical movements (fundamentalism and the conservative branches of evangelicalism) that were converging in this historical moment to form the modern religious right.

8. Roger Finke and Rodney Stark, *The Churching of America, 1776–1990: Winners and Losers in Our Religious Economy* (New Brunswick, NJ: Rutgers University Press, 1992), 15–16, 246–248.

9. Darren Dochuk, *From Bible Belt to Sunbelt: Plain-Folk Religion, Grassroots Politics, and the Rise of Evangelical Conservatism* (New York: W.W. Norton, 2011), xxiii.

10. Matthew Avery Sutton, "Was FDR the Antichrist? The Birth of Fundamentalist Antiliberalism in a New Deal Age," *Journal of American History* 98, no. 4 (March 2012): 1070–1071.

11. Randall Balmer and Joel Carpenter have both traced the development of evangelical subculture during these decades and argued that this subculture helped to facilitate conservative Protestants' retreat from mainstream American culture and politics after the Scopes Monkey Trial. However, although the books, tapes, conferences, and other forums developed in this subculture were often purportedly apolitical, they also shared a set of politically relevant assumptions about the universality of Christian morality, the Christian identity of the United States, and the importance of maintaining "traditional" family roles in order to preserve the nation.

Carpenter acknowledges that fundamentalists in this period were not apolitical "if one thinks of politics in broader terms as contests for power and influence," and Matthew Sutton takes that observation further, arguing that fundamentalists and conservative evangelicals remained deeply engaged with American political and cultural developments throughout the twentieth century. My analysis expands upon Sutton's while also arguing that this subculture's purportedly apolitical nature was a key component of its ability to attract audiences who thought of themselves as disengaged with mainstream politics in a more traditional sense. Randall Balmer, *The Making of Evangelicalism: From Revivalism to Politics and Beyond* (Waco, TX: Baylor University Press, 2010), 43–58; Joel A. Carpenter, *Revive Us Again: The Reawakening of American Fundamentalism* (New York: Oxford University Press, 1997), 118; Matthew Avery Sutton, *American Apocalypse: A History of Modern Evangelicalism* (Cambridge, MA: Harvard University Press, 2014), xi–xiv.

12. Matthew Avery Sutton, *Aimee Semple McPherson and the Resurrection of Christian America* (Cambridge, MA: Harvard University Press, 2007).

13. See, Catherine A. Brekus, *Strangers and Pilgrims: Female Preaching in America, 1740–1845* (Chapel Hill: University of North Carolina Press, 1998); Elizabeth Elkin Grammer, *Some Wild Visions: Autobiographies by Female Itinerant Evangelists in Nineteenth-Century America* (New York: Oxford University Press, 2002); Susan Hill Lindley, *You Have Stept Out of Your Place: A History of Women and Religion in America* (Louisville, KY: Westminster John Knox Press, 1996); Priscilla Pope-Levison, *Turn the Pulpit Loose: Two Centuries of American Women Evangelists* (New York: Palgrave Macmillan, 2004).

14. See especially Catherine E. Rymph, *Republican Women: Feminism and Conservatism from Suffrage through the Rise of the New Right* (Chapel Hill: University of North Carolina Press, 2006).

15. Nickerson, *Mothers of Conservatism*, xiii–xvi, 30.

16. Margaret Lamberts Bendroth, *Fundamentalism & Gender, 1875 to the Present* (New Haven, CT: Yale University Press, 1993); Ann Braude, "Women's History *Is* American Religious History," in *Retelling U.S. Religious History*, ed. Thomas A. Tweed (Berkeley: University of California Press, 1997), 87–107.

17. R. Marie Griffith, *God's Daughters: Evangelical Women and the Power of Submission* (Berkeley: University of California Press, 1997), 16–22. See also Brenda E. Brasher, *Godly Women: Fundamentalism and Female Power* (New Brunswick, NJ: Rutgers University Press, 1998).

18. Hugh Barbour (former executive at Revell), telephone interview with author, September 20, 2012; Bruce Barbour (former executive at Revell; nephew of Hugh Barbour), telephone interview with author, August 17, 2012; Allan Fisher, *Fleming H. Revell Company: The First 125 Years, 1870–1995* (Grand Rapids, MI: Fleming H. Revell, 1995), 23; "Book Ends: Religious Books," *New York Times Book Review*, Sunday, May 23, 1976, 53.

19. Janet Traylor Addison, "A History of *Today's Christian Woman*: 1978–1988" (M.A. Thesis, University of Mississippi, 1989), 7.

20. Griffith, *God's Daughters*, 183–184. The shift from submission doctrine to complementarianism is a significant one, though it is worth noting that complementarianism can also support a deeply conservative approach to gender roles. The Council on Biblical Manhood and Womanhood (CBMW) calls itself the "flagship organization for complementarianism," and its statements (along with books produced by founding member John Piper) serve as the foundational texts of the movement. Though complementarianism represented a softening of submission doctrine in terms of its emphasis on *mutual* submission and the different but equal roles of the sexes, CBMW has always defined its primary mission as helping "the church defend against the accommodation to secular feminism" and later to evangelical feminism ("Our Mission and Vision"). John Piper and Wayne A. Grudem, *Recovering Biblical Manhood and Womanhood: A Response to Evangelical Feminism* (Westmont, IL: Inter-Varsity Press, 1992); Council on Biblical Manhood and Womanhood (hereafter CBMW), "Mission and Vision," accessed November 22, 2017, https://cbmw.org/about/mission-vision/; CBMW, "Our History," accessed November 22, 2017, https://cbmw.org/about/history/.

CHAPTER 1

1. Sally Quinn, "Sex! Tears! Fried Chicken! The Saga of Marabel Morgan and 'Total Woman's' 3 Million Readers," *Washington Post*, January 27, 1978, D1–D2. See also Sally Quinn, "A Visit with Mr. and Mrs. 'Total Woman,'" *Los Angeles Times*, February 19, 1978, 10–12; Sally Quinn, " . . and the 'Total Woman's' View: She Just May Be, without Knowing It, the Most Avant Garde Feminist in America," *Boston Globe*, February 5, 1978, 38.

2. See, for example, "Fighting the Housewife Blues," *Time*, March 14, 1977, 62–70. Morgan also deployed the language of naïveté in her books, in talking about sex and in talking about her early expectations of marriage. See Marabel Morgan, *The Total Woman* (Old Tappan, NJ: Fleming H. Revell, 1973), 97; Marabel Morgan, *The Electric Woman: Hope for Tired Mothers, Lovers, and Others* (Old Tappan, NJ: Fleming H. Revell, 1985), 91.

3. This reference is often credited to *Total Woman* but actually came from a talk show appearance that Morgan made in the late 1970s. The book itself contained many other suggestions for erotic costumes and sexy after-work greetings. She attributed the Saran Wrap idea to a student in one of her Total Woman courses. See Rebecca L. Davis, "Eroticized Wives: Evangelical Marriage Guides and God's Plan for the Christian Family," in *The Embrace of Eros: Bodies, Desires, and Sexuality in Christianity*, ed. Margaret D. Kamitsuka (Minneapolis: Fortress Press, 2010), 166–167, 327 fn. 3.

4. See, for example, "How You Voted," *News Journal* [Mansfield, OH], March 20, 1977, 6A; Carol Kleiman, "Only Room for One Boss in the 'Total Woman's' Home," *Chicago Tribune*, March 23, 1975, D3.

5. "Best Seller List: General," *New York Times Book Review*, November 3, 1974, 77. This particular description did not appear in other promotions of Morgan's book, making it seem likely that this phrase was written by *New York Times* editorial staff rather than Morgan's publishers.

6. Marabel Morgan, interview with author at Morgan's home in Miami, FL, September 10, 2012.

7. See Peter Gardella, "Sex and Submission in the Spirit," in *Religions of the United States, in Practice*, ed. Colleen McDannell (Princeton, NJ: Princeton University Press, 2001). Morgan's exact birth year has been difficult to pin down, particularly because Hawk was her stepfather's name and not her birth name. She was likely born in 1936 or 1937. In 1977, she said that she was married at the age of twenty-eight (in 1964). (Quinn, "Sex! Tears! Fried Chicken!").

8. Interview with Morgan (2012). For stylistic reasons, I have chosen to refer to subjects by their first names when discussing periods of their lives (usually before and sometimes after their marriages) during which they did not use the surname most commonly associated with them.

9. Interview with Morgan (2012).

10. Interview with Morgan (2012).

11. For more on the centrality of the conversion narrative, and the testimonial script in general, in evangelical life, see Tanya Erzen, *Straight to Jesus: Sexual and Christian Conversions in the Ex-Gay Movement* (Berkeley: University of California Press, 2006), 1–14.

12. One contemporary source says that Morgan spent a year and a half at Ohio State University (OSU) before transferring, but the timeline that Morgan indicated during our interview made it seem more likely that she spent one year there. In any case, she did not spend very much time at OSU before leaving to go to Florida. "Fighting the Housewife Blues"; Interview with Morgan (2012).

13. "Fighting the Housewife Blues"; Interview with Morgan (2012). For an in-depth examination of the history and impact of Campus Crusade for Christ, see John G. Turner, *Bill Bright and Campus Crusade for Christ: The Renewal of Evangelicalism in Postwar America* (Chapel Hill: University of North Carolina Press, 2009).

14. "Fighting the Housewife Blues"; Louise Leyden, "She Sings His Praise," *Miami News*, Saturday, October 3, 1964, 5A; Interview with Morgan (2012).

15. Morgan, *Total Woman*, 15–18, 22–25.

16. Interview with Morgan (2012).

17. Quinn, "Sex! Tears! Fried Chicken!"; Quinn, "A Visit with Mr. and Mrs. 'Total Woman.'"

18. Morgan, *Total Woman*, 69.

19. Morgan, *Total Woman*, 22–23; Interview with Morgan (2012). In *Total Woman* (1973), Morgan describes reading widely on marriage and taking "self-help" courses, and her bibliography in *Total Woman* upholds that (see note 33 in this chapter). In our 2012 interview, she said that she was able to find very little written on marriage, except for two dense theoretical texts from the library (and the Bible). The discrepancy is a salient reminder of the potential limitations of oral histories, but it is also revealing, indicating an attempt on Morgan's part to make sense of the popularity of her book (by magnifying its novelty) as well as a growing willingness to situate herself as an innovator and an expert.

20. Interview with Morgan (2012).

21. Adjusted for inflation, $15 in January 1973 had approximately the "same buying power" as $87 in January 2018. Bureau of Labor Statistics, "Consumer Price Index (CPI) Inflation Calculator," accessed July 9, 2018, http://www.bls.gov/data/inflation_calculator.htm. Helen Andelin, whose similar "Fascinating Womanhood" concept is discussed below, initially charged $15 for her course but raised the fee to $30 in the mid-1970s. Virginia Lee Warren, "In This Day of Liberation, They Study How to Please Their Men," *New York Times*, June 28, 1975, 14.

22. Interview with Morgan (2012).

23. Total Cereal, "Keep Up with the House While You Keep Down Your Weight," *National Geographic* 138, no. 3 (September 1970).

24. Total Cereal, "Keep Up with Your Game While You Keep Down Your Weight." *National Geographic* 138, no. 2 (August 1970).

25. Of course, advertisements relying on gender role stereotypes have not disappeared from the cultural landscape even in the twenty-first century, and my intention is not to suggest that they have. Rather, it is to say that Morgan's claim not to have heard of feminism before the publication of her book and to have been surprised by the feminist backlash against her ideas is plausible given a cultural context in which Morgan and General Mills, among many others, still approached postwar domestic ideology as an unquestioned cultural ideal, though this discourse was rapidly changing.

26. Marabel Morgan, *Total Joy* (Old Tappan, NJ: Fleming H. Revell, 1976), 53; Interview with Morgan (2012).

27. Cycles of commitment and recommitment to God lie at the heart of evangelical ritual. Believers are asked to continually scrutinize themselves for sin and to confess any "backsliding" (out of a proper Christian life), often in public testimonials that mirror the conversion narrative. Altar calls, based on the ritual ending of revivals, ask audience members to come pray with a church leader or volunteer at the altar in the front of the worship space, either to accept God for the first time or to renew a commitment already made.

28. Morgan, *Total Woman*, 171–172.

29. Interview with Morgan (2012).

30. Interview with Morgan (2012). See also Joyce Maynard, "The Liberation of Total Woman: If It Is the Aim of the Steinems, Greers, and Milletts to Wage a War, It

Is the Aim of Marabel Morgan and Her Followers to Keep the Peace," *New York Times*, September 28, 1975, 10, 48–58, 63–65; Morgan, *Total Woman*, 188.

31. Interview with Morgan (2012). In 1976, Anita Bryant went on to gain further notoriety as the face of a national backlash against gay-rights legislation. Her career is the focus of Chapter 2.

32. Rebecca L. Davis, "Eroticized Wives: Evangelical Marriage Guides and God's Plan for the Christian Family," in *The Embrace of Eros: Bodies, Desires, and Sexuality in Christianity*, ed. Margaret D. Kamitsuka (Minneapolis: Fortress Press, 2010), 166; Patricia McCormack, "'Total Woman' Says Idea for Book Wasn't Totally Hers," *Montreal Gazette*, Saturday, June 26, 1976, 46; Morgan, *Total Woman*, 132, 136. McCormack's title is intentionally provocative; the text of the article explains that Morgan felt inspired by God in writing the book. Davis and McCormack cite the number of copies in *Total Woman*'s first run as 5,000 and 7,500, respectively. The precise number is less important than the implication that Revell, while interested in publishing Morgan's book, did not expect it to become a national bestseller. By the end of 1974, over three million copies of the book had been sold.

33. Some retelling of how Morgan's early unhappiness led to the Total Woman courses and eventually the book became standard not only in Morgan's published writing (*Total Woman* as well as its sequels) but also in most media accounts about Morgan. Even Morgan's 1980 cookbook contained a revised narrative that followed the same arc but centered on the kitchen. See, for example, Jo Ann Levine, "Housewife a Dodo? Not at All," *Christian Science Monitor*, March 24, 1975, 13; Bruce McCabe, "The Team Behind 'The Total Woman,'" *Boston Globe*, January 6, 1976, 14; Morgan, *Total Woman*, 15–27; Morgan, *Total Joy*, 16; Morgan, *Electric Woman*, 90–95; Marabel Morgan, *The Total Woman Cookbook: Marabel Morgan's Handbook for Kitchen Survival* (Old Tappan, NJ: Fleming H. Revell, 1980), 11–12.

34. Morgan, *Total Woman*, 191–192. Morgan drew widely from newspaper articles, classical philosophy, and literature, and she cited several self-help books in a short bibliography at the end of *Total Woman*. Most of these were Christian texts: James Dobson, *Dare to Discipline* (Wheaton, IL: Tyndale House, 1972); Tim LaHaye, *How to Be Happy though Married* (Wheaton, IL: Tyndale House, 1968); Herbert J. Miles, *Sexual Happiness in Marriage: A Positive Approach to the Details You Should Know to Achieve a Healthy and Satisfying Sexual Life* (Grand Rapids, MI: Zondervan, 1967); Cecil Osborne, *The Art of Understanding Your Mate* (Grand Rapids: Zondervan, 1970); Hannah W. Smith, *The Christian's Secret of Happy Life* (Old Tappan, NJ: Fleming H. Revell, 1968); Kenneth G. Smith, *Learning to Be a Woman* (Downers Grove, IL: Inter-Varsity Press, 1970); Paul Tournier, *To Understand Each Other* (Richmond, VA: John Knox Press, 1967). She also listed a few secular self-help books: Dale Carnegie, *How to Win Friends and Influence People* (New York: Simon and Schuster, 1936); William Glasser, *Reality Therapy* (New York: Harper and Row, 1965); W. Hugh Missildine, *Your Inner Child of the Past* (New York: Simon and Schuster, 1963).

35. Morgan, *Total Woman*, 95–96.
36. Morgan, *Total Woman*, 49–88.
37. Morgan, *Total Woman*, 65.
38. Morgan, *Total Woman*, 123.
39. Morgan, *Total Woman*, 126.
40. "Fighting the Housewife Blues."
41. See also Gillian Frank, "'Think about That Special Man Who's on His Way Home to You': Conservative Women's Sexualization of Marriage in the 1970s," in *Porno Chic and the Sex Wars: American Sexual Representation in the 1970s*, eds. Carolyn Bronstein and Whitney Strub (Amherst: University of Massachusetts Press, 2016), 178–195; Robert O. Self, *All in the Family: The Realignment of American Democracy since the 1960s* (New York: Hill and Wang, 2012), 314–315. Frank argues that other conservative Christian women would later take up these concerns in more explicitly politicized ways, directly blaming the feminist movement for its detrimental effects not only on women and children but also on the men who were supposed to head traditional families. Morgan never explicitly referenced the women's liberation movement in her books, but her frequent references to men's "tattered egos" reflected growing concerns among conservative Christians about the broad consequences of abandoning patriarchal family models.
42. Morgan, *Total Joy*, 95. Emphasis in original.
43. Morgan, *Total Woman*, 95–96.
44. Morgan, *Total Woman*, 56.
45. Morgan, *Total Joy*, 96.
46. Morgan, *Total Woman*, 45.
47. Davis, "Eroticized Wives," 166; McCormack, "'Total Woman' Says Idea for Book Wasn't Totally Hers."
48. "Fighting the Housewife Blues."
49. See, for example, "Tempo/TV Hour by Hour," *Chicago Tribune*, September 24, 1975, B8; "Morning Programs, Monday through Friday," *Chicago Tribune*, November 7, 1976, H11; "Tuesday: Morning," *Hartford Courant*, October 2, 1977, 17V; "Morning Programs, Monday through Friday," *Chicago Tribune*, June 3, 1977, 110; "Television and Radio," *Boston Globe*, February 16, 1978, 55; "Thursday's TV Talk," *Chicago Tribune*, March 30, 1978, A15; Morgan, *Total Joy*, 15, 21, 77, 128, 138; Morgan, *Electric Woman*, 145–147.
50. Interview with Morgan (2012); McCabe, "The Team behind 'The Total Woman.'"
51. Interview with Morgan (2012).
52. Ephesians 5:22–24 is the most commonly cited passage in this context. It reads, in the King James Version: "Wives, submit yourselves unto your own husbands, as unto the Lord. For the husband is the head of the wife, even as Christ is the head of the church; and he is the saviour of the body. Therefore as the church is subject unto Christ, so let the wives be to their own husbands

in every thing." The conservative interpretation of this verse—that "the husband is the head of the wife as Jesus is the head of the church"—was popularized in the postwar period by John R. Rice's *Bobbed Hair, Bossy Wives and Women Preachers: Significant Questions for Honest Christian Women Settled by the Word of God* (Murfreesboro, TN: Sword of the Lord Publishers, 1941) and by the evangelical family seminars of Bill Gothard. See Rebecca L. Davis, *More Perfect Unions: The American Search for Marital Bliss* (Cambridge, MA: Harvard University Press, 2010), 205.

53. Interview with Morgan (2012).
54. Morgan, *Total Woman*, 71.
55. Morgan, *Total Woman*, 69–70.
56. R. Marie Griffith, *God's Daughters: Evangelical Women and the Power of Submission* (Berkeley: University of California Press, 2000), 45, 183.
57. Morgan, *Total Woman*, 70.
58. Morgan, *Total Joy*, 93–94.
59. Morgan, *Total Joy*, 93–94. See also Kleiman, "Only Room for One Boss."
60. Betty Liddick, "An Affirmation of Homemakers' Values," *Los Angeles Times*, December 5, 1975.
61. Warren, "In This Day of Liberation, They Study How to Please Their Men."
62. The breezy style of Morgan's writing resembles her own style of speech (in our interview and other transcribed interviews and speeches), but it is also characteristic of a particular genre of advice written by and for women. This was a genre in which Revell excelled during the 1970s, as exemplified not only by Morgan's work but also by Anita Bryant's popular books, which are explored in more depth in Chapter 2.
63. Bruce Barbour, interview, August 17, 2012; Hugh Barbour, interview, September 20, 2012. In 1976, the *New York Times* reported that the "typical religious book buyer . . . is a married woman, age 28–35, which suggests the unconscious genius of Marabel Morgan, whose 'The Total Woman' hit that group right on the money, selling over 750,000 copies in hardcover." This was not "unconscious genius" on the part of Christian publishers but rather part of a deliberate strategy to tap into this market and increase sales. "Book Ends: Religious Books," *New York Times Book Review*, Sunday, May 23, 1976, 53.
64. These figures are taken from a comprehensive list of publications provided to me by Baker Publishing Group, the current owner of the Fleming H. Revell imprint. It is worth noting that during this period, while books by solo female authors always made up a larger percentage of total publications, the number of books by couples or mixed-gender groups also experienced a significant increase. In most cases, this reflected a trend toward hiring Christian couples (rather than just men or just women) to write books of marital and spiritual advice. On a smaller scale, it also reflected Revell's hiring of women and couples as ghostwriters for celebrity memoirs, especially in the late 1960s and onward. The total number

of publications for each decade was 233 (1940s), 229 (1950s), 338 (1960s), 471 (1970s), and 428 (1980s). My thanks to Marilyn Gordon and David Greendonner at Baker Publishing Group for their help in providing this information. David Greendonner, Baker Publishing Group Permissions Coordinator, email message to author (February 22, 2013).

65. Interview with Bruce Barbour (2012).

66. Helen Andelin, *Fascinating Womanhood: A Guide to a Happy Marriage* (Santa Barbara, CA: Pacific Press, 1963); Sylvia Morscher, *Fascinating Womanhood, or, The Art of Attracting Men: A Practical Course of Lessons in the Underlying Principles by Which Women Attract Men, Leading to the Proposal and Culminating in Marriage* (St. Louis, MO: Psychology Press, 1922). *Fascinating Womanhood* is currently in its fifth edition: Helen Andelin, *Fascinating Womanhood: How the Ideal Woman Awakens A Man's Deepest Love and Tenderness*, 5th ed. (Santa Barbara, CA: Pacific Press, 2007). See also Rebecca L. Davis, *More Perfect Unions*, 207–208.

67. Warren, "In This Day of Liberation, They Study How to Please Their Men."

68. "Fighting the Housewife Blues." For a discussion of similar contemporary courses and their reliance on "word-of-mouth publicity," see Russell Chandler, "Conservative Christian Women Resist Feminist Inroads: Men Urged to Reassert Authority but a Minority Stresses Equality," *Los Angeles Times*, December 29, 1974, B1–B2.

69. Griffith, *God's Daughters*, 183.

70. Thomas A. Harris, *I'm O.K., You're O.K.: A Practical Guide to Transactional Analysis* (New York: Harper and Row, 1969); Henry Raymont, "$1-Million Paperback Sale Sets Record," *New York Times*, July 27, 1972, 20; "Best Seller List: General," *New York Times Book Review*, April 16, 1972, 45; "Best Seller List: General," *New York Times Book Review*, August 19, 1973, 25. *Total Woman* spent seven weeks on the list, between November 3, 1974, and July 6, 1975. (The July 6, 1975, list erroneously says that the book had been on the list for five weeks, but it appeared seven times: November 11, 1974; April 27, 1975; May 11, 1975; May 18, 1975; June 8, 1975; June 29, 1975; and July 6, 1975.)

71. Harry Browne, *You Can Profit from a Monetary Crisis* (New York: Macmillan, 1974); "Best Seller List: General," *New York Times Book Review*, November 17, 1974, 61; Harry Lorayne and Jerry Lucas, *The Memory Book* (New York: Stein and Day, 1974); "Best Seller List: General," *New York Times Book Review*, March 23, 1973; Mildred Newman, Bernard Berkowitz, and Jean Owen, *How to Be Your Own Best Friend: A Conversation with Two Psychoanalysts* (New York: Lark, 1971); "Best Seller List: General," *New York Times Book Review*, February 17, 1974, 37.

72. Many of the short descriptions included on the *New York Times* bestseller list for nonfiction were similarly sharp-witted. For example, Charles Berlitz's *The Bermuda Triangle* (1975) was described as "uncritical theorizing about allegedly mysterious ship-plane disappearances"; Will and Ariel Durant's *The Age of Napoleon* (1975) as "popularized history that is more popularized than history"; (Charles Berlitz, *The Bermuda Triangle* 1975), "Best Seller List: General,"

New York Times Book Review, February 2, 1975, 33; (Will Durant and Ariel Durant, *The Age of Napoleon* 1975), "Best Seller List: General," *New York Times Book Review*, December 21, 1975, 21.

73. "Best Seller List: General," *New York Times Book Review*, February 17, 1974, 37. *The Joy of Sex* first appeared on the list December 3, 1972, but editorial descriptions were not included at that time.

74. The designation originated with author Tom Wolfe's cover story for *New York Magazine* in August 1976. See Tom Wolfe, "The 'Me' Decade and the Third Great Awakening," *New York Magazine*, August 23, 1976, accessed September 10, 2013, http://nymag.com/news/features/45938/. Most recent historiography about the 1970s disputes this view as an oversimplification (whether in terms of cultural, political, or class analysis), while still acknowledging the impact that this narrative has had on contemporary and historical interpretations of the decade. See Edward D. Berkowitz, *Something Happened: A Political and Cultural Overview of the Seventies* (New York: Columbia University Press, 2006), 158–177; Jefferson Cowie, *Stayin' Alive: The 1970s and the Last Days of the Working Class* (New York: New Press, 2010), 73, 217; Bruce Schulman, *The Seventies: The Great Shift in American Culture, Society, and Politics* (New York: Free Press, 2001), 145–146; Doug McAdam, *Freedom Summer* (New York: Oxford University Press, 1990), 201.

75. See especially Davis, *More Perfect Unions*, 196–197.

76. Morgan, *Total Woman*, 106.

77. For more on this history and an analysis of its legacy in the late twentieth century, see Krishan Kumar, "Home: The Promise and Predicament of Private Life at the End of the Twentieth Century," in *Public and Private in Thought and Practice: Perspectives on a Grand Dichotomy*, ed. Jeff Weintraub and Krishan Kumar (Chicago: University of Chicago Press, 1997), 204–236.

78. Elaine Tyler May, *Homeward Bound: American Families in the Cold War Era* (New York: Basic Books 2008).

79. May, *Homeward Bound*, xii–xvii.

80. The postwar emphasis on the suburban family and male breadwinner ideal was significant but never absolute. Postwar mass culture, including mass-market magazines, "expressed ambivalence about domesticity" and featured a surprising proportion of stories about women actively engaged in public life. See Joanne Meyerowitz, "Beyond the *Feminine Mystique*: A Reassessment of Postwar Mass Culture, 1946–58," *Journal of American History* 79, no. 4 (March 1993): 1455–1482.

81. See Susan Rimby Leighow, *Nurses' Questions/Women's Questions: The Impact of the Demographic Revolution and Feminism on United States Working Women, 1946–1986* (New York: Peter Lang, 1996), 2.

82. Natasha Zaretsky, *No Direction Home: The American Family and the Fear of National Decline, 1969–1980* (Chapel Hill: University of North Carolina Press, 2007).

83. Nena O'Neill and George O'Neill, *Open Marriage: A New Life Style for Couples* (New York: M. Evans, 1972); "Best Seller List: General," *New York Times Book Review*, January 21, 1973, 33.

84. O'Neill and O'Neill, *Open Marriage*, 76, 176, 256.

85. Morgan, *Total Woman*, 70; O'Neill and O'Neill, *Open Marriage*, 15–44.

86. See Davis, *More Perfect Unions*, 176–213. Though *Total Woman* was far and away the best selling of the conservative Christian marital and sexual manuals of this period, it was not alone in the genre, and indeed Morgan cited many of these other texts in *Total Woman*'s bibliography (see note 33 in this chapter).

87. I am following historian Beth Bailey here in pluralizing the term "sexual revolutions" to indicate and acknowledge the unevenness of contemporary changes in sexual culture and the variability of these changes across boundaries of class, race, gender, sexuality, region, and religion. See Beth Bailey, "Sexual Revolution(s)," in *The Sixties: From Memory to History*, ed. David Farber (Chapel Hill: University of North Carolina Press, 1994), 235–262. This is also reflected in Bailey's other work on postwar sexual culture—for example, Beth Bailey, *From Front Porch to Backseat: Courtship in Twentieth-Century America* (Baltimore: Johns Hopkins University Press, 1988); Beth L. Bailey, *Sex in the Heartland* (Cambridge, MA: Harvard University Press, 2002). For more from Bryant (and her husband/coauthor, Bob Green) on the contemporary sexualization of US culture, see Anita Bryant and Bob Green, *Bless This House* (Old Tappan, NJ: Fleming H. Revell, 1972), 15–19; Anita Bryant and Bob Green, *Raising God's Children* (Old Tappan, NJ: Fleming H. Revell, 1977), 17, 39, 98–99, 117, and dust jacket; Anita Bryant and Bob Green, *At Any Cost* (Old Tappan, NJ: Fleming H. Revell, 1978), 24. For examples in Beverly LaHaye's work, see Beverly LaHaye, "A Word from Beverly," *Concerned Women for America Newsletter* (hereafter *CWA Newsletter*), 1, no. 4 (November 1979), Wilcox Collection of Contemporary Political Movements, University of Kansas Special Collections, Lawrence, KS (hereafter Wilcox Collection), RH DL D3169; "New Radical Sex Education Curriculum," *CWA Newsletter* 2, no. 4 (April 1980), CWA Offices; Beverly LaHaye, *I Am a Woman by God's Design* (Old Tappan, NJ: Fleming H. Revell, 1980), 124. Whereas Bryant, Green, and Morgan emphasized the sexualization of American culture as a whole, LaHaye focused in particular on the feminist movement's emphases on legalized abortion, sexual liberation, and gay rights.

88. Rebecca Davis makes a similar argument in her essay "Eroticized Wives," emphasizing the woman's body as the focal point of this project.

89. Morgan, *Total Woman*, 57; see also Davis, "Eroticized Wives," 165–179.

90. Morgan, *Total Woman*, 147–149.

91. Morgan, *Total Woman*, 147–148.

92. Morgan, *Total Woman*, 148.

93. See, for example, Fred Fejes, "Murder, Perversion, and Moral Panic: The 1954 Media Campaign against Miami's Homosexuals and the Discourse of Civic Betterment," *Journal of the History of Sexuality* 9, no. 3 (July 2000): 307–334; James Burkhart Gilbert, *Men in the Middle: Searching for Masculinity in the 1950s* (Chicago: University of Chicago Press, 2005), 71–78; David K. Johnson, *The Lavender Scare: The Cold War Persecution of Gays and Lesbians in the Federal Government* (Chicago: University of Chicago Press, 2004), 95; Roel Van den Oever, *Mama's Boy: Momism and Homophobia in Postwar American Culture* (New York: Palgrave Macmillan, 2012).

94. Gay liberation activists in the 1960s and 1970s were not the first to organize in support of gay rights in the United States. However, putting forward a more assertive message of "gay pride" and drawing from the strategies of the civil rights movement, the New Left, and contemporary feminists, this movement did more than earlier homophile groups had done to draw national attention to the rights claims of sexual minorities. See John D'Emilio, *Sexual Politics, Sexual Communities: The Making of a Homosexual Minority in the United States, 1940–1970*, 2nd ed. (Chicago: University of Chicago Press, 1998), 129–239.

95. Bryant and Green, *Raising God's Children*, dust jacket.

96. Bryant and Green, *Raising God's Children*, 107.

97. Bryant and Green, *Bless This House*, 126.

98. Bryant and Green, *Bless This House*, 134.

99. Davis, *More Perfect Unions*, 206; Amy DeRogatis, "What Would Jesus Do? Sexuality and Salvation in Protestant Evangelical Sex Manuals, 1950 to the Present," *Church History* 74, no. 1 (March 2005): 108; Miles, *Sexual Happiness in Marriage*.

100. Tim LaHaye and Beverly LaHaye, *The Act of Marriage: The Beauty of Sexual Love* (Grand Rapids, MI: Zondervan, 1976). See also Barry Colman et al., *Sex and the Single Christian: Candid Conversations* (Ventura, CA: Regal Books, 1986); Tim LaHaye and Beverly LaHaye, *What Lovemaking Means to a Man: Practical Advice to Married Women about Sex* (Grand Rapids, MI: Zondervan, 1984); Tim LaHaye and Beverly LaHaye, *What Lovemaking Means to a Woman: Practical Advice to Married Men about Sex* (Grand Rapids, MI: Zondervan, 1984); Tim LaHaye and Beverly LaHaye, *Practical Answers to Common Questions about Sex in Marriage* (Grand Rapids, MI: Zondervan, 1984); "The Act of Marrriage," *Zondervan.com* (2014), accessed April 14, 2014, http://www.zondervan.com/the-act-of-marriage.html. *The Act of Marriage* has gone through several printings and updates since 1976 and has sold over 2.5 million copies as of 2014, according to the publisher's website. For more on the LaHayes and *The Act of Marriage*, see Chapter 3 of this book.

101. DeRogatis, "What Would Jesus Do?" 112.

102. DeRogatis, "What Would Jesus Do?" 108–112.

103. Morgan, *Total Woman*, 104.

104. LaHaye and LaHaye, *Act of Marriage*, 11.

105. DeRogatis, "What Would Jesus Do?" 112.

106. LaHaye and LaHaye, *Act of Marriage*, 21.
107. Morgan, *Total Woman*, 103.
108. Morgan, *Total Woman*, 104.
109. Gen. 1:27 (International Standard Version); DeRogatis, "What Would Jesus Do?" 110–113.

CHAPTER 2

1. Portions of this chapter appeared first in the article, Emily Suzanne Johnson, "God, Country, and Anita Bryant: Women's Leadership and the Politics of the New Christian Right," *Religion and American Culture* 28, no. 2 (Summer 2018): 238–268. Quotation from Anita Bryant, *The Anita Bryant Story: The Survival of Our Nation's Families and the Threat of Militant Homosexuality* (Old Tappan, NJ: Fleming H. Revell, 1977), 13–14.

2. Dade County Board of Commissioners, Commission Minutes for December 7, 1976, received in email attachment from Scott Rappleye, Commission Reporter, October 16, 2012.

3. Gillian Frank, "'The Civil Rights of Parents': Race and Conservative Politics in Anita Bryant's Campaign against Gay Rights in 1970s Florida," *Journal of the History of Sexuality* 22, no. 1 (January 2013): 126–160.

4. Bryant, *The Anita Bryant Story*, 146; Lynn Rosellini, "Anita Bryant's Battle with Gays Turns into a Holy War," *Chicago Tribune*, May 2, 1977, B1.

5. As early as the 1920s, some fundamentalists denounced homosexuality as a symptom of national moral degradation and a possible sign of the apocalypse. However, this did not become a central concern for most conservative Christians until the growing visibility of gay liberation movements in the 1970s. For more on homosexuality and early fundamentalists, see Matthew Avery Sutton, *American Apocalypse: A History of Modern Evangelicalism* (Cambridge, MA: Harvard University Press, 2014): 138–139.

6. Seth Dowland argues that political engagement has always been a central component of evangelical Christianity, given its emphasis on the "divine command to regulate morality in society." At the same time, he notes a long-standing hesitance among evangelicals to embrace political engagement, a trend that he traces to the Baptist emphasis on individualism and religious freedom. See Seth Dowland, *Family Values and the Rise of the New Christian Right* (Philadelphia: University of Pennsylvania Press, 2015), 16.

7. Michelle M. Nickerson, *Mothers of Conservatism: Women and the Postwar Right* (Princeton, NJ: Princeton University Press, 2012), 31.

8. Anita Bryant, *Mine Eyes Have Seen the Glory* (Old Tappan, NJ: Fleming H. Revell, 1970), 1–2.

9. Bryant, *Mine Eyes*, 5–9.

10. Bryant, *Mine Eyes*, 34–42.

11. Bryant, *Mine Eyes*, 33.

12. Bryant, *Mine Eyes*, 80–86. For a contemporary accounts of Bryant's appearances on the USO tours, see "Television Review: Bob Hope Buick Christmas Show," *Variety* 221, no. 8 (January 18, 1961); "NY Times Cable Re: Bob Hope: 'I Forgot to Burn My Draft Card,'" *Variety* 241, no. 6 (December 29, 1965); "Anita Bryant on USO B[oar]d," *Variety* 245, no. 5 (December 21, 1966); H. Viggo Andersen, "Another 'Joy Junket' Ends for Non-Stop Bob Hope," *Hartford Courant*, January 21, 1962, 2G; Herb Kelly, "Her Christmas in South Viet Nam," *Miami News*, January 7, 1963. Bryant appeared on the back of her 1992 book *A New Day* wearing the US Army jacket that a soldier gave to her during her USO tours, now decorated with patches from dozens of regiments. The same photo appears on the current website for Anita Bryant Ministries. See Anita Bryant, "Anita Bryant Ministries" (2006), accessed May 17, 2014, http://www.anitabmi.org/3.html; Anita Bryant, *A New Day* (Nashville, TN: Broadman Press, 1992).

13. Bob Green, interview with Adam Nagourney by telephone, April 28, 1995. Originally collected for Dudley Clendinen and Adam Nagourney, *Out for Good: The Struggle to Build a Gay Rights Movement in America* (New York: Touchstone, 1999). My thanks to Mr. Nagourney for sharing this transcript with me.

14. Bryant, *Mine Eyes*, 45–46.

15. Bryant, *Mine Eyes*, 69.

16. Bryant, *Mine Eyes*, 73.

17. Bryant, *Mine Eyes*, 96.

18. Bryant, *Mine Eyes*, 113–114. See, for example, "The Nation: Twins Arrive Early for Anita Bryant," *Los Angeles Times*, January 5, 1969, AA; Elizabeth Sullivan, "Anita Bryant on Christma Eve Special," *Boston Globe*, December 21, 1969, TV5.

19. Robert Cross, "Two Votes for Old-Fashioned Values," *Chicago Tribune*, April 18, 1976, G10. Emphasis in original.

20. Anita Bryant, *Bless This House* (Old Tappan, NJ: Fleming H. Revell, 1972), 53.

21. Anita Bryant, *Amazing Grace* (Old Tappan, NJ: Fleming H. Revell, 1971), 31.

22. Bryant, *Mine Eyes*, 79.

23. Bryant also penned another book—called *A New Day*—in 1992, twelve years after her divorce from Bob Green had made her a pariah in the evangelical communities upon which she had relied. A different Christian press, Broadman Books, published this memoir, which does not seem to have had the same success as her earlier work. Also not included in this count is Bryant's cookbook, *Bless This Food*, published by Doubleday in 1975.

24. Like other celebrity authors, Bryant had the help of a ghostwriter to create her books, though both she and the publisher worked to produce the illusion that Bryant was speaking directly to her readers. Whereas many contemporary evangelical authors openly credited their ghostwriters, Bryant did not acknowledge that she worked with one until much later. In her 1992 book *A New Day*, published by Broadman Press twenty-five years after Bryant's last publication

with Revell, Bryant gave special mention "to Charlotte Hale (Pinder) [who] from the beginning, starting with *Mine Eyes Have Seen the Glory* . . . for most of my past ten books and this one has gathered the information and has creatively put it into the proper form for public readership." (Notably, Bryant includes her 1975 cookbook, *Bless This Food*, in this count.) She went on to thank Hale for her "ability to convey my words and heart to the reader." However, Bryant's work with Hale by no means suggests that Bryant ever relinquished full authorial control. In fact, the publisher's foreword to Bryant's second book suggests an atypical level of authorial autonomy, stating that *Amazing Grace* was "like no other book published by the Fleming H. Revell company. . . . For one thing—there was no outline, no suggested order of chapters, no specific material to be covered." The conversational style of Bryant's first ten books, the author's in-text discussions of her own creative process, and the mention of a transcriber in the 1978 *Anita Bryant Story* all suggest that most of the material in the books was originated by Bryant, and at least some of it was taken from Bryant's extemporaneous speech. Bryant, *Amazing Grace*, 9; Bryant, *A New Day*, x.

25. See Tanya Erzen, *Straight to Jesus: Sexual and Christian Conversions in the Ex-Gay Movement* (Berkeley: University of California Press, 2006), 1–14.

26. For more on the history of this rhetorical practice, see Catherine A. Brekus, *Strangers and Pilgrims: Female Preaching in America, 1740–1845* (Chapel Hill: University of North Carolina Press, 1998), 39–42.

27. Bryant, *Bless This House*, 134.

28. Anita Bryant and Bob Green, *Running the Good Race* (Old Tappan, NJ: Fleming H. Revell, 1976), 44. All caps, italics, and ellipses in original.

29. Bryant, *Mine Eyes*, 61.

30. Cliff Jahr, "Anita Bryant's Startling Reversal," *Ladies Home Journal*, December 1980, 65; Circuit Court of the 11th Judicial Circuit in and for Dade County, Florida, *Anita Green vs. Robert Green* (August 15, 1980).

31. For an exploration of these trends in contemporary evangelical women's ministries, see R. Marie Griffith, *God's Daughters: Evangelical Women and the Power of Submission* (Berkeley: University of California Press, 1997).

32. Bryant and Green, *Running the Good Race*, 48.

33. Bryant and Green, *Running the Good Race*, 44.

34. Bryant, *Mine Eyes*, 5–6.

35. Bryant, *Bless This House*, 48, 113.

36. Bryant and Green, *Running the Good Race*, 48.

37. Feminist theories of embodiment have generally responded to this paradox by rejecting the notion of sex and gender as "natural" categories and insisting instead that both are culturally constructed and individually constituted through performances of culturally defined identities. Particularly influential here is the work of Judith Butler. See Judith Butler, *Gender Trouble: Feminism and the*

Subversion of Identity (New York: Routledge, 1990); and Judith Butler, *Undoing Gender* (New York: Routledge, 2004).

38. Bryant, *Mine Eyes*, 96–97.

39. Bryant described singing this song publicly for the first time "several years ago" in her 1970 book. She first recorded the song in 1967. See Bryant, *Mine Eyes*, 90; Anita Bryant, "Battle Hymn of the Republic," *Mine Eyes Have Seen the Glory* (Columbia CS-9373, 1967).

40. Bryant, *Bless This House*, 19.

41. This pattern of developing political awareness based on pre-existing assumptions about American values calls to mind historian Joan Scott's contention that "we need to attend to the historical processes that, through discourse, position subjects and produce their experiences. It is not individuals who have experiences but subjects that are constituted through experience." Joan Scott, "The Evidence of Experience," *Critical Inquiry* 17, no. 4 (Summer 1991): 779.

42. Scholars have traced concerns about imminent secularization and moral decline throughout US history, arguing that apocalyptic reasoning has been a consistent framework through which Americans have structured understandings of their nation and their future. See Michael Lienesch, *Redeeming America: Piety and Politics in the New Christian Right* (Chapel Hill: University of North Carolina Press, 1993), 223–245; Christopher McKnight Nichols and Charles Mathewes, "Introduction: Prophesies of Godlessness," in *Prophesies of Godlessness: Predictions of America's Imminent Secularization, from the Puritans to the Present Day*, ed. Charles Mathewes and Christopher McKnight Nichols (New York: Oxford University Press, 2008), 3–20.

43. Moral Majority, "The Moral Majority, Inc.: Fighting for a Moral America in This Decade of Destiny," [1980?], Contemporary Issues Pamphlet Collection, Wichita State University Special Collections, Wichita, KS, 81-07a. Pamphlet. Emphasis mine.

44. Edward B. Fiske, "Second Coming: There Are Those Who Think It Is Imminent," *New York Times*, Sunday, October 8, 1972, 8.

45. Ray Walters, "Paperback Talk," *New York Times Book Review*, Sunday, March 12, 1978, 45.

46. Bryant, *Mine Eyes*, 8.

47. Bryant, *Bless This House*, dust jacket.

48. Bryant, *Mine Eyes*, 74.

49. Historian Darren Dochuk speaks specifically about evangelical southerners' migrations to California, but Bryant's experience—migrating from a religious Oklahoma town and settling into a more prosperous, urban adulthood where she found a "Bible-believing" church but nonetheless felt frequently out of step with larger cultural developments—bears a strong resonance with the larger history that Dochuk relates. Further, historian Deborah Dash Moore has also used the framework of Sunbelt migration to discuss American Jewish migration to

both Los Angeles and Miami during the postwar period. See Darren Dochuk, *From Bible Belt to Sunbelt: Plain-Folk Religion, Grassroots Politics, and the Rise of Evangelical Conservatism* (New York: W. W. Norton, 2011); Deborah Dash Moore, *To the Golden Cities: Pursuing the American Jewish Dream in Miami and L.A.* (Cambridge, MA: Harvard University Press, 1994).

50. Nancy Tatom Ammerman, *Baptist Battles: Social Change and Religious Conflict in the Southern Baptist Convention* (New Brunswick, NJ: Rutgers University Press, 1990), 50–59.

51. See, for example, Kevin M. Kruse, *White Flight: Atlanta and the Making of Modern Conservatism* (Princeton, NJ: Princeton University Press, 2005); Robert O. Self, *American Babylon: Race and the Struggle for Postwar Oakland* (Princeton, NJ: Princeton University Press, 2003); Thomas J. Sugrue, *The Origins of the Urban Crisis: Race and Inequality in Postwar Detroit* (Princeton, NJ: Princeton University Press, 1996).

52. Matthew Lassiter, *The Silent Majority: Politics in the Sunbelt South* (Princeton, NJ: Princeton University Press, 2006): 1–5.

53. For more on discourses of race in Bryant's anti-gay-rights campaigning, see Frank, "'The Civil Rights of Parents.'"

54. Anita Bryant and Bob Green, *Fishers of Men* (Old Tappan, NJ: Fleming H. Revell, 1973), 75–79.

55. Bryant, *Bless This House*, 9.

56. Bryant, *Bless This House*, 18–19.

57. Anita Bryant and Bob Green, *Raising God's Children* (Old Tappan, NJ: Fleming H. Revell, 1977), 30–32.

58. The group and the campaign were originally called "Save Our Children" but were renamed within a year, after the international children's relief agency Save the Children brought suit. For clarity, this chapter refers to the campaign as "Protect America's Children" throughout. See "By Any Other Name, Cause Is Still Anita's" (March 4, 1978), Unidentified clipping in Anita Bryant collection, HistoryMiami Archives and Research Center, Miami, FL (Hereafter HistoryMiami); Joe Crankshaw, "Charity Sues Bryant Group to 'Save Their Children,'" *Miami Herald*, July 9, 1977.

59. "Bias against Homosexuals Is Outlawed in Miami," *New York Times*, January 19, 1977, 14.

60. Jeff Prugh, "Miami Kills Gay Rights Law," *Los Angeles Times*, June 8, 1977, 1.

61. See, for example, Lynn Charles Foley, "Anita Goes to War in the Gay Ghetto," *Observer* [London, UK], June 5, 1977, 16; Jean O'Leary and Bruce Voeller, "Anita Bryant's Crusade," *New York Times*, June 7, 1977, 35; William Raspberry, "Anita Bryant and Gay Rights: Bigotry or Prudence?," *Washington Post*, May 2, 1977, A23; Rosellini, "Anita Bryant's Battle with Gays Turns into a Holy War," *Chicago Tribune*, May 2, 1977, B1; Jonathan Steela, "Miami Puts Gay Rights on Test," *Guardian* [London, UK], June 6, 1977, 4; "Anita Bryant Takes On 'Gay' Activists,"

Los Angeles Times, February 15, 1977, A1; "County to Hold Vote on Homosexual Law," *Globe and Mail* [Toronto, ON], March 16, 1977, 13; "Miami Votes on Gay Rights," *Jerusalem Post*, June 8, 1977, 4; "Vote Is Set on Gay Rights Law Opposed by Anita Bryant," *Sun* [Baltimore, MD], March 16, 1977, A3.

62. "Anita Bryant Hails Vote in St. Paul," *Boston Globe*, April 27, 1978, 40; "Anita Bryant Has Scheduled Her Second Visit to Wichita," *Gay Chicago News*, December 2, 1977, Bryant Collection, Stonewall National Museum and Archives, Ft. Lauderdale, FL; "Bryant to Wichita," *Gay Community News*, December 3, 1977, See Thomas L. Higgins Papers, P2155, Minnesota History Center, Gale Family Library, St. Paul, MN (hereafter "Higgins Papers"), Box 4, "Pie File."; Muriel Dobbin, "Calif. Anti-Gay Petition Likely," *Sun* [Baltimore, MD], May 30, A7.

63. Anita Bryant and Bob Green, "Anita and Bob Announce New Counseling Services Program," *Protect America's Children Newsletter* (July, 1978), Wilcox Collection, RH WL D2982; Alice Murray, "Ex-Homosexual Claims He Was Saved by Jesus," *Protect America's Children Newsletter* (July, 1978), Wilcox Collection, RH WL D2982. The volume numbers on the Protect America's Children (PAC) and Anita Bryant Ministries (ABM) newsletters are inconsistent, making it difficult to know how many issues of each periodical were produced. The Wilcox Collection at the University of Kansas has PAC newsletter holdings for February 1978, April 1978, and May–June 1978 (designated as volumes 1, 2, and 3, respectively), as well as for June 1978 and July 1978 (both also designated as volume 1). Both issues of the ABM newsletter held in the Wilcox Collection (from September 1978 and October 1978) are also designated as volume 1 of that periodical. For more on the development of the "ex-gay movement," see Tanya Erzen, *Straight to Jesus*.

64. Anita Bryant Ministries, "When the Homosexuals Burn the Holy Bible in Public," August 6, 1979, 1, Wilcox Collection, RH WL Eph 606, fundraising letter.

65. Anita Bryant Ministries, Letter to the Internal Revenue Service: Attention 720-2, EP/EO Division—Warnick, July 10, 1978. Cornell University Special Collections, Larry Bush Papers, Collection #7316 23/5/1, Box 2, Folder 40, 1.

66. Jahr, "Bryant's Startling Reversal," 63.

67. Jahr, "Bryant's Startling Reversal."

68. The full resolution is reprinted in Jerry Sutton, *A Matter of Conviction: A History of Southern Baptist Engagement with the Culture* (Nashville: B&H Publishing Group, 2008), 220–221. See also Elizabeth H. Flowers, *Into the Pulpit: Southern Baptist Women and Power since World War II* (Chapel Hill: University of North Carolina Press, 2012), 55–58; Daniel K. Williams, *God's Own Party: The Making of the Christian Right* (New York: Oxford University Press, 2012), 150.

69. "Miss Bryant Loses in Baptist Post Bid," *New York Times*, June 14, 1978, B8.

70. Bryant, *Bless This House*, 13.

71. Bryant, *Bless This House*, 58. Bryant openly wrestled with her decision to employ household staff, worrying in particular that she was shirking her duties as a

mother. This struggle served to underscore the overwhelming difficulty of being a working mother, and (although Bryant did not ultimately give up her career) to remind readers that their own roles as mothers should always be paramount.

72. Bryant, *Bless This House*, 14. My count of Bryant's books here includes only the volumes that she published with Revell. Green also appears on the cover of Bryant's 1975 cookbook, but not on the post-divorce book that she published in 1992. Bryant, *Bless This Food*; Bryant, *A New Day*.

73. Bryant, *Mine Eyes*, 134–136; Bryant, *Amazing Grace*, 14–15.

74. Bryant, *Bless This House*, 14, 18, 36–42, 137–143; Bryant and Green, *Raising God's Children*, 22, 130–131.

75. See, for example, Bryant, *Bless This House*, 71–80; Bryant and Green, *Raising God's Children*, 115–134.

76. Margaret Lamberts Bendroth, *Fundamentalism and Gender, 1875 to the Present* (New Haven, CT: Yale University Press, 1993), 83–87.

77. Bryant, *Bless This House*, 69; Anita Bryant and Bob Green, *Light My Candle* (Old Tappan, NJ: Fleming H. Revell, 1974), 149–153.

78. Brekus, *Strangers and Pilgrims*, 162–167; Matthew Avery Sutton, *Aimee Semple McPherson and the Resurrection of Christian America* (Cambridge, MA: Harvard University Press, 2007), 12–13.

79. See, for example, Bryant, *Mine Eyes*, 134–136.

80. Bryant, *Amazing Grace*, 9.

81. Bryant, *Bless This House*, 19, emphasis in original.

82. Bryant and Green, *Raising God's Children*, 38–41.

83. Bryant, *The Anita Bryant Story*, 14.

84. Bryant, *The Anita Bryant Story*, 16.

85. Bryant, *The Anita Bryant Story*, 57.

86. Bryant, *The Anita Bryant Story*, 58. Emphasis in original.

87. Bryant and Green, *Fishers of Men*, 139.

88. Bryant and Green, *At Any Cost* (Old Tappan, NJ: Fleming H. Revell, 1978), 51.

89. Dochuk, *From Bible Belt to Sunbelt*, 365; "Counting Souls," *Time*, October 4, 1976, 75.

90. Susan Friend Harding, *The Book of Jerry Falwell: Fundamentalist Language and Politics* (Princeton, NJ: Princeton University Press, 2000), 21–25, 112–113.

91. Beverly LaHaye, *Who but a Woman?* (Nashville, TN: Thomas Nelson, 1984), 121.

92. A group of Christian students organized the rally in March 1969 in response to a controversial concert during which the singer Jim Morrison had allegedly exposed himself to a Miami crowd. Bryant told the story over two pages of her first autobiography in the context of her return to show business after her twins were born. Bryant, *Mine Eyes*, 118–119.

93. Bryant, *Bless This House*, 44.

94. Bryant and Green, *Raising God's Children*, 41.

95. Bryant and Green, *Raising God's Children*, 41. Emphasis in original.

96. Bryant, *Bless This House*, 44.

97. Bryant and Green, *Raising God's Children*, 41.

98. Bryant, *Bless This House*, 45.

99. Marlee Schwartz and Kenneth J. Cooper, "Equal Rights Initiative in Iowa Attacked," *New York Times* August 23, 1992, A15.

100. See, for example, "3,000 in Houston Protest Anita Bryant Appearance," *New York Times*, June 17, 1977, A12; Marjorie Hyer, "Outside, Angry Protests; Inside, Baptists Cheer Anita Bryant," *Washington Post*, June 12, 1978, A2.

101. The protestor, Thom Higgins, was a leader of the gay-rights movement in Minnesota and his papers have been archived by the Minnesota Historical Society. Higgins Papers, Box 4, "Pie File."

102. National Gay Task Force, "1977: The Year in Review" (1977), 4–5, Glenda Mattoon Papers, Entry 946, Western History Collection, University of Oklahoma, Norman, OK (hereafter "Mattoon Papers"), Box 2, Folder 9.

103. "Amsterdam Gays Rally Anti-Bryant," *Gaysweek*, October 24, 1977, Higgins Papers; "Dutch Disk Protests Anti-Gay Campaigns," *Billboard* 89, no. 46 (November 19, 1977); "Thousands March to Support Equal Rights for Homosexuals," *Boston Globe*, June 27, 1977, 8; Bryant and Green, *At Any Cost*, 97; Theo Van Der Meer, interview with author by telephone, May 23, 2014."

104. Ken Kelley, "*Playboy* Interview: Anita Bryant—A Candid Conversation," *Playboy* 25, no. 5 (May 1978): 73. For more on Bryant's impact on gay-rights activism, see Tina Fetner, "Working Anita Bryant: The Impact of Anti-Gay Activism on Lesbian and Gay Movement Claims," *Social Problems* 48, no. 3 (August 2001): 411–428; Tina Fetner, *How the Religious Right Shaped Lesbian and Gay Activism* (Minneapolis: University of Minnesota Press, 2008).

105. Billy Masters, "Billy Masters," *Windy City Times*, April 2, 2014, 29; Robert Sutton, "Names in the News," *Toronto Star*, May 30, 1977, C6.

106. The Stonewall National Museum and Archives (SNMA) in Ft. Lauderdale, Florida, houses a rich collection of documents and ephemera related to gay communities' response to Anita Bryant, including pins, T-shirts, and posters bearing these slogans.

107. "Nation," *Chicago Tribune*, February 25, 1977, 16.

108. "Bryant Says Gays Caused Cancellation," *Hartford Courant*, February 25, 1977, 3; Jay Clarke, "Gay Rights Dispute Stops Bryant's Show," *Washington Post*, February 25, 1977, B1; Jennings Parrott, "Anita Bryant Drive Costs Her a Show," *Los Angeles Times*, February 25, 1977, 2.

109. "The Anita Bryant Show," *Washington Post*, March 2, 1977, A18; Garry Wills, "Banning Artists for Views, Even Anita Bryant, Is Bad," *Sun* [Baltimore, MD], March 9, 1977, A15.

110. Advertising and Merchandising Committee, Meeting Minutes, November 16, 1977, S1782, p. 8762, Florida Citrus Commission, Department of

Citrus Records, State Archives of Florida. Tallahassee, FL (hereafter Citrus Commission records).

111. Public Relations Committee, Meeting Minutes, July 20, 1977, S1782, p. 8404, Citrus Commission records.

112. Advertising and Merchandising Committee, Meeting Minutes, July 19–20, 1977, pp. 8347–8349, Citrus Commission records.

113. Barry Bearak, "Turmoil within Ministry: Bryant Hears 'Anita, . . . Please Repent,'" *Miami Herald*, June 8, 1980; Jeff Golden, "Anita Bryant Asks Court for Divorce," *Miami Herald*, May 23, 1980.

114. Ken Campbell, "'A Lament for Anita Bryant': Being the Essence of a Message (with Supporting Documentation), Preached by Evangelist Ken Campbell in the Evening Service of the Churchill Heights Baptist Church, Agincourt, Ontario, Sunday, June 1, 1980," 26, National Religious Broadcasters Collection, Billy Graham Center Archives, Wheaton, IL (hereafter NRB collection), BGC 309, Series III.

115. Anita Bryant, fundraising letter on behalf of James Robison (December 1981); Ken Campbell, letter to Anita Bryant (February 4, 1982); Ken Campbell, letter to James Robison (February 4, 1982); both in NRB collection, BGC 309, Series III. In Robison's book *Attack on the Family* (first published in October 1981), Robison mentioned "Bryant's 'Save Our Children' endeavor" briefly, apparently assuming that his readers would already be familiar with the campaign. He did not mention the conflict with Campbell in subsequent books, but he also did not mention Bryant again. See James Robison, *Attack on the Family* (Wheaton, IL: Tyndale House, 1981), 63.

116. Jahr, "Anita Bryant's Startling Reversal," 67.

117. Marie-Amelie George, "Expressive Ends: Understanding Conversion Therapy Bans," *Alabama Law Review* 68, no. 3 (2017): 793–853.

CHAPTER 3

1. Beverly LaHaye, *I Am A Woman by God's Design* (Old Tappan, NJ: Fleming H. Revell, 1980), back cover. LaHaye commonly employed similar language in early fund-raising efforts. See Beverly LaHaye, "Your Support Is Making CWA the Leading Women's Lobby!" (September 2, 1980), Wilcox Collection, RH WL Eph 1352.2, direct-mail letter; Beverly LaHaye, "Women Must Never Be Drafted in America!" (February 1980), Wilcox Collection, RH WL Eph 1352.2, direct-mail letter.

2. Beverly LaHaye, *The Restless Woman* (Grand Rapids: Zondervan, 1984), 123.

3. Beverly LaHaye, *Who but a Woman?* (Nashville, TN: Thomas Nelson, 1984), 122.

4. LaHaye, *Who but a Woman?* 121; Sally Bedell Smith, "Film on a Nuclear War Already Causing Wide Fallout," *New York Times*, November 17, 1983, A20. Some scholars as well as feminist opponents of CWA have suggested that the organization's membership numbers have consistently been inflated by a practice

of including anyone who has ever been a member of the organization regardless of their current status. Even given this possibility, however, these numbers suggest that CWA garnered significant interest in its first half decade of existence that probably put it at least on par with the older Eagle Forum. For commentary on CWA membership numbers, see Jill A. Irvine, "Exporting the Culture Wars: Concerned Women for America in the Global Arena," in *Women of the Right: Comparisons and Interplay across Borders*, ed. Kathleen M. Blee and Sandra McGee Deutsch (University Park: Pennsylvania State University Press, 2012), 49 fn. 5; Deane A. Rohlinger, "Framing the Abortion Debate: Organizational Resources, Media Strategies, and Movement-Countermovement Dynamics," *Sociological Quarterly* 43, no. 4 (Autumn 2002): 505 fn. 2.

5. Darren Dochuk, *From Bible Belt to Sunbelt: Plain-Folk Religion, Grassroots Politics, and the Rise of Evangelical Conservatism* (New York: W. W. Norton, 2011).

6. See Lisa McGirr, *Suburban Warriors: The Origins of the New American Right* (Princeton, NJ: Princeton University Press, 2001); Michelle M. Nickerson, *Mothers of Conservatism: Women and the Postwar Right* (Princeton, NJ: Princeton University Press, 2012).

7. LaHaye, *Who but a Woman?* 129–130; Beverly LaHaye, "Women Must Never Be Drafted in America!" (February, 1980), Wilcox Collection, RH WL Eph 1352.2, direct-mail letter. Note: throughout this book, I refer to Beverly LaHaye in short-form notes as "LaHaye" and Tim LaHaye as "T. LaHaye," with the exception of books coauthored by the couple, which appear under "LaHaye and LaHaye."

8. 1930 United States Federal Census, "Beverly Davenport," Southfield, Oakland, Michigan, accessed through Ancestry.com; 1940 United States Federal Census, "Beverly Jean Ratcliffe," Southfield, Michigan, accessed through Ancestry.com; Jennifer Jean McGee, "Rocking the Cradle/Ruling the World: Beverly LaHaye's Rhetorical Dilemma and Rhetorical Strategies" (M.A. Thesis, University of Minnesota, 1994). Beverly's mother's name is recorded as Melie in the 1930 census and Nellie in the 1940 census; I have followed McGee's lead here in referring to her as Elie. When Beverly's mother remarried, Beverly and her older sister Aileen both took their stepfather's last name, which was Ratcliffe.

9. McGee, "Rocking the Cradle," 9.

10. Over the course of the twentieth century, U.S. divorce and marriage rates (as a percentage of the total population) have tended to rise and fall together, though not always at the same pace. One notable exception to this trend was during the late 1920s, when divorce rates continued to climb steadily despite a sharp drop-off in marriages at the same time. In the years immediately following the Second World War—formative years for Morgan (b. 1937), Bryant (b. 1940), LaHaye (b. 1929), and Bakker (b. 1942)—marriage and birth rates peaked, bringing with them an intensive cultural focus on marital ideals and failures. During the second half of the twentieth century, divorce and marriage trends continued to mirror one another but the gap between them steadily narrowed. The panic over

rising divorce rates was one central concern of New Christian Right authors, but it was also a focal issue in mainstream media throughout the last half of the twentieth century. See Kristin Celello, *Making Marriage Work: A History of Marriage and Divorce in the Twentieth Century* (Chapel Hill: University of North Carolina Press, 2009): 2; Elaine Tyler May, *Homeward Bound: American Families in the Cold War Era*, rev. ed. (New York: Basic Books, 1999): xii–xvi, 35–36, 95.

11. Nancy Skelton, "Tim LaHaye—Waging War against Humanism," *Los Angeles Times*, February 22, 1981, SD_A1.

12. McGee, "Rocking the Cradle," 5.

13. In a 1987 book of interviews with the wives of prominent evangelists, authors James Schaffer and Colleen Todd present a range of acceptable roles for pastors' wives ranging from Tammy Faye Bakker's role as televangelical co-star alongside her husband to Macel Falwell's intense desire for privacy. They suggest, however, that a more moderate position between the two is much more normative, with the wife offering encouragement and assistance to her husband and playing a supporting role in a ministry that is nonetheless distinctly his. See Colleen Todd and James Schaffer, *Christian Wives: Women behind the Evangelists Reveal Their Faith in Modern Marriage* (Garden City, NY: Doubleday, 1987), 27.

14. Beverly LaHaye, *The Spirit-Controlled Woman* (Irvine, CA: Harvest House, 1976), 13.

15. Daisy Hepburn, *Why Doesn't Somebody Do Something? What 20 Women Are Doing about Government, Education, Leadership, Decency, Morality* (Wheaton, IL: Victor Books, 1981), 135; Tim LaHaye and Beverly LaHaye, *Spirit-Controlled Family Living* (Old Tappan, NJ: Fleming H. Revell, 1978), 10; McGee, "Rocking the Cradle," 6. Tim LaHaye wrote in the foreword to Beverly LaHaye's 1976 *The Spirit-Controlled Woman*: "I can testify that since you surrendered yourself completely to God some thirteen years ago, your temperament has been controlled by the Holy Spirit. I have witnessed a sweet, soft-spirited worry machine that was afraid of your own shadow become transformed into a gracious, outgoing, radiant woman that God has used to inspire thousands of women to accept Him and the abundant life He offers through your lectures on the Spirit-filled life. It has been fun to watch you burn the midnight oil writing this book. Thirteen years ago you would have been frightened off the first page. Now you have trusted Him who is able to do exceedingly abundantly above all we can ask or think—and it is finished." In LaHaye, *The Spirit-Controlled Woman*, 7–8.

16. LaHaye, *The Restless Woman*, 121, 129–130.

17. Nancy Skelton, "Tim LaHaye" A3. For more on Family Life Seminars (FLS), see Tim LaHaye, *The Bible's Influence on American History* (El Cajon, CA: Christian Heritage College, 1976), 84; Tim LaHaye, "Family Life Seminars for Missionaries: Curriculum and Post-Seminar Evaluation" (D. Min., Western Conservative Baptist Seminary, 1978). A sampling of materials produced by FLS include Tim LaHaye, *Biblical Counseling* (El Cajon, CA: Family Life Seminars,

[1979?]); Tim LaHaye, *A Christian View of Radical Sex Education* (San Diego, CA: Family Life Seminars, [1970s]); Tim LaHaye, *How to Be All You Were Meant to Be* (El Cajon, CA: Family Life Cassette of the Month Club, 1978); Tim LaHaye, *How to Face Success and Persecution* (El Cajon, CA: Family Life Cassette of the Month Club, 1978); Tim LaHaye, *How We Got Our Bible* (El Cajon, CA: Family Life Seminars, [1970s]); Tim LaHaye, *A Marriage Ceremony in the Heavens* (El Cajon, CA: Family Life Cassette of the Month Club, 1979); Tim LaHaye, *Overcoming Your Personal Weaknesses* (El Cajon, CA: Family Life Cassette of the Month Club, 1978); Tim LaHaye, *Understanding the Male Temperament* (El Cajon, CA: Family Life Cassette of the Month Club, [1970s]); Tim LaHaye, *The Christian after the Resurrection* (El Cajon, CA: Family Life Cassette of the Month Club, 1979); Tim LaHaye and Beverly LaHaye, *Coping with Hostility* (El Cajon, CA: Family Life Distributors, 1978); Tim LaHaye, *Eternal Rewards* (El Cajon, CA: Family Cassette of the Month Club, 1979); Tim LaHaye and Beverly LaHaye, *Why You Do the Things You Do* (El Cajon, CA: Family Life Distributors, 1978).

18. LaHaye and LaHaye, *Spirit-Controlled Family Living*, 12; Tim LaHaye, *The Battle for the Mind* (Old Tappan, NJ: Fleming H. Revell, 1980); William C. Martin, *With God on Our Side: The Rise of the Religious Right in America* (New York: Broadway Books, 2005), 196.

19. LaHaye rarely mentions her children in her public speaking or writing, but public records indicate that they were born in approximately 1948–1949 (Linda), 1951 (Larry), 1952–1954 (Lee), and 1958 (Lori). See Christian High School, "Council," *Patriot 1968* (1968 Yearbook), (San Diego, CA: Christian High School, 1968), 15; "Linda LaHaye and Gerald M. Murphy," California Marriage Index, 1960–1985 (San Diego, CA: June 28, 1969); "Larry Kent LaHaye," US Public Records Index, 1950–1993, Vol. 1; "Larry K. LaHaye and Kathleen M. Stuard," California Marriage Index 1960–1985 (San Diego, CA: October 17, 1971); "Lori K. LaHaye," California Birth Index, 1905–1995 (San Diego, CA: September 14, 1958). Lee LaHaye appears in the 1968 yearbook for Christian High School, making him between fourteen and eighteen years old that year. He is younger than Larry and so must have been born between 1952 and 1954. All records accessed through the Ancestry database.

20. LaHaye, *The Spirit-Controlled Woman*, 8.

21. LaHaye, *The Spirit-Controlled Woman*, 7.

22. Tim LaHaye and Beverly LaHaye, *The Act of Marriage: The Beauty of Sexual Love* (Grand Rapids, MI: Zondervan, 1976), 8.

23. See Catherine A. Brekus, *Strangers and Pilgrims: Female Preaching in America, 1740–1845* (Chapel Hill: University of North Carolina Press, 1998); Elizabeth Elkin Grammer, *Some Wild Visions: Autobiographies by Female Itinerant Evangelists in Nineteenth-Century America* (New York: Oxford University Press, 2002); Susan Hill Lindley, *You Have Stept Out of Your Place: A History of Women and Religion in America* (Louisville, KY: Westminster John Knox Press, 1996);

Priscilla Pope-Levison, *Turn the Pulpit Loose: Two Centuries of American Women Evangelists* (New York: Palgrave Macmillan, 2004).

24. LaHaye and LaHaye, *Spirit-Controlled Family Living*, 12–13.

25. LaHaye and LaHaye, *Act of Marriage*, 8.

26. The book sold over 1.4 million copies by 1983, and its revised edition (1998) is still in print from Zondervan. It has been translated into at least ten languages (including Arabic, Afrikaans, Chinese, and Spanish) and has inspired spinoffs by the LaHayes, including *What Lovemaking Means to a Man* (1984), *What Lovemaking Means to a Woman* (1984), *The Act of Marriage after 40: Making Love for Life* (2001). George W. Cornell, "Dealers Protest 'Silent Censorship' of Religion Books," *Washington Post*, September 17, 1983, B6.

27. This was a serious concern. A spokesman for Zondervan told the *Christian Science Monitor* that the bestselling *Act of Marriage* was "so explicit" that "it would 'have been wrapped in brown paper five years ago.'" David T. Cook, "Religious, Inspirational Book Sales Mounting Fast," *Christian Science Monitor*, August 12, 1976, 11.

28. Marabel Morgan, *The Total Woman* (Old Tappan, NJ: Fleming H. Revell, 1973), 122–123.

29. LaHaye and LaHaye, *Act of Marriage*, 92.

30. LaHaye and LaHaye, *Act of Marriage*, 11–21, 47–61; Morgan, *The Total Woman*, 106–107.

31. LaHaye and LaHaye, *Act of Marriage*, 105.

32. LaHaye and LaHaye, *Act of Marriage*, 97.

33. The LaHayes mentioned Morgan's *Total Woman* in the text of their book but did not include her in their bibliography. Morgan listed Tim LaHaye's *How to Be Happy though Married* in her 1973 book and his *How to Win over Depression* in the 1976 sequel. Other books appearing in both the LaHayes' and Morgan's bibliographies include Herbert J. Miles, *Sexual Happiness in Marriage: A Positive Approach to the Details You Should Know to Achieve a Healthy and Satisfying Sexual Life* (Grand Rapids, MI: Zondervan, 1967) and Marie N. Robinson, *The Power of Sexual Surrender* (New York: New American Library, 1962).

34. This count includes all books for which Beverly LaHaye is listed as author or coauthor. It does not count translations of earlier works as unique works. It also does not count republications of earlier works (including by new publishers) unless the work was substantially updated, revised, or truncated.

35. LaHaye, *The Spirit-Controlled Woman*, 71–72.

36. LaHaye, *The Spirit-Controlled Woman*, 71.

37. During the 1970s, Tim LaHaye was instrumental in helping to build the institutional bases of the emerging New Christian Right. Along with the prominent creationist Henry M. Morris, Tim LaHaye founded Christian Heritage College in El Cajon, California, in 1970, which became the base for their Institute for Creation Research in 1972. Over the decade, his political interests grew beyond Christian education and creationism to include a broader platform of family values and

opposition to secular humanism. He joined the newly founded Christian Voice in the late 1970s, and in 1979 was among the founders of the Moral Majority. In the early 1980s, he retired from full-time preaching to focus on his political work, public speaking, and writing. He helped to found the lobbying group Council for National Policy in 1981, as well as the American Coalition for Traditional Values and the Coalition for Religious Freedom in 1983. In 1976, the same year that the couple published *The Act of Marriage*, Tim also published *The Bible's Influence on American History*, in which he asserted that the United States was rightfully a Christian nation, that it was built on Christian principles, and that it had recently lost its way. In particular, he asserted that recent Supreme Court decisions removing prayer and Bible reading from public schools did not honor the First Amendment's Establishment Clause so much as they violated it—stripping American institutions of their intended Christian influences and establishing a new religion of secular humanism in their place. Similar assumptions would become foundational in Tim and Beverly's later political work, and in the rhetoric of the New Christian Right more broadly. See Bruce David Forbes, "How Popular Are the Left Behind Books . . . and Why? A Discussion of Popular Culture," in *Rapture, Revelation, and the End Times: Exploring the Left Behind Series*, ed. Bruce David Forbes and Jeanne Halgren Kilde (New York: Macmillan, 2004), 12–14; Tim LaHaye, *The Bible's Influence on American History* (El Cajon, CA: Christian Heritage College, 1976), 33, 49–53, 61, 75; Michael Standaert, *Skipping towards Armageddon: The Politics and Propaganda of the Left Behind Novels and the LaHaye Empire* (Brooklyn, NY: Soft Skull Press, 2006), 38–58, 111–112.

38. LaHaye, *Who but a Woman?* 136–137.

39. LaHaye, *The Restless Woman*, 10; Betty Friedan, *The Feminine Mystique* (New York: W. W. Norton, 1963)

40. McGirr, *Suburban Warriors*, 17.

41. "New Organization Formed," *CWA Newsletter* (Spring 1979), Wilcox Collection, RH WL D3169.

42. Beverly LaHaye, "For the sake of our children and grandchildren, please help me" (n.d. [1984]), Wilcox Collection, RH WL Eph 1352.6, direct-mail letter. See also Holly G. Miller, "Concerned Women for America: Soft Voices with Clout," *Saturday Evening Post*, October 1985; Beverly LaHaye, "Does this liberal women's organization represent you?" (n.d. [1979–1980s]), Wilcox Collection, RH WL Eph 1352.6, direct-mail letter.

43. LaHaye, *Who but a Woman?* 24.

44. LaHaye, *Who but a Woman?* 25.

45. LaHaye, *Who but a Woman?* 26.

46. LaHaye, *Who but a Woman?* 25. All-caps in original. I have not found evidence of an "enemy list" in any archive, but it is evident that feminist organizers and even some media outlets were overtly hostile to conservative delegates and especially to the protesters who organized a right-wing counter-conference outside the convention center. One *Baltimore Sun* report began by identifying the

conservative respondents to the conference as "The Ku Klux Klan, John Birch Society, and militant groups of Catholics, Mormons and Baptists [who] are out to insert their own thinking into the fall convention." A relatively sympathetic *Chicago Tribune* report noted that only about 20 percent of the delegates to the conference were "conservatives" and "while they were occasionally able to make debating points from the convention floor, they were not successful in getting any changes in the national action plan itself." The official report released by conference organizers made reference to conservatives' concerns only in sections that covered opposition to feminist and conference goals, where these concerns were generally dismissed as "myths" or "misunderstandings." See "Antifeminists Plan 'Women's Year' Role," *Sun* [Baltimore, MD], August 23, 1977, A5; "Who Represents Women?" *Chicago Tribune*, November 27, 1977, A4; National Women's Conference Organizers, "Woman: 1977, The Status of American Women" (1977), Mattoon Papers, Box 1, Folder 7, p. 5, IWY Conference Report. Marjorie Spruill's in-depth examination of the IWY conference makes it clear that feminist and antifeminist groups considered each other to be "enemies," both implicitly and explicitly. See: Marjorie J. Spruill, *Divided We Stand: The Battle Over Women's Rights and Family Values That Polarized American Politics* (New York: Bloomsbury, 2017).

47. LaHaye, *Who but a Woman?* 29.

48. LaHaye, *Who but a Woman?* 31. Emphasis in original.

49. LaHaye, *Who but a Woman?* 15–23. See also Hepburn, *Why Doesn't Somebody Do Something?* Hepburn's book—which LaHaye mentioned in *Who but a Woman?* and advertised in CWA newsletters—discusses LaHaye and CWA as well as the work of nineteen other women active in political organizing around issues of "government, education, leadership, decency, [and] morality." See, for example, "Recommended Reading," *Concerned Women for America Newsletter* 5, no. 5 (October 1983): 6, Wilcox Collection, RH WL D3169.

50. Briggs quoted in "Initiative Aimed at Firing Homosexual Teachers Filed," *Los Angeles Times*, August 4, 1977, OC1. Protect America's Children shared its contributor list with Briggs for use in rally support for his own efforts. For more on the Briggs Initiative, including Tim LaHaye's and Anita Bryant's support for the measure, see Tina Fetner, *How the Religious Right Shaped Lesbian and Gay Activism* (Minneapolis: University of Minnesota Press, 2008), 23–25; Craig A. Rimmerman, *From Identity to Politics: The Lesbian and Gay Movements in the United States* (Philadelphia: Temple University Press, 2002), 15, 127–130; Daniel K. Williams, *God's Own Party: The Making of the Christian Right* (New York: Oxford University Press, 2012), 151–153, 164.

51. Daniel Horowitz, *Betty Friedan and the Making of the Feminine Mystique: The American Left, the Cold War, and Modern Feminism* (Amherst: University of Massachusetts Press, 1998).

52. Beverly LaHaye, "A Word from the Director," *CWA Newsletter* 1, no. 3 (September 1979): 1, CWA Offices, Washington, D.C. (hereafter "CWA Offices"). By January

1980, the organization had developed a handbook and standard procedure for establishing a prayer chapter, and by February 1982, CWA was advertising a new "slide presentation with cassette tape to educate women on the need for establishing prayer chains across the country." Shirley Peters, untitled column in *CWA Newsletter* 2, no. 1 (January 1980): 3, CWA Offices; "New CWA Presentation Available," *CWA Newsletter* 4, no. 1 (February 1982): 5, CWA Offices.

53. Shirley Peters, untitled column in *CWA Newsletter* 2, no. 1 (January 1980): 3, CWA Offices; "CWA Appoints Field Director," *CWA Newsletter* 5, no. 1 (February/March 1983): 6, CWA Offices.

54. Shirley Peters, "CWA Prayer Chapters," *CWA Newsletter* 2, no. 3 (March 1980): 4, CWA Offices.

55. "CWA Appoints Field Director," *CWA Newsletter* 5, no. 1 (February/March 1983): 6, CWA Offices.

56. Rhode Island was the only state that did not have a Prayer/Action Chapter by 1986 according to newsletter records. In late 1984 or early 1985, Eloise Correa established the first Prayer/Action Chapter outside the United States, at the US military base in Pirmasens, West Germany. "New Prayer Chapter Leaders," *CWA Newsletter* 7, no. 1 (December 1984/January 1985): 7, CWA Offices.

57. Farris was identified in CWA literature as "legal counsel for CWA" as early as December 1981. The establishment of the Educational and Legal Defense Foundation was not announced in this newsletter, however it was first mentioned in the December 1982/January 1983 issue, where it was presented as being already established. Michael Farris, "ERA—Only Three More States?" *Concerned Women for America* 3, no. 6 (December 1981): 1, CWA Offices; Michael Farris, "CWA Helps in Three Lawsuits," *Concerned Women for America Newsletter* 4, no. 5 (December 1982/January 1983): 2, CWA Offices. Also see Sarah Barringer Gordon, *The Spirit of the Law: Religious Voices and the Constitution in Modern America* (Cambridge, MA: Belknap Press of Harvard University Press, 2010), 168.

58. Gordon, *Spirit of the Law*, 133–168.

59. "CWA Opens Office in Washington, D.C.," *Concerned Women for America Newsletter* 5, no. 4 (September 1983): 1, Wilcox Collection, RH WL D3169. See also "CWA Arrival on Capitol Hill Blacked Out by Most Major Media," *Concerned Women for America Newsletter* 5, no. 6 (November 1983): 1–2, Wilcox Collection, RH WL D3169.

60. Beverly LaHaye, "A Word from Beverly: Moving to Washington," *CWA Newsletter* 7, no. 2 (February 1985): 2, CWA Offices.

61. Barrie Lyons, "From the Editor's Desk," *CWA Newsletter* 7, no. 3 (March 1985): 2, Wilcox Collection, RH WL D3168.

62. "CWA's '535,'" *CWA Newsletter*, vol. 6, no. 3 (April 1984): 2, CWA Offices.

63. CWA, "How to Lobby from Your Kitchen Table" (Washington, DC: Concerned Women for America, [1985?]), CWA Offices, pamphlet; "Who Is Beverly LaHaye? Questions and Answers" (Washington, DC: Concerned Women for America, [1985]), Wilcox Collection, RH WL Eph 1352.3, enclosure with Beverly LaHaye,

"Here is the pamphlet you requested," (July 1985), Wilcox Collection, RH WL Eph 1352.3, direct-mail letter.

64. See, for example, "CWA Testifies at FEC," *CWA Newsletter*, vol. 5, no. 4 (September 1983): 2, Wilcox Collection, RH WL D3169; "CWA Testifies at Hearings on Family Violence," *CWA Newsletter*, vol. 6, no. 2 (March 1984): 1, CWA Offices; "Unisex Insurance Bill Faces Defeat," *CWA Newsletter*, vol. 6, no. 5 (June 1984): 6, CWA Offices; Jordan Lorence, "CWA Attorney Visits Rumania," *CWA News*, vol. 7, no. 2 (February 1985): 4, CWA Offices.

65. Concerned Women for America, "Biography: Beverly LaHaye" (Washington, DC: Concerned Women for America, [1990s?]), Information Sheet, CWA Offices; Edward Walsh and Lou Cannon, "Bork Hearings End; Reagan Rallies Backers: President Focuses on Law and Order Issue," *Washington Post*, October 1, 1985, A3; Miranda S. Spivack, "Public Hearings on Judges End," *Hartford Courant*, August 7, 1986, A8; John E. Yang and Lynne Duke, "Outside the Hearing, It Was Cheers, Jeers: Thomas's Supporters Were Most Vocal, Visible," *Washington Post*, October 12, 1991, A9.

66. See, for example, Beverly LaHaye, "What Can a CWA Member Do?" *CWA Newsletter*, vol. 4, no. 5 (December/January 1983): 4, CWA Offices; Beverly LaHaye, "CWA—Back Again?" *CWA Newsletter*, vol. 5, no. 2 (April/May 1983): 1, CWA Offices; Frank York, "The Humanists Seek to Destroy Religious Freedom in America," *CWA Newsletter*, vol. 5, no. 3 (June/July 1983): 1–2, Wilcox Collection, RH WL D3169; Michael Jameson, "ACLU Attacks President Reagan," *CWA Newsletter*, vol. 5, no. 5 (October 1983): 2, Wilcox Collection, RH WL D3169; Beverly LaHaye, "Letters from CWA Presented to President Reagan," *CWA Newsletter*, vol. 6, no. 4 (May 1984): 1–2, CWA Offices.

67. "CWA Leads the Way in Parents' Rights," *CWA News*, vol. 7, no. 10 (October 1985): 1, 11–13, CWA Offices.

68. Kathy Hogancamp, "NEA Attacks Parents' Rights," *CWA Newsletter*, vol. 7, no. 2 (February 1985): 8, CWA Offices; Dennis Laurence Cuddy, "The Grab for Power: A Chronology of the NEA (National Education Association)," (Washington, DC: Concerned Women for America, 1993), pamphlet, CWA Offices.

69. "International Year of the Child," *Eagle Forum Newsletter* (January 1979), 1, Wilcox Collection, RH WL E608; "The International Year of the Child, 1979," *Concerned Women for America* (Special Issue, [July 1979?]), Wilcox Collection, RH WL Eph 1352.1.

70. Donald T. Critchlow, *Phyllis Schlafly and Grassroots Conservatism: A Woman's Crusade* (Princeton, NJ: Princeton University Press, 2005), 3–4, 25.

71. See especially Chritchlow, *Phyllis Schlafly*, 12–15, 212–242; Donald G. Mathews and Jane De Hart, *Sex, Gender and the Politics of the ERA: A State and the Nation* (New York: Oxford University Press, 1990), 50–69.

72. For an overview of the theological battles between American evangelicals and American Catholics in the nineteenth and twentieth centuries, see William M. Shea, *The Lion and the Lamb: Evangelicals and Catholics in America* (New York: Oxford University Press, 2004).

73. Thomas F. Zimmerman, "If a Roman Catholic is elected President—what then?" (1960), John F. Kennedy Pre-Presidential Papers, Presidential Campaign Files, 1960, John F. Kennedy Presidential Library, Boston, MA, 14, Folder on Religious Literature, National Association of Evangelicals. Available online at http://www.jfklibrary.org/Asset-Viewer/Archives/JFKCAMP1960-1021-002.aspx. Emphasis in original.

74. LaHaye and LaHaye, *Act of Marriage*, 98.

75. Frank Clifford, "Kemp Defends Campaign after Bias Incident," *Los Angeles Times*, December 9, 1987, 5; Mark Matthews, "Kemp Co-Chairman Backs Away from Writings on Religion," *Baltimore Sun*, December 5, 1987, 12A; Mark Matthews, "Co-Chairman Quits Kemp Campaign: LaHaye Defends Religious Writings," *Baltimore Sun*, December 8, 1987, 18A; Ted Vollmer, "Principal's Firing, Bias Charges Shake Christian High: Politics, Hiring of Catholics Involved in School Turmoil," *Los Angeles Times*, April 30, 1981, SD A1, 6–7. The controversy surrounding LaHaye's involvement in the Kemp campaign centered on his book *Revelation: Illustrated and Made Plain*, first published in 1973. In the midst of the controversy, he distanced himself from statements made in the book (and exaggerated its age), telling a *Baltimore Sun* reporter that he "had a 'better understanding' and 'a greater respect for the moral concerns of Catholics of all walks of life today than 20 years ago.'" Interestingly, Beverly LaHaye—also a co-chair of the campaign—continued to work for Kemp even after Tim's resignation.

76. Neil J. Young, *We Gather Together: The Religious Right and the Problem of Interfaith Politics* (New York: Oxford University Press, 2016), 172–173; Stephen P. Miller, *The Age of Evangelicalism: America's Born-Again Years* (New York: Oxford University Press), 53.

77. Francis A. Schaeffer, *Plan for Action: An Action Alternative Handbook for Whatever Happened to the Human Race?* (Old Tappan, NJ: Fleming H. Revell Company, 1980), 68.

78. Francis A. Schaeffer, *The Complete Works of Francis A. Schaeffer: A Christian Worldview*, 2nd ed., vol. 4 (Westchester, IL: Crossway Books, 1985), 30.

79. LaHaye, *Who but a Woman?* 13.

80. LaHaye, *Who but a Woman?* 51.

81. See, for example, "Books Available," *CWA Newsletter* 1, no. 7 (August/September 1981), CWA Offices; "Educational Resources," *CWA Newsletter* 9, no. 5 (May, 1987), CWA Offices; "Suggested Reading List," *CWA Newsletter* 1, no. 1 (Spring 1979), Wilcox Collection, RH WL D3169; Michael Jameson, "Update on News," *CWA Newsletter* 4, no. 2 (April/May 1982), CWA Offices; Beverly LaHaye, "The Unequal ERA Lawsuit," *CWA Newsletter* 2, no. 1 (January 1980), CWA Offices;

Beverly LaHaye, "A Word from Beverly: Remember, They Are Still Communists," *CWA Newsletter* 8, no. 2 (October 1986), CWA Offices.

82. LaHaye, *Who but a Woman?* 44. Spencer Fluhman's work on anti-Mormonism in American history deals primarily with the nineteenth century but also offers insight into evangelicals' persistent anti-Mormon views into the twentieth century. See J. Spencer Fluhman, *"A Peculiar People": Anti-Mormonism and the Making of Religion in Nineteenth-Century America* (Chapel Hill: University of North Carolina Press, 2012), 4–8, 127, 146.

83. LaHaye, *Who but a Woman?* 51. After decades of difficulty, by the early twenty-first century, the language of a shared commitment to (Christian) "religious freedom" proved to be one of the most successful bases for political cooperation between conservative evangelicals, Catholics, and Mormons. See Young, *We Gather Together*, 282–285.

84. "Speakers' Calendar," *CWA Newsletter* 2, no. 4 (April, 1980), CWA Offices.

85. Jo Ann Levine, "Housewife a Dodo? Not at All," *Christian Science Monitor*, March 24, 1975, 13.

86. LaHaye, *Who but a Woman?* 53.

87. As Chapter 5 of this book explores, modern conservative Christian women have tried to resolve this problem in part by reclaiming the legacy of feminism as pro-life and pro-family.

88. "CWA Prayer Chapters," *CWA Newsletter* 1, no. 4 (November, 1979), Wilcox Collection, RH WL D3169.

89. "CWA Prayer Chapters," *CWA Newsletter* 1, no. 4 (November, 1979), Wilcox Collection, RH WL D3169. In her 1981 book on prominent conservative women, Daisy Hepburn also recognized the centrality of prayer in CWA's message and strategies, as evidenced in her decision to title the chapter on Beverly LaHaye and CWA "Prayer Is Paramount." See Hepburn, *Why Doesn't Somebody Do Something?* 135–141.

90. Beverly LaHaye, "Effective Prayers of CWA Women," *CWA Newsletter* 4, no. 2 (April/May 1982), CWA Offices.

91. In the King James Version of the Bible, II Chronicles 7:14 reads: "If my people, who are called by my name, will humble themselves and pray and seek my face and turn from their wicked ways, then I will hear from heaven, and I will forgive their sin and heal their land."

92. Beverly LaHaye, *Prayer: God's Comfort for Today's Family* (Nashville, TN: Thomas Nelson, 1990), 196.

93. Concerned Women for America, "Beverly LaHaye Institute," accessed May 6, 2017, https://concernedwomen.org/resources/beverly-lahaye-institute/about-the-beverly-lahaye-institute/.

94. Concerned Women for America, "Issues," accessed May 4, 2017, https://concernedwomen.org/issues/.

CHAPTER 4

1. Art Harris and Michael Isikoff, "Tammy Bakker's Tearful Vow; Evangelists' Security Guard Quits over Their Efforts to Keep House," *Washington Post*, June 18, 1987, C01.

2. The Bakkers' South Carolina home was reportedly worth $435,000 in 1987. According to the Consumer Price Index published by the United States Bureau of Labor Statistics, this amount of money in 1987 would have had approximately the same buying power as $970,000 in 2018. See Bureau of Labor Statistics, "Consumer Price Index Inflation Calculator" (2013), accessed July 11, 2018, http://www.bls.gov/data/inflation_calculator.htm. The couple also owned a $650,000 home in Palm Springs, California (~$1.4 million in 2018 dollars) and bought a $148,000 home in Gatlinburg, Tennessee, in the midst of the scandal (~$330,000 in 2018 dollars). See Art Harris and Michael Isikoff, "The Bakkers' Tumultuous Return; Hundreds at PTL Greet Couple; Length of Their Stay is Unclear," *Washington Post*, June 12, 1987, D01; "Head East to Smoky Mountains Chalet; Jim, Tammy Bakker Move Out of Palm Springs Home," *Los Angeles Times (Southland Edition)*, July 29, 1987, 23.

3. Harris and Isikoff, "Tammy Bakker's Tearful Vow," C01.

4. For example, in their foundational work on televangelism, sociologists Jeffrey Hadden and Charles Swann assess Tammy Faye's contributions to the Bakkers' ministry in a single line: "Tammy Faye Bakker is also a regular on the show." See Jeffrey K. Hadden and Charles E. Swann, *Prime Time Preachers: The Rising Power of Televangelism* (Reading, MA: Addison-Wesley, 1981), 33.

5. Tammy Faye was born with the surname La Valley, took the name Bakker when she married Jim in 1961, and then took the name Messner (sometimes going by Tammy Faye Messner and other times by Tammy Faye Bakker Messner) after she remarried in 1993. This chapter refers to her primarily by her given names and by her best-known surname, Bakker. To avoid confusion, it therefore refers to Jim by his first name.

6. For more on the late twentieth-century culture wars, see Andrew Hartman, *A War for the Soul of America: A History of the Culture Wars* (Chicago: University of Chicago Press, 2015).

7. Pentecostalism (which emerged in the early twentieth century) is derived from evangelicalism (whose history dates to the eighteenth century). Both focus on the importance of a distinct conversion experience, a personal relationship with God, and the duty to share one's faith in order to convert others. Pentecostalism differs from other branches of evangelicalism in its emphasis on modern-day miracles including the ability of believers to prophecy, speak in tongues, and become possessed by the Holy Spirit. Like fundamentalists, most Pentecostals adhere to some degree of biblical literalism although this is often mixed with a pronounced belief in the possibility of receiving personal messages directly from God. For

this reason, fundamentalists have historically been wary of Pentecostals (an animosity that is apparent in Jerry Falwell's statements during the 1987 PTL scandal)
but their overlapping political priorities, especially since the 1970s, have complicated this relationship. Pentecostalism is rooted in particular denominations (the
largest being the Assemblies of God, to which the Bakkers belonged), but the
influence of Pentecostal theologies and their associated "charismatic" worship
styles can now be seen in other evangelical Protestant and even some Catholic
congregations. See Vinson Synan, *The Holiness-Pentecostal Tradition: Charismatic
Movements in the Twentieth Century* (Grand Rapids, MI: W. B. Eerdmans, 1997).

8. Minnesota Department of Health, "Tamara Fay La Valley" (March 7, 1942),
Minnesota Birth Index, 1935–2002, Ancestry.com, File Number 1942-MN-
023327. Though Bakker later spelled her middle name with an "e," it is absent
from this birth record.

9. Tammy Faye Bakker, *I Gotta Be Me* (Harrison, AK: New Leaf Press, 1978), 13,
19. Although the six younger siblings were biologically half siblings, Bakker said
that this did not occur to her until years later and that even in adulthood she
would "always get aggravated if someone mentions the word half."

10. Bakker, *I Gotta Be Me*, 13.

11. John Wigger, *PTL: The Rise and Fall of Jim and Tammy Faye Bakker's Evangelical
Empire* (New York: Oxford University Press, 2017), 9.

12. Jim Bakker with Robert Paul Lamb, *Move that Mountain!* (Plainfield, NJ: Logos,
1976), 2–4.

13. Jim Bakker, *Move that Mountain!* 8. Throughout this chapter, short notes refer to
Jim Bakker by his full name, and use "Bakker" to refer to Tammy Faye.

14. Jim Bakker, *Move that Mountain!* 2.

15. Bakker, *I Gotta Be Me*, 15–16.

16. Bakker, *I Gotta Be Me*, back cover; Tammy Faye Bakker with Cliff Dudley, *Run to
the Roar* (Harrison, AR: New Leaf Press, 1980).

17. See, for example, Jim Bakker, "California, Monday Night," [March 1987], Flower
Pentecostal Heritage Center, Springfield, MO (hereafter iFPHC), direct-mail
letter; Jim Bakker and Tammy Faye Bakker, "Tammy's Drug Problem," PTL
Club (March 9, 1987), iFPHC, T848, audio cassette; Charles E. Shepard, "Bakker
Treated for Drug Dependency," *Charlotte Observer*, March 7, 1987, 1A.

18. Bakker, *I Gotta Be Me*, 34.

19. Bakker, *I Gotta Be Me*, 34.

20. Bakker, *Run to the Roar*, 22.

21. Bakker, *I Gotta Be Me*, 35.

22. Bakker, *I Gotta Be Me*, 26.

23. Bakker, *I Gotta Be Me*, 27.

24. Anita Bryant, for example, insisted throughout her campaigning that "I have
never stood in hate or anything other than love. If you love someone, you love
them enough to tell the truth," she reasoned. "You don't do anyone a favor by

condoning their lifestyle if it's immoral but at the same time, you stand on God's righteousness and you share with them the hope that they will come out of that lifestyle." Michele Horaney, "Crusader Bryant," *Daily Illini*, November 12, 1977, Bryant Collection, Stonewall National Museum and Archives, Ft. Lauderdale, FL.

25. Synan, *The Holiness-Pentecostal Tradition*, 192.

26. Kate Bowler, *Blessed: A History of the American Prosperity Gospel* (New York: Oxford University Press, 2013), 11, 41–76.

27. David Harrington Watt, *A Transforming Faith: Explorations of Twentieth-Century American Evangelicalism* (New Brunswick, NJ: Rutgers University Press, 1991), 49–50.

28. Bakker, *I Gotta Be Me*, 43–44.

29. Bakker, *I Gotta Be Me*, 44.

30. Bakker, *I Gotta Be Me*, 50–51; Colleen Todd and James Schaffer, *Christian Wives: Women behind the Evangelists Reveal Their Faith in Modern Marriage* (Garden City, NY: Doubleday, 1987), 8–9.

31. Todd and Schaffer, *Christian Wives*, 9.

32. For more on women's preaching in Pentecostal traditions, see Synan, *The Holiness-Pentecostal Tradition*, 190–194.

33. Bakker, *I Gotta Be Me*, 53–54.

34. The Bakkers later sold Allie and Susie records and mass-produced dolls and they had a concession stand at their Heritage USA theme park called "Susie's Ice Cream Parlor." See "Shopping Is a Delight at Heritage USA," *Heritage USA Herald* 6, no. 12 (March, 1987), iFPHC; "Shopping Enjoyable at Heritage USA," *Heritage USA Herald* 5, no. 17 (October 12–25, 1985), iFPHC.

35. Wigger, *PTL*, 27–29.

36. Wigger, *PTL*, 28.

37. Bakker, *I Gotta Be Me*, 76.

38. Bakker does not quote the verse but specifies the *Living Bible* translation, which is quoted here.

39. Bakker, *I Gotta Be Me*, 85–86.

40. For more on this conflict, see Wigger, *PTL*, 28–32.

41. Bakker, *I Gotta Be Me*, 93.

42. Wigger, *PTL*, 35–37.

43. Bakker, *I Gotta Be Me*, 95.

44. Bakker, *I Gotta Be Me*, 110.

45. See, for example, "Heritage USA Church Activities," *Heritage USA Herald* 6, no. 12 (March 1987), iFPHC; Jim Bakker, "Dear PTL Partner," *Action* (July 1977), iFPHC; Jim and Tammy Faye Bakker, "Merry Christmas," *Action* (December, 1977), iFPHC; Jim Bakker and Tammy Faye Bakker, *The PTL Family Devotional* (Charlotte, NC: PTL Television Network, 1982), iFPHC. The *Heritage USA Herald* was a newspaper for visitors to the Heritage USA theme park that listed activities at the park and included stories on PTL's ministries. *Action* was a glossy newsletter sent out to PTL

supporters that included updates about PTL along with daily devotional readings. Frequent references to the "PTL" family drew on more generic theological terms like "church family" or "Family of God" but also had a special resonance in the context of PTL, where the Bakkers' constant presence and candid dispositions cultivated a particular intimacy with their audience and especially with regular viewers.

46. Bakker, *I Gotta Be Me*, 94.

47. See, for example, "Doll Restorer Has Special Ministry," *Heritage USA Herald* 5, no. 17 (October 12–25, 1985), iFPHC; "Workshops Help to Repair Lives," *Heritage USA Herald* 6, no. 12 (March 1987), iFPHC.

48. See, for example, PTL Television Network, *Action* 5, no. 17 (March 1978), iFPHC.

49. See, for example, "Home Missions Programs of PTL Minister to Many," *Heritage USA Herald* 4, no. 25 (February 2-15, 1985), iFPHC.

50. Jim Bakker, *Move That Mountain!*; Bakker, *I Gotta Be Me*; Jim Bakker and Tammy Faye Bakker, *How We Lost Weight and Kept It Off!* (Charlotte, NC: Jim Bakker, 1979).

51. Bakker, *I Gotta Be Me*, 126–127.

52. Stewart M. Hoover, *Mass Media Religion: The Social Sources of the Electronic Church* (Newbury Park, CA: Sage, 1988), 131. Emphasis mine.

53. Hoover, *Mass Media Religion*, 222–223, 234.

54. J. Brooks Flippen, *Jimmy Carter, the Politics of Family, and the Rise of the Religious Right* (Athens: University of Georgia Press, 2011), 1–24; William C. Martin, *With God on Our Side: The Rise of the Religious Right in America* (New York: Broadway Books, 2005), 212.

55. Jack Houston, "Religion: Chicagoans to Attend Capital Prayer Rally," *Chicago Tribune*, April 26, 1980, A30; Barbara T. Roessner, "Crowd Praises Lord, Decries Immorality at Rally in Capital," *Hartford Courant*, April 30, 1980, 3. Both news reports use this exact phrase though neither attributes it directly to Gimenez.

56. "Religious Rally on Mall in the Capital Draws Support and Criticism," *New York Times*, April 27, 1980, 64. These quotations are directly attributed to Gimenez.

57. Jim Bakker, "Dear Friends," *Action* (April, 1980), iFPHC, 2–3; Jim Bakker, "We Must Vote," *Action* (November 1980), iFPHC, 2; Jim Bakker, "'God Is Always There for Me'—Ronald Reagan," *Action* (November 1980), iFPHC, 3–5.

58. Jim Bakker, "We Must Vote," *Action* (November 1980), iFPHC, 2.

59. Todd and Schaffer, *Christian Wives*, 85.

60. Kristin McMurran, "If Jesus Were Preaching Today, Says His TV Apostle Rex Humbard, 'He Would Never Get into Politics,'" *People*, May 11, 1981, http://www.people.com/people/article/0,,20079235,00.html.

61. PTL Ministries, "Tender Loving Care Adoption Agency," (n.d. [1980s]), Jeffrey K. Hadden Papers, University of California at Santa Barbara Special Collections, ARC Mss 24, Box 3, Folder 36, pamphlet.

62. Jim Bakker and Tammy Faye Bakker, "Jim and Tammy Ask for Restoration," *The Jim and Tammy Newsletter* 27 (Summer, 1988), iFPHC, direct-mail letter; Tammy

Faye Bakker, "It is a BEAUTIFUL . . . sunny day here in Florida!" (April 29, 1991), iFPHC, direct-mail letter.

63. The opening of maternity homes for pregnant teenagers marked a new strategy among pro-life evangelical leaders at this time, which scholar Susan Harding argues was a complicated response to contemporary feminism. See Susan Friend Harding, *The Book of Jerry Falwell: Fundamentalist Language and Politics* (Princeton, NJ: Princeton University Press, 2000), 186–187, 202–209; Susan Harding, "If I Should Die before I Wake: Jerry Falwell's Pro-Life Gospel," in *Uncertain Terms: Negotiating Gender in American Culture*, eds. Faye Ginsberg and Anna Lowenhaupt Tsing (Boston, MA: Beacon Press, 1990), 76–97; Alix M. Freedman, "Special Deliveries: Anti-Abortion Forces, in a Change of Tactics, Offer Alternative Care," *Wall Street Journal*, March 10, 1986, 1. I found three instances in PTL publications in which abortion was mentioned outside the context of the Bakkers' homes for pregnant women, two by Jim and one by another writer. In Jim Bakker's interview with Ronald Reagan, Bakker mentions abortion (alongside "abolishment of school prayer") in a list of legislative trends that concern him. In an unusually politically focused direct-mail letter written two months before the Washington for Jesus rally, Jim lists "abortion-on-demand" as evidence that ministries like PTL are necessary in order "to turn our nation and our world back to God." In the April 1980 issue of *Action*, a rise in the abortion rate in Italy is cited as one reason that PTL wants to establish a ministry in that country. See Jim Bakker, "Reagan Interview," *Action* (November 1980), iFPHC, 4; Jim Bakker, "PTL Partners" (February 19, 1980), iFPHC, direct-mail letter; Anton Marco, "Unto the Ends of the Earth," *Action* (April, 1980), 24, iFPHC.

64. Bakker, *I Gotta Be Me*, 122–124.

65. See Michael Lienesch, *Redeeming America: Piety and Politics in the New Christian Right* (Chapel Hill: University of North Carolina Press, 1993), 124–138.

66. Lawrence Grossberg, *We Gotta Get Out of This Place: Popular Conservatism and Postmodern Culture* (New York: Routledge, 1992), 276. Tammy Faye's over-the-top gender performance also came up in interviews that sociologist Mary Jo Neitz conducted with "post-patriarchal" Neo-pagan women in the mid-1990s, many of whom consciously constructed their own identities in contrast to mainstream religious and gender norms. Neitz quotes one of her informants as saying: "There are too many women in this lifetime who have an artificial view of what feminine is, as what the patriarchy has told them feminine is, and they are doing *this Tammy Faye Bakker number*. And, that doesn't work, and then they think the answer to that is like, 'if this isn't working, if this is an uncomfortable mode, then my answer is to wear business suits and carry a briefcase.' And that probably isn't real comfortable either, Reeboks aside (laughs). So, perhaps what the pagan woman is trying to do for women, and for men, is to help them find an expression of the masculine or the feminine, on the surface—externally—that they can present that they're comfortable with." See Mary Jo Neitz, "Queering

the Dragonfest: Changing Sexualities in a Post-Patriarchal Religion," *Sociology of Religion* 61, no. 4 (Winter 2000). Emphasis mine.

67. Todd and Schaffer, *Christian Wives*, 8.

68. Todd and Schaffer, *Christian Wives*, 24.

69. Todd and Schaffer, *Christian Wives*, 24.

70. Todd and Schaffer, *Christian Wives*, 24. Ellipsis in original.

71. Mirko D. Grmek, *History of AIDS: Emergence and Origin of a Modern Pandemic* (Princeton, NJ: Princeton University Press, 1990), 32.

72. Cathleen Decker, "Robertson Opens '88 Bid amid Jeering Protesters," *Los Angeles Times*, October 2, 1987, B21; Maralee Schwartz, "Robertson Disputes Doctors on AIDS," *Washington Post*, December 20, 1987, A12. See also Anthony Petro, *After the Wrath of God: AIDS, Sexuality, and American Religion* (New York: Oxford University Press, 2015).

73. Myra MacPherson, "The Pulpit and the Power: '700 Club's' Pat Robertson, Preaching the Gospel and Eyeing the White House," *Washington Post*, October 18, 1985, D1, D8. Ellipsis mine.

74. Tammy Faye Bakker, "Interview with Steve Pieters: Part Three," *Tammy's House Party* (Charlotte, NC: PTL, 1985), Streaming Video, 5:32–5:54, accessed March 20, 2009, http://www.youtube.com/watch?v=tJVUj-MFB-0.

75. Tammy Faye Bakker, "Interview with Steve Pieters: Part One," *Tammy's House Party* (Charlotte, NC: PTL, 1985), Streaming Video, 2:43–3:07, accessed March 20, 2009, http://www.youtube.com/watch?v=eC2BD6JnuIc; Tammy Faye Bakker, "Interview with Steve Pieters: Part Two," *Tammy's House Party* (Charlotte, NC: PTL, 1985), Streaming Video, 2:34–3:09, accessed March 20, 2009, http:// www.youtube.com/ watch?v=AuR65eSqYno&NR=1.

76. Bakker, "Pieters Interview: Part One," 6:55–7:00.

77. Bakker, "Pieters Interview: Part One, 2:43–3:07; Bakker, "Pieters Interview: Part Two," 2:34–3:09.

78. I am using the term "affirming" here to denote Christian theologies that affirm the practice of homosexuality, in contrast to "accepting" or "welcoming" churches that accept homosexuals as members but condemn homosexuality as a sin, and ask homosexual Christians to lead heterosexual or celibate lives. This vocabulary is borrowed from Stanley James Grenz, *Welcoming but Not Affirming: An Evangelical Response to Homosexuality* (Louisville, KY: Westminster John Knox Press, 1998).

79. Jerry Falwell, *The Spiritual Renaissance in America* (Temple Baptist Church, Redford, Michigan, 1986), sermon. Quoted in Harding, *The Book of Jerry Falwell*, 160. Falwell denied that he believed "AIDS is God's judgment against homosexuals" (asserting instead that he believed "it is God's judgment against the whole society") but it seems unlikely that his reference to "immorality" with regard to an epidemic that especially affected gay men did not encompass some judgment of homosexuality. Indeed, historian William Martin argues: "So

seriously is sexual sin regarded in evangelical circles that, when the term 'immorality' is used without elaboration, it almost always refers to intimate sexual relations outside of the bonds of one's own marriage. And to many conservative Christians, even 'immorality' seems too gentle a term when speaking of homosexual behavior." See Martin, *With God on Our Side*, 100.

80. Bakker, "Pieters Interview: Part Two," 6:43–7:22.
81. Bakker, "Pieters Interview: Part Two," 7:38–9:08.
82. Bakker, "Pieters Interview: Part One," 6:16–6:25.
83. See Janet R. Jakobsen and Ann Pellegrini, *Love the Sin: Sexual Regulation and the Limits of Religious Tolerance* (New York: New York University Press, 2003), 1–17.
84. Bakker, "Pieters Interview: Part One," 6:25–6:55.
85. Bakker, "Pieters Interview: Part One," 5:52–6:15; Bakker, "Pieters Interview: Part Two," 1:57–2:30.
86. Bakker, "Pieters Interview: Part Two," 3:31–4:07.
87. See Tanya Erzen, *Straight to Jesus: Sexual and Christian Conversions in the Ex-Gay Movement* (Berkeley: University of California Press, 2006); Martin, *With God On Our Side*, 248.
88. Bakker, "Pieters Interview: Part One," 7:28–7:57.
89. Anita Bryant and Bob Green, *Raising God's Children* (Old Tappan, NJ: Fleming H. Revell, 1977), 153.
90. Bakker, "Pieters Interview: Part Two," 1:22–1:29.
91. Bakker, "Pieters Interview: Part Two," 1:29–1:56.
92. See, for example, Seth Dowland, "'Family Values' and the Formation of a Christian Right Agenda," *Church History* 78 (2009): 606–631; Lienesch, *Redeeming America*, 11–12, 52–53, 84–85; Martin, *With God on Our Side*, 100–101; Robert O. Self, *All in the Family: The Realignment of American Democracy since the 1960s* (New York: Hill and Wang, 2012), 353–355, 393.
93. Wigger, *PTL*, 205. Wigger also argues that by the mid-1980s, Tammy Faye resented PTL for taking all of Jim's time and interfering with her marriage and family life. He asserts that this resentment may have played a role in Tammy Faye's willingness to take risks on the air.
94. See, for example, "Falwell: Bakker Set to Meet Accusers," *Chicago Tribune*, May 19, 1987, 6; "Falwell Planning to Quit PTL Post as Bakker Denies New Allegations," *Globe and Mail* [Toronto, ON], April 27, 1987, A12; "Tapes Cite 3 Homosexual Acts by Bakker, Falwell Says Church Leaders Received Testimony on Encounters," *Los Angeles Times*, May 28, 1987, 2; Art Harris, "Falwell Takes Control, Bars Bakker from PTL; Board Cuts Off All Payments to Evangelist," *Washington Post*, April 29, 1987, A01; Art Harris and Michael Isikoff, "Holy War Heats Up; Bakker Accuses Falwell of Stealing Ministry," *Washington Post*, May 27, 1987, D01.
95. Susan Wise Bauer, *The Art of the Public Grovel: Sexual Sin and Public Confession in America* (Princeton, NJ: Princeton University Press, 2008), 139.

96. Hahn described a violent and forcible sexual encounter well within the legal definition of rape, but the issue of criminal assault never became a substantial focus of the scandal, which instead revolved around Jim's sexual hypocrisy and financial misdeeds. For her part, Jessica Hahn told historian John Wigger in a 2014 interview: "I can't call it rape. I just can't. Everybody else does, though, and it bothers me for some reason." I have tried to write about this incident in a way that is both forthright and respectful of Hahn's experience. Wigger, *PTL*, 124.

97. See, for example, Jim Bakker, "Dear Partners in Jesus Christ," [July 1987?], iFPHC, direct-mail letter; Jim Morrill, "Live from Pineville: The Bakkers Return to TV with New Show," *Charlotte Observer*, [December 1988?], iFPHC, news clipping.

98. See, for example, Michael Isikoff and Art Harris, "Falwell Hits Back: Bakkers Respond as 'Holy War' Intensifies," *Washington Post*, May 28, 1987; Martin Steinberg, "Swaggart Lashes Out against Bakker, Roberts," *Associated Press*, March 25, 1987; Harris and Isikoff, "Tammy Bakker's Tearful Vow; Evangelists' Security Guard Quits over Their Efforts to Keep House," *Washington Post*, June 18, 1987, C01; "Falwell: Bakker Set to Meet Accusers," *Chicago Tribune*, May 19, 1987, 6; Art Harris, "Falwell Takes Control, Bars Bakker from PTL; Board Cuts Off All Payments to Evangelist," *Washington Post*, April 29, 1987, A01.

99. For more on this, see Hoover, *Mass Media Religion*, 67.

100. Wigger, *PTL*, 79, 98–105.

101. Examples abound throughout the Bakkers' autobiographies and self-help books. See Jim Bakker, *Move That Mountain!* 32–35; Bakker and Bakker, *How We Lost Weight*, ix; Bakker, *I Gotta Be Me*, 65–68.

102. Bakker, *I Gotta Be Me*, 67; Todd and Schaffer, *Christian Wives*, 13–14.

103. Bakker, *I Gotta Be Me*, 80–81; Todd and Schaffer, *Christian Wives*, 15.

104. Jim Bakker and Tammy Faye Bakker, "Tammy's Drug Problem," PTL Club (March 9, 1987), iFPHC T848, audio cassette.

105. Jim Bakker, "California, Monday Night," [March 1987], iFPHC, direct-mail letter.

106. The Bakkers had also concealed Tammy Faye's drug addiction for years, but this was easier to justify to supporters as a private matter. Tammy Faye was the most obvious victim of her own addiction, and her scandal did not involve payoffs and bribes, as Jim's did.

107. See, for example, "Bakker's Lawyer Denies Hahn's Story of Encounter," *Chicago Tribune*, September 24, 1987, 18; Art Harris, "The Jessica Hahn Tape: Adviser Recalls Her Tearful Account of the Episode with Jim Bakker," *Washington Post*, April 9, 1987, C01; Jay Mathews, "The Jessica Hahn 'Confession': Adviser Says PTL Forced Her to Take Blame for Bakker Episode," *Washington Post*, March 28, 1987, B01. Jessica Hahn also famously posed in both *Playboy* and *Penthouse*, appearing regularly in *Playboy* especially during the late 1980s and early 1990s. See "I Was Jessica Hahn's Madam," *Penthouse*, January 1988; "Jessica Hahn: Born Again, in Words and Pictures," *Playboy*, November 1987; "Jessica Hahn: Her Affair with a 19-Year-Old," *Penthouse*, March 1988; Jessica Hahn: Her

Own Story," *Penthouse*, October 1987; "Jessica Hahn, Part Two: The Cover Up," *Playboy*, December 1987; "The New Jessica Hahn: The Photos You've Been Waiting For," *Playboy*, September 1988; "The New Jessica Hahn, She's Naughty and Nice Enough to Be In Santa's Dreams," *Playboy*, December 1992.

108. Phil Donahue, "Phil Donahue Interviews Patti Roberts Thompson; Cal Thomas, Syndicated Columnist; and Paul Roper about TV Evangelists," *Donahue* (April 17, 1987), iFPHC, video cassette.

109. See, for example, Sean Cronin, "Bakker Guilty of Fraud," *Irish Times*, October 6, 1989, 6; Tom Durkin, "Study to Eye Tammy's Mascara," *Los Angeles Times*, June 14, 1989, 2; May Lee, "Bakker Guilty of Fleecing His TV Flock of Millions," *Los Angeles Times*, October 6, 1989, 1; Nancy Wride, "'39 Rolls, Other PTL Items to Be Auctioned," *Los Angeles Times*, May 22, 1987, 3.

110. Isikoff and Harris, "Falwell Hits Back: Bakkers Respond as 'Holy War' Intensifies," *Washington Post*, May 28, 1987; Steinberg, "Swaggart Lashes Out against Bakker, Roberts," *Associated Press*, March 25, 1987.

111. Wigger, *PTL*, 3, 181–188; "Bakker Found Guilty," *Telegram and Gazette*, October 5, 1989, A1; Cronin, "Bakker Guilty of Fraud," *Irish Times*, October 6, 1989, 6; Lee, "Bakker Guilty of Fleecing His TV Flock of Millions," *Los Angeles Times*, October 6, 1989, 1.

112. "Bakker Gets New Shorter Sentence," *Atlanta Daily World*, August 27, 1991, 2; Charles E. Shepard, "A Testament to Unfinished Business: As New Owners Attempt to Resurrect Heritage USA, Jim Bakker Begins Life after Prison," *Washington Post*, December 11, 1994, A03.

113. "'Lonely' Tammy Bakker Says She Will Seek Divorce," *Globe and Mail*, March 13, 1992, A10; "Tammy Faye Bakker Gets Divorce, Custody of Son, 16," *Los Angeles Times*, March 14, 1992, 13.

114. Tammy Faye Messner, *I Will Survive . . . and You Will, Too!* (New York: Jeremy P. Tarcher/Penguin, 2003), 265–272. Accessed at https://www.youtube.com/watch?v=ySVCvOmQMC0

115. Messner, *I Will Survive. . . and You Will, Too!* 325–327.

116. Larry King, "Tammy Faye Messner and Jay Baker [*sic*]," *Larry King Live* (New York: CNN, 2006), Streaming Video, 0:14–0:24.

117. "Her Advice: Be Proud," *USA Today*, May 16, 2002, 8; Joseph Adalian, "Worlds to Collide in 'Surreal Life 2,'" *Daily Variety*, October 21, 2003; Michael Applebaum, "My Ex-Husband Sinned, but I'm Back!" *Brandweek* 45, no. 1 (January 5 2004); Tammy Faye Messner, *Tammy: Telling It My Way* (New York: Villard, 1996), 29–31; Tammy Faye Messner, "Christians Should Accept Gays," *XY* (May 2002): 112–113; Tammy Faye Messner, "Let Your Light Shine," *XY* (December 2002); Tammy Faye Messner, "Welcome *XY* Advice Columnist Tammy Faye," *XY* (March 2002): 120–121.

118. *The Eyes of Tammy Faye*, directed by Fenton Bailey and Ryan Barbato (Hollywood, CA: World of Wonder Productions, 1999), DVD.

119. Neal Broverman, "No Dry Eyes for Tammy Faye," *Advocate*, no. 991 (August 28 2007).

CHAPTER 5

1. Susan Faludi, *Backlash: The Undeclared War against American Women* (New York: Crown, 1991). In the revised and updated edition, Faludi describes conservative women as "cross-dressers" who appropriate the language of women's liberation in service of antifeminist ends. See Susan Faludi, *Backlash: The Undeclared War against American Women*, rev. ed. (New York: Three Rivers Press, 2009), xii–xiii.

2. Suffragist Victoria Woodhull was the first woman to run for the United States presidency, which she did under the auspices of the Equal Rights Party in 1872, well before women gained national suffrage through the ratification of nineteenth amendment to the US Constitution in 1920. Nearly a century later, in 1964, Republican congresswoman Margaret Chase Smith became the first woman to appear on the ballot for the presidential nomination at a major party's convention. Smith had been mentioned as a possible vice-presidential pick on Dwight Eisenhower's 1952 ticket, though that nomination never materialized. Instead, Geraldine Ferraro was the first woman nominated to the vice-presidential slot on a major party ticket, alongside Walter Mondale in 1984. Sarah Palin, in 2008, was only the second woman to run for the office on behalf of a major party, and she was the first Republican. For more on this history, see Richard L. Fox and Zoe M. Oxley, "Why No Madame President? Gender and Presidential Politics in the United States," in *Women as Political Leaders: Studies in Gender and Governing*, eds. Michael A. Genovese and Janie S. Steckenrider (New York: Routledge, 2013), 307–311.

3. McCain did not use the term "maverick" during this speech, but it was widely applied to the McCain-Palin ticket and had been used to refer to McCain since his 2000 bid for the Republican presidential nomination. See Richard L. Berke, Adam Nagourney, and Alison Mitchell, "The Voters: The Maverick Fate of McCain Campaign Rests on Today's Vote," *New York Times*, February 1, 2000, A1.

4. John McCain, "Transcript: McCain Announces Sarah Palin Is VP," *National Public Radio*, August 29, 2008, accessed December 15, 2016, http://www.npr.org/templates/story/story.php?storyId=94116743.

5. William Safire, "The Maverick Ticket," *New York Times*, September 7, 2008, WK10.

6. Elisabeth Bumiller and David D. Kirkpatrick, "Romney Is Out; McCain Emerges as G.O.P. Choice," *New York Times*, February 8, 2008, A1; Nicholas D. Kristof, "The World's Worst Panderer," *New York Times*, February 17, 2008, WK13; David Kirkpatrick, "Christian Right Labors to Find an '08 Candidate," *New York Times*, February 25, 2007, 1; Adam Nagourney and Michael Cooper, "McCain's

Conservative Model? Roosevelt (Theodore, That Is)," *New York Times*, July 13, 2008, 1, 30.

7. Conservatives also worried about McCain's criticisms of President George W. Bush's tax cuts and of the US military's use of torture, as well as McCain's moderate stance on federal welfare spending.

8. Carl Hulse, "Senators Block Initiative to Ban Same-Sex Unions: Amendment, Endorsed by Bush, Fails after Days of Debate," *New York Times*, July 15, 2004, A1. McCain advocated a state-by-state approach rather than a federal amendment.

9. David Barstow, "McCain Denounces Political Tactics of Christian Right," *New York Times*, February 29, 2000, A1; Kevin Sack, "Remarks Rally Christian Right against McCain," *New York Times*, March 3, 2000, A1.

10. John McCain, "Liberty University Commencement Address," Liberty University, Lynchburg, VA, May 13, 2006, accessed December 17, 2016, http://www.mc-cain.senate.gov/public/index.cfm/2006/5/post-780c520d-739f-46d7-831a-8155c8doad28. For his part, Falwell emphasized that his invitation to McCain was "not an endorsement" in a *New York Times* opinion piece that positioned McCain as an example of ideological diversity among Liberty University commencement speakers. (He also said that McCain was "the kind of conservative candidate that I would have no trouble supporting," but this was not the overall tone of the piece). Jerry Falwell, "An Invitation, Not an Endorsement," *New York Times*, May 7, 2006, D13. See also Paul Krugman, "John and Jerry," *New York Times*, April 3, 2006, A17.

11. Adam Nagourney, "McCain Emphasizing His Conservative Bona Fides; Strategy Puts His Independent Image at Risk," *New York Times*, April 9, 2006, 33; Jon Meacham, "A Nation of Christians Is Not a Christian Nation," *New York Times*, October 7, 2007, C15. McCain also made some notable missteps along this path. for example, enthusiastically accepting endorsements from televangelist John C. Hagee and megachurch pastor Rod Parsley and then publicly renouncing those endorsements after recordings surfaced of Parsley's anti-Muslim sermons and Hagee's remarks that the Holocaust was a part of God's plan to drive Jews from Europe and into Palestine. See Neela Banerjee and Michael Luo, "McCain Cuts Ties to Pastors Whose Talks Drew Fire," *New York Times*, May 23, 2008, A1.

12. Michael Luo, "McCain Extends His Outreach, but Evangelicals Are Still Wary," *New York Times*, June 9, 2008, A1; Michael Luo, "Religious Right Divides Its Vote: At Meeting, 2 Are Close, Guiliani Is Praised," *New York Times*, October 21, 2007, 1; Frank Rich, "Rudy, the Values Slayer," *New York Times*, October 28, 2007, C12. Mitt Romney won the poll with 27.6 percent of the 5,775 votes; former Arkansas governor Mike Huckabee was a close second with 27.1 percent. McCain finished directly behind former New York City mayor Rudy Guiliani, who received only 1.85 percent of the vote. See also Jill Zuckman, "A Bitter Pill for Conservatives," *Chicago Tribune*, February 18, 2008, 1, 20.

13. Robert Novak, "McCain Facing Trouble from Evangelical Block," *Asheville Citizen-Times* [NC], June 12, 2008, A7. By July 2008, Dobson seemed to be ready to take a "lesser-of-two-evils approach" to McCain. See "Dobson Might Endorse McCain," *Los Angeles Times*, July 21, 2008, A16.

14. Michael Luo, "Evangelicals See Dilemmas in GOP Presidential Field: Leaders Haven't Won over a Key Group," *New York Times*, July 8, 2007, 15.

15. Palin has attended a variety of churches over her lifetime, following her Catholic mother's conversion to Protestant evangelicalism when Sarah was a child. She has tended toward Pentecostal congregations, spending most of her teenage years in an Assemblies of God church. This is the same denomination to which Jim and Tammy Faye Bakker belonged, and she speaks a similar language of experiencing God's personal guidance and presence in her life. See, for example, Sarah Palin, *Going Rogue: An American Life* (New York: HarperCollins, 2009), 21–22.

16. Bob Smietana, "McCain's VP Choice Thrills Conservatives," *Tennessean* [Nashville], August 29, 2008.

17. Elisabeth Bumiller and Michael Cooper, "McCain Has Made His Pick and Is Set to Tell on Friday," *New York Times*, August 28, 2008, A24; *New York Times* columnist William Kristol mentioned Sarah Palin (alongside former Ebay CEO Meg Whitman and former secretary of state Condoleezza Rice) as a possible pick if the McCain camp wanted a female running mate to "appeal to . . . anguished Hillary supporters." However, even Kristol focused on Romney, Pawlenty, and Lieberman as the likely frontrunners: William Kristol, "A Joe of His Own?" *New York Times*, August 25, 2008, A19. See also William Kristol, "How to Pick a VP," *New York Times*, August 4, 2008, A19.

18. Craig L. Foster, "Mitt Romney, the 2008 Vice-Presidential Selection Process, and the Continuing Impact of the Mormon Question," *John Whitmer Historical Association Journal* 29 (2009): 161–168. See also David E. Campbell, John C. Green, and J. Quin Monson, "The Stained Glass Ceiling: Social Contact and Mitt Romney's 'Religion Problem,'" *Political Behavior* 34, no. 2 (June 2012): 277–299; Gary S. Selby, "'Where Mitt Romney Takes His Family to Church': Mike Huckabee's GOP Convention Speech, the 'Mormon Hurdle,' and the Rhetoric of Proportion," *Rhetoric and Public Affairs* 16, no. 2 (Summer 2013): 385–387.

19. Although scholars have shown that media outlets focused more on the historicity of Barack Obama's campaign (in terms of race) than that of Clinton's (in terms of gender), the sense that either campaign would be historically significant was a dominant theme in media coverage of the 2008 Democratic primaries. See Regina G. Lawrence and Melody Rose, *Hillary Clinton's Race for the White House: Gender Politics and Media on the Campaign* Trail (Boulder, CO: Lynne Rienner, 2010).

20. David S. Broder, "Clinton Takes Women a Long Way," *Palm Beach Post*, June 13, 2008, A15. Broder was a long-time columnist for the *Washington Post*, and this column was syndicated nationally. In another nationally syndicated column, *Boston Globe* writer Ellen Goodman penned the speech that she wished Barack Obama would give, acknowledging the role of gender in the campaign and reaching out to erstwhile Clinton supporters: Ellen Goodman, "A Gender Talk We'd Like to Hear," *Boston Globe*, June 1, 2008, 10.

21. Thomas Fitzgerald, "Experts: Clinton Advanced Women's Cause, On Balance," *Philadelphia Inquirer*, June 8, 2008, A1, A6. This column was nationally syndicated.

22. In August 2008, Gallup polling indicated that overall, male voters favored McCain by a six-point margin (42 percent to 48 percent) while female voters favored Obama by a ten-point margin (39 percent to 49 percent). White women, however, favored McCain by a small margin (4 points), and white female independents (those who did not identify as either Democrat or Republican when asked) were split, with 41 percent favoring Obama and 42 percent favoring McCain. Further, in an analysis of polling data grouped by race, gender, and party affiliation, it was this group (white female independents) that was most closely split, indicating that the right choice of running mate might make the most difference in swaying these voters to one candidate or the other. Palin's appearance on the McCain ticket seems to have briefly boosted the popularity of the Republican choice, but that gain was short-lived, peaking in the week of September 8 at an eleven-point (40 percent to 51 percent) lead over the Democratic ticket. By the following week, the gap had narrowed to a mere two-point lead (47 percent to 45 percent) in McCain's favor. Frank Newport et al., *Winning the White House 2008: The Gallup Poll, Public Opinion, and the Presidency* (New York: Infobase, 2009), 476–477, 514–515.

23. Hillary Clinton, "Text of Clinton's 2008 Concession Speech," *Guardian*, June 7, 2008, accessed December 18, 2016, https://www.theguardian.com/commentisfree/2008/jun/07/hillaryclinton.uselections20081.

24. Sarah Palin, "Transcript: Palin's Speech in Dayton, Ohio," *National Public Radio*, August 29, 2008, accessed December 18, 2016, http://www.npr.org/templates/story/story.php?storyId=94118910.

25. Gail Collins, "McCain's Baked Alaska," *New York Times*, August 30, 2008, A19.

26. Gloria Steinem, "Wrong Woman, Wrong Message," *Los Angeles Times*, September 8, 2008, accessed December 18, 2016, http://articles.latimes.com/2008/sep/04/news/OE-STEINEM4.

27. For example: On gay marriage: as of 2008, both McCain and Clinton spoke positively about private ceremonies and civil unions for same-sex couples but did not support new federal legislation on gay marriage. McCain framed this as a states' rights issue whereas Clinton implied that states would be quicker to

legalize gay marriage. Palin's position was similar to McCain's, in keeping with her strong preference for state-level rather than federal intervention, but most commentators assumed that she would take a harder line with regard to gay marriage due to her association with the Christian Right. On crime: McCain tended to favor expanding the carceral state more than Clinton did, but both supported the death penalty as well as expanded community policing. On Climate: in 2006, McCain and Clinton co-led a congressional delegation to witness the effects of polar warming in Alaska and spoke out about the need to address climate change. On foreign policy: both supported a strong military and tended to favor US intervention in foreign affairs. For a distillation of each candidates' position on these and other issues, see the websites updated and maintained by the nonprofit, nonpartisan organization On the Issues: http://www.ontheissues. org/John_McCain.htm and http://www.ontheissues.org/Hillary_Clinton.htm, accessed May 13, 2017.

28. See Anne E. Kornblut, *Notes from the Cracked Ceiling: What It Will Take for a Woman to Win* (New York: Broadway Paperbacks, 2011, [Crown Publishing, 2009]), 21.

29. Robin Morgan, "Goodbye to All That (#2)," *Women's Media Center* (February 2, 2008), accessed December 20, 2016, http://www.womensmediacenter.com/feature/entry/goodbye-to-all-that-2. Emphasis in original. See also Kornblut, *Notes from the Cracked Ceiling*, 13–17; Kate Zernike, "Post-Feminism and Other Fairy Tales," *New York Times*, March 16, 2008, WK1.

30. Steinem, "Wrong Woman, Wrong Message."

31. Cintra Wilson, "Pissed about Palin," *Salon*, September 10, 2008, accessed December 20, 2016, http://www.salon.com/2008/09/10/palin_feminism/. Emphasis mine. Wilson's critique in particular was connected to a presumption that Palin's pro-life commitments were inauthentic to her experience as a woman and must therefore arise from cynical political ambition rather than sincere and considered belief. Conservative columnist Jonah Goldberg rounded up these and other feminist critiques of Palin in his own syndicated column. Jonah Goldberg, "Palin Exposes Feminism," *Herald and Review* [Decatur, IL], 5. See also Cathy Young, "Why Feminists Hate Sarah Palin," *Wall Street Journal*, September 15, 2008, accessed December 20, 2016, http://www.wsj.com/articles/ SB122143727571134335.

32. Wendy Doniger, "All Beliefs Welcome, Unless They Are Forced on Others," *OnFaith.co* (September 9, 2008), https://www.onfaith.co/onfaith/2008/09/09/ all-beliefs-welcome-unless-the/578. OnFaith is a blog that was at the time jointly operated by the *Washington Post* and *Newsweek*. Some commentators mistakenly claimed that Doniger's comments were written in one or the other of these flagship publications.

33. In his recent examination of the twentieth-century culture wars, intellectual historian Andrew Hartman declares: "The logic of the culture wars has been exhausted. The metaphor has run its course." Andrew Hartman, *A War for the Soul*

of America: A History of the Culture Wars (Chicago: University of Chicago Press, 2015), 285. The political ground has certainly shifted substantially, but I would argue that the metaphor—and particularly its implication of deep division over basic assumptions and fundamental visions of the nation—continues to resonate as an apt description of American political culture.

34. *New York Times* columnist Bob Herbert wrote, "The idea that the voters of the United States might install someone in the vice president's office who is too insecure to appear on, say, 'Meet the Press' or 'Face the Nation' is mind-boggling." Bob Herbert, "Palin's Words Raise Red Flags," *New York Times*, September 27, 2008, A21.

35. Katie Couric, interview with Sarah Palin and John McCain conducted on September 29, 2008, and broadcast on September 30, 2008. Transcript accessed at http://www.cbsnews.com/news/transcript-palin-and-mccain-interview/.

36. Maureen Dowd, "Sound, but No Fury," *New York Times*, September 27, 2008.

37. Herbert, "Palin's Words Raise Red Flags."

38. Kathleen Parker, "The Palin Problem," *Washington Post*, September 28, 2008. Emphasis (capitalization) in original.

39. Stephanie Condon, "Sarah Palin: I Was 'Annoyed' by Katie Couric's Newspaper Question," *CBS News*, November 16, 2009, accessed May 12, 2017, http://www.cbsnews.com/news/sarah-palin-i-was-annoyed-by-katie-courics-newspaper-question/.

40. Palin, *Going Rogue*, 207. She also referred to the interview as a whole as a "seemingly endless serial chat with the lowest-rated news anchor in network television" (270).

41. This narrative was on display when Couric questioned why Palin hadn't been more accessible to media. Palin responded: "I think this may be a little bit more about a campaign of reform, where just because maybe someone in the *media elite* hasn't had the access that maybe they're demanding, because we're running the campaign the way that we believe will best result in a good result for America—and that is a victory for John McCain. And maybe some are kind of put off by that. But that's all part of no more politics as usual; no more business as usual. I'm out there talking to the American people, those who I so dearly love and care about. I'm doing these rope-lines. I'm talking to every individual American that I can, in every hour that I have in my day. That's who I will be serving, that's who I'm connecting with today." Couric, interview with Palin and McCain, 2008.

42. As governor of Alaska, Palin had a mixed record on abortion. In keeping with her priority of curtailing government spending, Palin leaned heavily on her line-item veto and cut—among many other things—funding for day care and other programming aimed at helping young and at-risk mothers. Though Palin said elsewhere that programs should be in place to make it easier for women to choose to carry their pregnancies to term, she—like many social and fiscal

conservatives—apparently preferred that these be funded through private charity
rather than state spending. In 2007, the Alaska Supreme Court overturned a
twenty-year-old law requiring girls under sixteen to get parental consent in order
to obtain an abortion. Palin vocally opposed the court's decision, but her opposition had no immediate effect. See Katie Paul, "Sarah Palin's Real Record on
Abortion," *Newsweek*, September 5, 2008.

43. On evolution: Couric asked whether Palin thought that "evolution should
be taught as an accepted scientific principle or one of several theories." Palin
responded that as the daughter of a science teacher, she believed that "it should
be taught as an accepted principle" and that "science should be taught in science
class" though she added: "I won't ever deny that I see the hand of God in this
beautiful creation that is earth." Couric pressed Palin on whether creationism
should also be taught in schools and Palin reiterated her position that curriculum decisions should be matters for local school boards. Couric, interview with
Palin and McCain, 2008.

44. Conservative talk radio host Dennis Prager echoed many Palin supporters in
accusing Couric of "set[ting] out to humiliate Palin with a series of 'gotcha'
questions," asserting that this was a "tactic—rarely employed with major liberal candidates." The conservative Media Research Center was more measured, conceding that "most observers agree that Palin did not perform well
in the Couric interview" but also faulting the major news networks for basing
"so many 'news' reports" on replays of the interview's "worst moments,
making Palin looked as unprepared and inexperienced as possible." See
Dennis Prager, "Gotcha Questions for Katie Couric (and Her Colleagues),"
Townhall, October 7, 2008, accessed May 13, 2017, https://townhall.com/
columnists/dennisprager/2008/10/07/gotcha-questions-for-katie-couric-
and-her-colleagues-n834366; Media Research Center, "A Study in Character
Assassination: How the TV Networks Have Portrayed Sarah Palin as Dunce
or Demon," October 29, 2008, accessed May 13, 2017, https://www.mrc.
org/special-reports/study-character-assassination-how-tv-networks-have-
portrayed-sarah-palin-dunce-or.

45. *Saturday Night Live*, "Cold Open: Palin-Couric Interview," Season 34, Episode 3
(Anna Farris/Duffy), performed by Amy Poehler and Tina Fey, NBC, September
27, 2008, transcript accessed at http://snltranscripts.jt.org/08/08cpalin.phtml.

46. Wolf Blitzer, John King, *CNN News: Late Edition*, September 28, 2008, accessed
https://www.youtube.com/watch?v=zeMypXCUWMw.

47. Jason Linkins, "SNL's Palin Mockery Used the Candidate's Own Words,"
Huffington Post, October 30, 2008, accessed at http://www.huffingtonpost.com/
2008/09/29/snls-palin-mockery-used-t_n_130363.html.

48. *Saturday Night Live*, "A Non-Partisan Message from Sarah Palin and Hillary
Clinton," Season 34, Episode 1 (Michael Phelps/Lil Wayne), written by Seth
Myers, with Tina Fey and Amy Poehler, NBC, September 13, 2008.

49. Charles Gibson, "Interview with Sarah Palin," *World News*, ABC News, September 11–12, 2008, transcript, accessed March 23, 2017, http://abcnews. go.com/Politics/Vote2008/full-transcript-gibson-interviews-sarah-palin/ story?id=9159105.

50. See, for example, Frank Rich, "Could She Reach the Top in 2012? You Betcha," *New York Times*, November 21, 2010, WK8.

51. Sarah Palin, *Going Rogue: An American Life* (New York: HarperCollins, 2009); Sarah Palin, *America by Heart: Reflections on Faith, Family, and Flag* (New York: HarperCollins, 2010); Sarah Palin, *Good Tidings, Great Joy: Protecting the Heart of Christmas* (New York: Broadside Books, 2013); Sarah Palin, *Sweet Freedom: A Devotional* (Washington, DC: Regnery Faith, 2015).

52. Jay Newton-Small, "Why Sarah Palin Quit: The Five Best Explanations," *Time*, July 6, 2009, accessed March 23, 2017, http://content.time.com/time/politics/ article/0,8599,1908800-2,00.html.

53. Huma Kahn, "Sarah Palin's Endorsements See New Bag," *ABC News*, November 3, 2010, accessed March 23, 2017, http://abcnews.go.com/Politics/vote-2010-election-sarah-palins-endorsements-mixed-bag/story?id=12041219; Staff Writers, "Palin Endorsement Tracker," *Washington Post*, November 22, 2010, accessed March 23, 2017, http://www.washingtonpost.com/wp-srv/special/ politics/palin_tracker/. According the *Washington Post*'s "Palin Endorsement Tracker," forty-one of Palin's sixty-four endorsements went to candidates with "Tea Party ties" and twenty-three to "establishment" candidates. Palin also endorsed a remarkable twenty-seven women (and thirty-seven men). Just over half (thirty-three of sixty-four) of Palin's endorsed candidates won their races.

54. Jay Newton-Small, "How Sarah Palin Compounds the Donald Trump Effect," *Time*, January 20, 2016, accessed December 13, 2017, http://time.com/4186428/ donald-trump-sarah-palin-endorsement-2016-election/.

55. See, for example, Palin, *Going Rogue*, 139–140.

56. Couric, Interview with Palin, September 2008; Janice Shaw Crouse, "Obamacare: Payback Time for All the Single Ladies," *Concerned Women for America Website* (May 21, 2010), http://concernedwomen.org/obamacare-payback-time-for-all-the-single-ladies/.

57. Kornblut, *Notes from the Cracked Ceiling*, 125–126.

58. Amanda Terkel, "Palin Was a Feminist before She Wasn't," *ThinkProgress*, October 24, 2008, accessed May 31, 2017, https://thinkprogress.org/palin-was-a-feminist-before-she-wasnt-8bf085a856d1; Jessica Valenti, "Opinion: The Fake Feminism of Sarah Palin," *Washington Post*, Sunday, May 30, 2010, accessed May 12, 2010, http://www.washingtonpost.com/wp-dyn/content/article/2010/05/ 28/AR2010052802263.html.

59. Sarah Palin, Speech at Susan B. Anthony List's "Celebration of Life" Breakfast, Ronald Reagan Building and International Trade Center, Washington, DC, May 14, 2010, accessed at http://www.p2012.org/photos10/palin051410spt.html.

60. This debate has received extensive media coverage over the past decade. Conservative groups Feminists for Life and the Susan B. Anthony List are the most vocal proponents of the idea that Susan B. Anthony firmly opposed abortion, although this idea is now also supported by a display at the Susan B. Anthony Birthplace and Museum in Massachusetts. The most prominent opponents of this idea are journalist and Stanton biographer Lynn Sherr and Ann Gordon, professor emerita at Rutgers University and editor of the six-volume *Selected Papers of Elizabeth Cady Stanton and Susan B. Anthony* (Rutgers University Press). Cat Clark, "The Truth about Susan B. Anthony: Did One of America's First Feminists Oppose Abortion?" *Feminists for Life,* June 17, 2008, accessed May 13, 2017, http://www.feministsforlife.org/the-truth-about-susan-b-anthony/; Ruth Graham, "The Battle over Susan B. Anthony: Behind a Quiet House Museum Are Anti-Abortion Activists with a Mission: To Claim America's Most Famous Historical Feminist as Their Own," *Slate.com,* May 8, 2017, accessed May 13, 2017, www.slate.com/articles/double_x/doublex/2017/05/susan_b_anthony_anti_abortion_heroine_how_activists_are_claiming_her_for.html; Lynn Sherr and Ann D. Gordon, "No, Susan B. Anthony and Elizabeth Cady Stanton Were Not Antiabortionists," *Time,* November 10, 2015, accessed May 13, 2017, http://time.com/4106547/susan-b-anthony-elizabeth-cady-stanton-abortion/.

61. Meghan Daum, "Sarah Palin, Feminist," *Los Angeles Times,* May 20, 2010, accessed May 12, 2017, http://articles.latimes.com/2010/may/20/opinion/la-oe-0520-daum-fword-20100520.

62. Valenti, "The Fake Feminism of Sarah Palin."

63. For more information, see Know Your Meme, "Who Needs Feminism?" accessed May 12, 2017, http://knowyourmeme.com/memes/who-needs-feminism#fn4. "Know Your Meme" is a user-generated web-based encyclopedia hosted by the Cheezburger Network and dedicated to tracing the history of popular internet memes. Given the nature of its sourcing, the information on it should be approached with some degree of skepticism, but it is nonetheless the best resource for information of this kind.

64. Jessica Valenti, "Feminism Makes Women 'Victims'? I Think You've Mistaken Us for the Sexists," *Guardian,* Wednesday, July 30, 2014, accessed May 12, 2017, https://www.theguardian.com/commentisfree/2014/jul/30/feminism-makes-women-victims-sexist-women-against-feminism.

65. Valenti may be right that these Twitter accounts were set up by men to exaggerate the meme's popularity among women. It is also possible that they were fake accounts set up by conservative women for the same purpose, or that they were authentic accounts created by women who were inspired by this meme to take to Twitter for the first time. What is significant here is Valenti's implication that women's support for conservative antifeminism must be exaggerated, an argument that has deep roots in the history that this chapter traces.

66. Beverly LaHaye, "Why Feminism No Longer Sells," speech given to the Heritage Foundation in Washington, DC, on March 10, 1987. Transcript published by the Heritage Foundation and accessed at the CWA Offices in Washington, DC.

67. Her closest competitor was libertarian Ron Paul with 27.7 percent of the vote, but he was one of only two candidates besides Bachmann to receive more than 10 percent. Tim Pawlenty, who came in third with 13.6 percent, dropped out of the race three days later. See Donna Schill et al., "Bachmann Struts Stuff in Iowa, Pawlenty Falls Behind," *IowaWatch.org*, August 14, 2011, accessed May 12, 2017, http://iowawatch.org/2011/08/14/bachmann-struts-stuff-in-iowa-pawlenty-falls-behind-4/.

68. For more on the Tea Party, and Palin's and Bachmann's relationship to it, see Melissa Deckman, *Tea Party Women: Mama Grizzlies, Grassroots Leaders, and the Changing Face of the American Right* (New York: New York University Press, 2016).

69. Michele Bachmann, *Core of Conviction: My Story* (New York: Sentinel, 2011), 201.

70. Bachmann, *Core of Conviction*, 5. For more on the concept of "servant leadership" and its development in twentieth-century evangelicalism, see Bethany Moreton, *To Serve God and Wal-Mart: The Making of Christian Free Enterprise* (Cambridge, MA: Harvard University Press, 2009), 101–124, 132, 144, 186.

71. Bachmann, *Core of Conviction*, 200.

72. Bachmann, *Core of Conviction*, 200.

73. The state's "profile of learning" rule went into effect in 1998 and focused on requiring high school students to "expand their knowledge and skill beyond the state's basic standards" in ten core areas including subject areas like math, literature, and science and skills including reading, writing, decision making, and "resource management." Conservative groups also worried that the standards' vague language could be used to resurrect controversial diversity standards promoted by progressive reformers. See "Minnesota's 'Profile of Learning,'" *Education Reporter: The Newspaper of Education Rights* no. 147 (Eagle Forum: April 1998), accessed May 13, 2017, http://eagleforum.org/educate/1998/apr98/chaos.html; Lisa Larson, "Information Brief: Profile of Learning and the State's High School Graduation Rule" (St. Paul, MN: Minnesota House of Representatives, September 1998), accessed May 13, 2017, http://www.house.leg.state.mn.us/hrd/pubs/profile.pdf; "Minnesota's 'Profile of Learning,'" *Education Reporter: The Newspaper of Education Rights* no. 147 (Eagle Forum: April 1998), accessed May 13, 2017, http://eagleforum.org/educate/1998/apr98/chaos.html.

74. Michele Bachmann, "Fed Ed in Minnesota's Classrooms: 'Smaller Learning Communities' Prepare Workers for a State-Planned Economy," *Education Reporter* no. 205 (Eagle Forum: February 2003), accessed May 13, 2007, http://eagleforum.org/educate/2003/feb03/MN-classrooms.shtml; Ryan Lizza, "Leap of Faith: The Making of a Republican Front-Runner," *New Yorker*, August 15,

2011, accessed May 13, 2017, http://www.newyorker.com/magazine/2011/08/15/leap-of-faith-ryan-lizza.

75. Bachmann, *Core of Conviction*, 200.

76. The video has repeatedly been removed from Youtube, but has remained accessible as an embedded video file in Jill Lawrence, "Michele Bachmann's Bible Submissiveness: Is It a Problem?" *Daily Beast*, July 10, 2011, accessed May 12, 2017, http://www.thedailybeast.com/articles/2011/07/10/michele-bachmann-s-bible-submissiveness-is-it-a-problem.

77. Brian Montopoli, "Bachmann: 'Submissive' Doesn't Mean Subservient," *Face the Nation*, CBS News, August 15, 2011, accessed May 12, 2017, http://www.cbsnews.com/news/bachmann-submissive-doesnt-mean-subservient/.

78. Marabel Morgan, *The Total Woman* (Old Tappan, NJ: Fleming H. Revell, 1973), 71.

79. R. Marie Griffith, *God's Daughters: Evangelical Women and the Power of Submission* (Berkeley: University of California Press, 1997), 45, 183.

80. Roland S. Martin, "Bachmann 'Submission' Question Was Offensive," CNN News, August 12, 2011, accessed May 12, 2017, http://www.cnn.com/2011/OPINION/08/12/martin.bachmann.submission/.

81. Morgan, *Total Woman*, 70.

82. Leslie Bennetts, "Michele Bachmann Deflects 'Submissive' Question at GOP Debate: The Tea Party Queen Deflects the Now-Famous 'Submissive' Question," *Daily Beast*, August 12, 2011, accessed May 12, 2017, http://www.thedailybeast.com/articles/2011/08/12/michele-bachmann-deflects-submissive-question-at-gop-debate.html. See also D. Gregory Smith, "Michele Bachmann—(Submissive) Theologian?" *LGBTQ Nation*, Sunday, August 21, 2011, accessed May 13, 2017, https://www.lgbtqnation.com/2011/08/michele-bachmann-submissive-theologian/.

CONCLUSION

1. Leslie Ludy, *Set-Apart Feminity: God's Sacred Intent for Every Young Woman* (Eugene, OR: Harvest House, 2008).

2. Leslie Ludy, *Set Apart Girl* (2014), accessed May 16, 2014, http://setapartgirl.com/magazine/issue/2014/mayjun.

3. For more on Christian romance literature, see Lynn S. Neal, *Romancing God: Evangelical Women and Inspirational Fiction* (Chapel Hill: University of North Carolina Press, 2006).

4. Christianity Today, "her.meneutics: Christian Women. Cultural Comment," accessed May 16, 2014, http://www.christianitytoday.com/women/.

5. An excellent introduction to this subculture is the list of the "Top 10 Blogs for Christian Women" put out by the popular evangelical blog *Devotional Diva*. See

Maggie Winterton, "Top 10 Blogs for Christian Women," *Domestic Diva* (2013), accessed May 16, 2014, http://www.devotionaldiva.com/2013/08/top-10-blogs-for-christian-women/.

6. See Sheila Wray Gregoire, *To Love, Honor, and Vacuum: When You Feel More Like a Maid than a Wife and Mother* (Grand Rapids, MI: Kregel, 2003); Sheila Wray Gregoire, *How Big Is Your Umbrella?: Weathering the Storms of Life* (Winnipeg, MB: Word Alive Press, 2003); Sheila Wray Gregoire, *Honey, I Don't Have a Headache Tonight: Help for Women Who Want to Feel More in the Mood* (Grand Rapids, MI: Kregel, 2004); Sheila Wray Gregoire, *The Good Girl's Guide to Great Sex (And You Thought Bad Girls Have All the Fun)* (Grand Rapids, MI: Zondervan, 2012).

7. Jessica Warner, "Praise the Lord. Let's Fornicate," *Globe and Mail*, February 12, 2011, F5.

8. Mitchell Smyth, "Orange Juice Queen Bounces Back," *Toronto Star*, August 14, 1988, D4.

9. Mitchell Smyth, "Whatever happened to . . . Anita Bryant," *Toronto Star*, May 15, 1994, B11.

10. For more on Branson and evangelical tourism, see Aaron K. Ketchell, *Holy Hills of the Ozarks: Religion and Tourism in Branson, Missouri* (Baltimore: Johns Hopkins University Press, 2007).

11. Anita Bryant, "Anita Bryant Ministries" (2006), accessed May 17, 2014, http://www.anitabmi.org/3.html. Attempts to contact Bryant through the ministry's webpage resulted in infrequent responses from an assistant, and ultimately no response from Bryant herself.

12. For a few recent examples, see Susan Henking, "Drawn to Uncertainties," *New York Times*, August 25, 2013, BU.7; Chris Johnson, "40 Years Later, Bella Abzug's Daughter Recalls Mother's Support for Equality Act," *Washington Blade*, May 14, 2014; Alex Press, "The Power of Three Words—Almost 2 Milllion 'One Human Family' Stickers Distributed," *Keys Weekly* (2014), accessed May 19, 2014, http://keysweekly.com/42/the-power-of-three-words-almost-2-million-one-human-family-stickers-distributed/; Jonathan Rauch, "The Case for Hate Speech," *Atlantic* 312, no. 4 (November 2013).

13. Jeremy W. Peters, "The Decline and Fall of the 'H' Word," *New York Times*, March 23, 2014, ST.10.

14. *Milk*, directed by Gus Van Sant (Los Angeles: Focus Features, 2008).

15. Concerned Women for America, "Beverly LaHaye: Founder and President of Concerned Women for America," [1994?]. CWA Offices, Washington, DC, Information Sheet.

16. Concerned Women for America, "Beverly LaHaye: Founder and President of Concerned Women for America," [1994?], CWA Offices, Washington, DC, Information Sheet; Leslie Dorrough Smith, *Righteous Rhetoric: Sex, Speech, and*

the *Politics of Concerned Women for America* (New York: Oxford University Press, 2014), 55.

17. Gail Collins, "Michele Bachmann's Holy War," *Rolling Stone*, July 7–July 21, 2008, 53–54, 56–58.

18. Sally Jesse Raphael, "Tammy Faye and Roe Messner," *Sally Jesse Raphael*, November 23, 1993, Flower Pentecostal Heritage Center, Springfield, MO, V324, Video Recording.

19. The Jim Bakker Show at Morningside Church, "The Jim Bakker Show Website," accessed May 18, 2014, http://www.jimbakkershow.com.

20. Concerned Women for America, "Core Issues: Biblical Foundations," *CWFA. org* (2014), accessed May 19, 2014, http://www.cwfa.org/core-issues-biblical-foundations/.

Index

Printed in the USA/Agawam, MA
May 18, 2020

755211.009